Documentary in the Digital Age

Maxine Baker

Focal Press
Taylor & Francis Group

NEW YORK AND LONDON

First published 2006

This edition published 2013
by Focal Press
70 Blanchard Road, Suite 402, Burlington, MA 01803

Simultaneously published in the UK
by Focal Press
2 Park Square, Milton Park, Abingdon, Oxon OX14 4RN

Focal Press is an imprint of the Taylor & Francis Group, an informa business

Notices

Practitioners and researchers must always rely on their own experience and knowledge
in evaluating and using any information, methods, compounds, or experiments described
herein. In using such information or methods they should be mindful of their own safety
and the safety of others, including parties for whom they have a professional responsibility.

To the fullest extent of the law, neither the Publisher nor the authors, contributors, or
editors, assume any liability for any injury and/or damage to persons or property as a matter
of products liability, negligence or otherwise, or from any use or operation of any methods,
products, instructions, or ideas contained in the material herein.

British Library Cataloguing in Publication Data
A catalogue record for this book is available from the British Library

Library of Congress Cataloguing in Publication Data
A catalogue record for this book is available from the Library of Congress

ISBN-13: 978-0-240-51688-2 (pbk)

Transferred to Digital Printing in 2015

Contents

Acknowledgements

I would like to thank Georgia Kennedy of Focal Press for her patience, guidance and support. Also Beth Howard, who originally commissioned the book, and the editor who took over from her, Emma Baxter. I am especially grateful to Alex Cooke, who read the manuscript and offered excellent advice and support throughout. Mark Boulos researched and compiled the sections advising on documentary festivals and funding, and Pierre Haberer offered his great technical expertise with the new technology. I thank them both for their efficiency, patience and constant good humour.

The book could not have been written without the support of the UK's National Film and Television School at Beaconsfield. Special thanks to Roger Crittenden, the Academic Director, and to the knowledgeable and courteous film library staff, Noel Greenwood and Simon Aylward. Also to the Documentary Department, Dick Fontaine and the many students who helped with this project, particularly Simon Chambers, Julie Moggan and Piers Sanderson. Also, my attitudes throughout have been influenced by my work at the Cuban International Film and Television School. The perspective from Latin America is always so important and often so different from the Anglo-Saxon consensus. I have learned a lot from both staff and students, and I really appreciate their patience in explaining to me their different world view.

Peter Dale at Channel 4 and Nick Fraser at BBC's *Storyville* were both supportive to the project, intellectually stimulating, full of great ideas and always ready to help. Both are distinguished film-makers in their own right. With commissioners, this is not always the case, so we are lucky.

Looking back over my long and very happy life in documentary, I realize there is one other group of people I should thank – Clem Attlee and the Labour government of 1945. Without them I would never have been able to go to university or to write this book. On behalf of myself and my generation, I salute their memory!

Finally, of course, I thank my long-suffering friends. And I would like to dedicate the book to my godmother and aunt, Kate Ford, to my brother Roy and to the memory of my parents, Margaret and Wilfred Baker.

Maxine Baker
London

Introduction: Life on the run

There are very few clearly definable turning points in history. One of those rare moments happened in Paris in December 1895, when the Lumière brothers introduced their brand new moving picture show to a paying audience. That was the day that cinema was born. All the experiments, the invention of different systems to project moving pictures in different parts of the world, had been of great interest, technologically, but cinema requires an audience. And that first cinema show, run by the Lumières, was pure documentary. They described their scenes of everyday life, filmed around their home and factory near Lyons, as 'life on the run'. I have always thought this a perfect description of those vibrant fragments of French life at the turn of the nineteenth/twentieth century; a great definition, as well, of the word 'documentary'. The phrase is so much more evocative than John Grierson's clinically precise description of the genre, 'the creative treatment of actuality'.

This book looks at life on the run, twenty-first century style, Documentary in the Digital Age. The Lumières' brilliant invention, the cinematograph, was a machine which filmed, processed, projected and also, being portable, it could be taken anywhere with a minimum of fuss and used to record and display to an audience the world in which they lived. The Lumières chose to film real people in real situations, never showing any interest in dramatic stories. That is why I think that they are the true fathers of the documentary form.

It has taken film technology 100 years to catch up and overtake them. A century after that first screening in Paris, we finally have a camera which can rival and outstrip the cinematograph. Granted, the digital video camera cannot project its pictures to an audience – but it can play them back in the camera. And it can keep filming for long periods without having to change tapes. And it records sound. It is cheap, it is lightweight, the picture and sound quality are constantly improving, and it is user friendly. A single operator can take it anywhere and record our own contemporary lives on the run.

The invention of the DV camera has had a massive influence on documentary. So too has the development of digital video editing, sound recording and post-production, and of course also digital tools for animation. This book will not be concentrating on the camera or indeed any other particular aspect of the technology, although the technology is fundamental to the story.

It is my considered opinion that all new aesthetic developments in documentary have followed on from technical breakthroughs. In the 1930s and 1940s, for example, some of the most compelling and beautiful documentaries were made, but they only really became possible after sound came to the movies. In the 1960s, the invention of 16 mm cameras with sync sound shepherded in the movements known variously as *cinéma vérité*, direct cinema or fly on the wall. Now we have the digital technology which has liberated film-making in so many ways. In documentary, the effect has been immense.

I believe that we are now in the middle of a new golden age of documentary. What makes this one different and therefore, for me, more exciting is that there are so many people working in different styles with different approaches to the documentary genre. For years, the *vérité* aesthetic dominated documentary production and this, as a form, was often unduly restrictive and creatively stifling. Of course, some brilliant films came out of that whole movement, but I am convinced that some other brilliant films, stylistically different films, were not being made when they could and should have been made. After all, film-making was a very expensive business until recently, so the small number of television commissioning editors – still the main source of funding for most documentarists – had a great deal of power. Some of them were very narrow-minded, even conservative, in their approach.

Things are different now. Because of the lightweight, relatively inexpensive digital equipment, more and more people are funding their own films, which gives them the creative freedom that my generation never had. These people, the mavericks who want to express themselves without censorship or who have projects with no obvious big audience appeal, are now leading the way, creatively speaking. Their films are often purchased after they are shot, even, sometimes, after they have finished editing. Only at that stage are schedulers prepared to admit that the film-makers were right in the first place. The maverick films are everywhere. They refresh the television schedules, often get international distribution deals in cinemas and win major awards.

The situation for the documentary film-maker now is completely changed and those with a belief in their own ideas have everything to gain. Each chapter in this book examines the work of one director. They are all people with strong convictions and they are all very different. I have chosen them, first, because I admire their work and, second, because they all represent a different approach, style and attitude in their films. It seems to me that documentary now has many sub-categories, or sub-genres, to use an accurate but ugly constructed expression. Each director in the book makes work that belongs in one of these sub-categories. Some of them still shoot on film, some on DigiBeta or DV. All of them work digitally on sound and in editing and mixing. So the emphasis in the book is not on the technology itself but on what these people do with the technology.

The film-makers come from very different backgrounds and countries. Two are American, one is Polish, one Russian, one French, one German resident, one Irish-Portuguese, one Scot, three English. Through looking at the work of these very different people, I want to encourage others to open themselves up to the many possibilities that are out there today in documentary production. It is an exciting time to be working in factual film and a great time for taking risks, as all of the directors in the book regularly do.

Documentary has been my passion all my working life and it has been a stimulating experience for me to write this book. I worked, myself, as a documentary film-maker for many years, mostly for television companies – the BBC, CBC Canada, Granada, Scottish Television. I have been a researcher, producer, director, executive producer and commissioning editor. Apart from a short spell as

Chief Executive of the Scottish Film Council, I have always worked in documentary and never wanted to do anything else. The siren calls of the fiction film industry never appealed to me.

Now I restrict myself to executive producing and teaching documentary direction. I am a Visiting Senior Tutor at the National Film and Television School in the UK and Visiting Professor at the Escuela International de Cine y Television in Cuba. My students in both schools come from all over the world and I also teach workshops in other countries, most recently in Ghana, where the students came from all over sub-Saharan Africa, and in the Philippines. I have written about the aspects of the work of the directors in the book that I know will interest film school students, because I know what questions they invariably ask. But I think the book will be useful also for other film-makers, indeed for anybody who is interested in documentary.

Having spent so many years working as a documentary producer/director in television, it is wonderful for me to now see the growing popularity of documentaries in the cinema. I had always believed that audiences would not be prepared to pay out good money to watch documentaries when they could watch them for nothing on television. The obvious exception to this rule for me was the USA, but only because their television is so limited in its scope and seriously talented people, both factual and fiction film-makers, tend to gravitate towards the cinema. Now, even in the UK, that situation is changing and I hear on a regular basis how friends and colleagues have got themselves international distribution deals in the cinema for their documentaries. More and more, films shot on DV cameras are being blown up to 35 mm. Ten years ago, I never would have believed that was even possible.

I wanted to write this book because I wanted to share my passion for the documentary film. This is not an objective or analytical book. It is not a book of academic theory and it is not comprehensive – which would probably be an impossible task in any case. So what is it? It is a book by a film-maker for other film-makers. And it is a salute to the featured documentarists and to the many categories and sub-genres that they so creatively subvert. Put simply, it is a fan letter – to the factual film – from a lifelong supporter.

1 Errol Morris
American iconoclast

Errol Morris

Errol Morris, the American documentary film-maker, is a complex character. At university, he studied the History and Philosophy of Science, an unlikely sounding background for a popular film-maker. But these academic influences inform all of his work. His films are always stylish but also packed with innovative ideas. They work on a number of levels and at the same time they are highly entertaining. Often, they interrogate the very form of the documentary genre in which they belong. Maybe that is the reason why it took many years before the American Academy of Motion Pictures finally gave him the Oscar he deserves, for *The Fog of War* (2003), his film about Robert McNamara. The Academy is conservative in its judgements and in its ideas about form.

For years, American documentary was dominated by the style of film-making once described as 'direct cinema', now more commonly known by the French expression, *cinéma vérité*. Errol says that when he first started making movies he made a conscious attempt to break with the *vérité* tradition. He says:

> *You take any of the principles of* vérité, *I was interested in doing the exact opposite. Perhaps because of a certain contrary inclination by nature, but also it seemed to me that the idea of* vérité, *the metaphysical baggage of* vérité, *seemed to be quite false. I have nothing against* vérité *as a style of shooting but, to me, the idea that if you adopt a certain style of shooting, that would make what you do more truthful, strikes me as utter nonsense.*

Vérité, he says, developed 'a crazy set of rules'. You are supposed to handhold the camera, use only available light and remain as unobtrusive as possible. He says that, from the beginning, his films broke those rules. He tells a story about a book that influenced him. The book was about imaginary numbers, the usual light reading you would expect from a person with postgraduate degrees in the history and philosophy of science. The book discussed the difficulty of introducing the idea of the square root of minus one. It quoted Gabriel Garcia Marques, who described how influenced he had been by Kafka when he first read him as a teenager. Errol says that Kafka has the best opening lines in the business. Marques read the first paragraph of *Metamorphoses*, 'One fine day, Gregor woke up and found himself transformed into a giant dung beetle.' Marques said, 'I didn't know you were allowed to do that.'

As far as breaking the *vérité* rules was concerned, Errol did not know you were allowed to do that. But he did it anyway. He says about his early films:

> *In* Gates of Heaven, Vernon, Florida, The Thin Blue Line, *we always put the camera on a tripod, we tried to be as obtrusive as possible, we used the heaviest equipment we could find, people looked directly into the camera, which is considered to be the great 'no-no'. To break that* cinéma vérité *notion of observing without being observed, I lit everything. I can't think of a single instance where I used 'available*

light'. For me, available light is anything you can produce, anything you have at hand.

Errol points out that *The Thin Blue Line*, which examined the case of Randall Adams, a man who had been wrongly convicted and sent to jail for a murder he did not commit, would have had no evidentiary value at all if *vérité* was correct in its claims. Yet, he says, he is hard pushed to name another movie which resulted in a man being released from prison, not because the movie had drawn attention to the case and raised a public outcry, but because there was evidence recorded during the making of the movie that could be produced in a court of law and used to prove that the major witnesses in the l977 trial had committed perjury.

The Thin Blue Line has become one of the most influential films in recent documentary history, not only in factual film-making but also in fiction. It has become fashionable these days for fiction films to use the language of documentary, and the influence of Errol Morris can easily be spotted, particularly in films coming out of Hollywood. At the same time, *The Thin Blue Line* also uses many of the techniques of fiction. At the time of its release this caused great controversy and was mainly responsible, Errol was told, for stopping the film from being nominated for an Oscar. The re-enacted sequences, highly cinematic in their execution, were said to make the film 'not a proper documentary'. Nowadays, the techniques are commonly used in documentary though, it should be said, rarely as skilfully as in *The Thin Blue Line*.

The movie opens with a simple credit sequence, with Philip Glass music playing over the graphics. The first three shots of the film show the Dallas skyline at night, lights flickering, the back sky blue. The scene is vaguely familiar. Something about it is reminiscent of the television series *Dallas*, still hugely popular all over the world when *The Thin Blue Line* was made. The Glass music emphasizes the feeling that something dramatic is about to happen. Over the third shot, a voice-over begins. A man tells how he and his brother were driving to California from Ohio and stopped in Dallas. One more cityscape shot and then the picture cuts to the person talking. He is not identified, in the conventional manner, with a caption or commentary. The background picture gives no clues. He simply tells his story. He is looking directly at

3

the audience. He says he got a job within half a day of arriving in the city, 'as if I was meant to be here'. With the Glass music still running quietly under the picture, it cuts to a revolving red light, a police car light. Another man, younger, wearing a red shirt, is now talking. He tells how he ran away from home a couple of times, at 16 took a pistol and a shotgun, stole a neighbour's car and ended up coming to Dallas.

The young man describes a night out with the first man – who he names as Randall Adams – and his brother. There was a lot of drinking, marijuana and a movie, no suggestion of anything unusual. The only hint of menace up until now has been the softly playing music of Philip Glass. Randall Adams then appears, expressing what sounds like an internal monologue. He got up and went to work on Saturday morning. Why did he meet that kid? Why did he run out of gas at that time? He doesn't know. Suddenly, the film cuts to a dramatized reconstruction. This, the first of a number of re-enactments of the crime, fundamental to the story, is carried on picture and music alone. The first shot shows a car pulled up at the roadside, a police vehicle behind it. The scene continues with very short shots, dramatically lit. The point of view seems to be that of the driver of the car, looking through his rear view mirror, seeing a policeman getting out of the police car and coming up to him. We only see the driver's hand. When the policeman is level with the car of the driver who has been stopped, a hand clutching a gun begins to shoot. The cutting is now very fast. From the gun to police artists' line drawings of the bullet wounds the police victim suffered. The dead policeman lies by the side of the road, a foot stamps on an accelerator and there is the sound of a car driving off at speed. Now a police-woman jumps out of the police car and shoots at the disappearing vehicle.

A morgue photograph of the dead policeman is cut with pictures of his bullet-riddled uniform and a colour picture of him smiling, in uniform, a handsome young man. There follows a rostrum sequence, cleverly conceived. A newspaper front page, the camera tracks in to the headline: 'Officer's killer sought'. Then the picture story: 'Officer killed Sunday. Robert Woods.' The camera roams around, picking out key words: '12.30 a.m.'; 'Oh my gosh'. Then, a hugely enlarged, grainy picture of the victim. Another quote, 'The description could not be the assailant.' The date 'November 29' mixes into 'December 22 1976'. The camera pans down to a picture of an official-looking guy, holding onto the arm of a hapless arrestee. A voice-over interview begins. The picture cuts to the man we saw at the beginning of the film, Randall Adams. He is the man in the newspaper photograph, but no longer resembles him. He has been in jail for many years.

The film now begins a detailed analysis of what actually happened on that night, 27 November 1976. There are a number of interview-ees, police and public, lawyers, witnesses, all talking to, or just past, the camera. They are all framed the same way, head and shoulders shots, no camera movement. There are no name captions but it is obvious from the content of the interviews what role each person plays in the story. It is a painstaking investigation, tracing and retracing, step by step, the events of that night and the backgrounds of the convicted man and the chief witness for the prosecution. Randall Adams is convicted but is he really guilty? Ultimately, the mystery is solved. Adams is innocent and the real killer is the young man in the red shirt, David Harris.

While the story itself is utterly absorbing, I am just as interested in the visual, musical and graphic techniques that Morris uses to drive his story along. The simply framed interviews are compelling because the people talking are articulate and lively characters with a murder mystery to tell. In principle, however, we can see a good factual cop story on television any day. What distinguishes this film from investigative television is the skilful storytelling and the juxtaposition of interview, reconstruction and other diverse visual illustration. The key images in the film revolve around the scene of crime itself. As the story progresses, the point of view of the camera changes as different witnesses discuss what they claim actually happened. The murder of the policeman is shown over and over again, but each time it is filmed from a different angle and each time the audience is being given new, usually contradictory, information. Errol says, 'It is a re-enactment of lies. Not reality. It is unreality, falsehood. Based on the point of view of the witnesses, you are treated to the spectacle of imagery which you are told shows you something of the real world but which is untrue.' The high production values of these episodes, stylishly shot like a Film Noir movie, enhance the feeling that this cannot be real, we are watching fiction. Then the picture cuts back to a simply shot interviewee and we realize that it is indeed a factual account we are hearing. But which of the people in this film are lying and who is telling the truth?

Sometimes the visual material is used in an almost satirical way, debunking what an interviewee has said, or is about to say. At one point, the lawyers for the defence explain that the judge at Adams's trial would not let them introduce evidence about a crime spree that David Harris had been on. One of them says that she felt that the reason why the judge was determined to put Randall Adams on trial and not David Harris was because Adams was 28 and could be given the death sentence, while Harris was only 16 and could not. An artist's impression of a scene in the courtroom shows a picture of the trial judge. So we recognize him when he appears as the next interviewee, talking about how he learned to respect the law from his father, who was an FBI man in Chicago in the 1930s. As he speaks, the picture cuts to an old black and white movie showing a man in 1930s clothes shooting a rifle. The judge is still talking when a classic movie episode, in which John Dillinger is assassinated, is shown. He says his father was there when it happened and tells with glee how, as a child, he had been told about the people who dipped their handkerchiefs in Dillinger's blood for souvenirs. On the picture, guns are blazing, there is absolute mayhem on screen but no soundtrack, only the voice-over interview with the judge and Philip Glass's music. The sequence is vintage Errol Morris, acutely perceived and wittily executed. It is also a very effective way of underlining the casual attitude to the death penalty that prevails in the state of Texas, a penalty that could be handed down to the unfortunate Randall Adams.

Adams was convicted in May 1977, on the basis of evidence given by David Harris and two other key witnesses who came forward very late in the day and perjured themselves. He was still in jail in December 1986, when Errol interviewed David Harris about the murder, for the last time, on sound only. The final shots in this richly cinematic film are of a cassette recorder, filling the frame and filmed from every conceivable angle. The starkness of the image makes the content of the interview even more shocking.

EM: Is he innocent?
DH: Did you ask him?
EM: Well he has always said he is innocent.
DH: There you go. Didn't believe him huh? Criminals always lie.
EM: Well what do you think about whether or not he's innocent?
DH: I'm sure he is.
EM: How can you be sure?
DH: Because I'm the one who knows.
EM: Were you surprised that the police blamed him?
DH: They didn't blame him. I did. A scared 16-year-old kid. Sure would like to get out of it if you can.

The interview ends with Harris asserting that Adams is probably only in jail because he would not give Harris a place to sleep for the night after he had helped him when he ran out of gas.

A final caption reveals that Adams has been in jail for 11 years. David Harris is on death row in Huntsville, Texas for a murder he committed in 1985. Material recorded for *The Thin Blue Line* was introduced as evidence at an appeal by Randall Adams. The witnesses who lied were proved to be perjurers and Randall Adams was finally set free.

Mr Death (2000) is another film which caused a great deal of controversy. It is subtitled *The Rise and Fall of Fred A. Leuchter Jr.* The opening credit sequence owes something to the Hammer House of Horror genre of movie making. The music, composed by Caleb Sampson, is pure Ealing Studios, circa 1955. A series of images, intercut with black flash frames, show what looks like a mad scientist's laboratory lit up by the lightning that comes with an electric storm. It is obviously a set, elaborately dressed and lit. Almost subliminally, we see a man is sitting there. This must be Mr Death. You get the feeling that Errol and his regular collaborator, production designer Ted Bafaloukos, had a lot of fun putting this elaborate pastiche together.

In the last shot in the sequence, a light shines directly on the man and we see him more clearly, albeit briefly. The picture cuts to black for a full five seconds. Then, we see a man's eyes reflected in the mirror of a moving car. He is wearing glasses. It is the man we just saw in the laboratory. Cut to a hand on the driving wheel. These two shots are in black and white. Soothing, contemporary music plays over the pictures and the man's voice-over begins. He says, 'I became involved in the manufacture of execution equipment because I was concerned with the deplorable condition of the hardware that's in most of the state's prisons, which generally results in torture, prior to death.' Cut again, this time to colour footage, back of head shot, the driver suddenly seems like a rather ordinary-looking fellow. He carries on talking. 'A number of years ago I was asked by a state to look at their electric chair. I was surprised at the condition of the equipment and I indicated to them what changes should be made to bring the equipment up to the point of doing a humane execution.'

A humane execution? Who is this man and what sort of a world is Errol Morris inviting us to join him in? When I spoke to him, Errol asked the questions himself:

> What is going on in Leuchter's head? He has a whole set of beliefs which one could honestly describe as being utterly repellent. He is in love with the death penalty. I think that is the best way to describe it. He loves execution devices. Loves them. And he has become a Holocaust denier. One question I have, is he for real? Is this just some whacky joke or has he really invested in these beliefs? Is he an anti-Semite or a Nazi, who is this man? And is it possible to hold a set of utterly wrong, ridiculous, pernicious beliefs and still imagine oneself to be a good guy?

And this is where I suddenly begin to understand why this philosopher/film-maker wanted to make this film. He says:

> It is an endlessly interesting story to me because people, after all, do generally believe in their own rectitude, do not think of themselves as bad people or evil agents. They see themselves as acting from the best of all possible motives. Leuchter sees himself as having a collection of genuine heroic traits. He is the Florence Nightingale of Death Row. He is Galileo besieged by the forces of repression and ignorance. A true scientist. People said that they were appalled by my suggestion that Leuchter could be an example of Everyman. I loved the idea.

In the early part of the film, we are invited into the life of this 'true scientist'. He talks directly to camera, in the style Errol Morris has made his own. He talks about his research, his experiments and his quest to perfect the art of killing prisoners humanely. While the to-camera interviews are always static, the camera roams around him in other scenes, often tilting at an extreme angle, suggesting the off-centre view of the world that Leuchter holds. In one truly bizarre sequence, he talks about his health routine. It starts with him addressing the audience directly, 'I have often been asked, generally by some kind of adverse party, whether I sleep at night, or how well I sleep at night. My answer is always the same. I sleep very well at night and I sleep with a comforting thought, knowing that those persons who are being executed with my equipment have a better chance of having a painless, more humane and dignified execution.' The picture cuts to a silhouette shot, a hand pulls down a handle, the sounds are reminiscent of the echo in a prison hall. The next shot is a close-up of a spoonful of coffee. So, maybe it was the lever on a coffee machine we saw, not an execution after all.

Errol and cameraman Peter Donahue at Auschwitz-Birkenau

The film now moves, visually, into the style that is pure commercial advertising. Turn the sound down and you are looking at a slick, beautifully produced cinema advertisement. The sound is something else. Leuchter, in voice-over, is saying he loves coffee and it does not bother his ulcer. He tells the story about how he went to see his doctor years ago and was asked how much coffee he drank a day. He said 40 cups. The doctor repeated the question, thinking he was joking. He was not. The doctor then asked how many cigarettes he smoked in a day. He said six packs. The doctor told him he should be dead. Now Fred is sitting at a counter in a café; he is talking about a woman who came into his life. She was a waitress and he was a good tipper. The woman's voice takes over. She says he came into the café on his way to the gun club. He taught her to shoot. This is the woman who married him.

They had only been married a month when he took her to Poland, the only honeymoon she had. They stayed at the Auschwitz Hotel, once the headquarters of the German officers who ran the infamous wartime concentration camp. A man called Ernst Zundel had invited Fred to carry out some research for him. Zundel was a Holocaust denier who was on trial in Canada as a result of his publication, 'Did Six Million Really Die?' Described in one of the film's captions as 'Revisionist Publisher/Broadcaster', he says in an interview that you cannot just open up a phone book and find an expert on gas chambers. 'Fred Leuchter was our only hope.' So Fred went to Auschwitz to take samples from the walls of what he called 'presumed gas chambers' to test later and establish whether any trace of cyanide gas could be found in the fabric of the buildings. His every move was recorded by a Canadian video cameraman. His wife of one month, Carol, was given the job of lookout, standing in the doorway in the freezing cold. Fred did not want to get caught violating these internationally sensitive historic sites.

Leuchter made detailed drawings of the buildings and kept notes also. These, together with the video footage, were produced in evidence at the trial of Zundel. Fred sent his samples, chiselled from the walls of the Auschwitz gas chambers, to a laboratory for testing for traces of cyanide gas. The lab found no traces, not surprisingly, because, as one of the laboratory experts explains later in the film, the samples were taken from too deep into the wall faces. Fred stood by his findings and for a time became internationally notorious, the expert witness defending the Holocaust deniers.

It is in this section of the film that it seems to depart from the integrated style and form that it had at the beginning. Understandably, use is made of the roughly shot video footage showing Fred at work in Auschwitz, which was produced in court. This is necessary because it had been exhibited as evidence, but it jars slightly because it is visually less stylish and imaginative than the camerawork in the early parts of the film. More surprisingly, however, this clever and elegant film now makes an unlikely gear shift and becomes, just for a while, something else. A historian, Robert Jan van Pelt, appears, talking to camera, saying how important it was for him to follow in the footsteps of Leuchter and to check his every result, his every move. This is a standard device, familiar to news or current affairs televison audiences. The expert witness, the voice of reason, is there to provide the other point of view, what we used to call 'balance'. He makes an efficient job of proving that the physical and documentary evidence for the truth of the historical claims about the murder of millions during the Nazi Holocaust are verifiably and demonstrably true. The sequences with him are skilfully conceived and edited, but for a while Leuchter is no longer the dominant voice in the movie.

The film now introduces a number of voices. As we learn that the Canadian court has brought in a verdict of guilty, other witnesses, for and against the line that Fred has espoused, appear. While his own star seems to be on the rise, he is invited to attend meetings of extreme right parties in other parts of the world; other voices condemn and dismiss him. This part of the film combines interviews, archive film and simple graphics. For Errol Morris, this is close to conventional documentary television in its approach, but he clearly finds it necessary to make the point and clarify the storyline.

When Fred does return to dominate the film again, the glorious sense of surreality combines with a sad, almost tragic, sense of pity for a man who got it so wrong that he wrecked his own life. Again addressing the audience directly, he tells how he cannot get work because of his testimony in Canada. In a moment of almost unbelievable dislocation from the attitudes of normal people, Fred explains that because prison authorities would no longer employ him, he was reduced to putting an unfinished device, a lethal injection machine, up for sale in the *Want Advertiser*. After a lot of negative publicity, he says that the Attorney General had to announce that it was not illegal to sell such a machine. So Fred, still talking to camera, says that if any of us, the audience, would like to buy half a lethal injection machine, we should contact him.

At the end of the film Fred is in California, having gone there with the offer of a job which did not materialize. His wife has left him, he is totally broke, has had his rental cars taken away from him, his hotel room has been locked up with all his belongings in it. He is wandering along the side of a busy motorway when the voice of British Holocaust denier, David Irving, is heard. Irving says of Leuchter's research at Auschwitz, 'It was an act of criminal simplicity. He had no idea of what he was blundering into.'

I asked Errol why he felt it necessary to include the fact-based historian or, for that matter, the interviews both for and against the Holocaust argument. Surely every halfway conscious human being on this earth knows all about the Holocaust and only a tiny bunch of weirdos doubt that it happened? He explained. Before the film was finished, he showed it to students at Harvard. (This was before the 'balance' material had been included.) He says that some of the students asked why Leuchter had not found trace cyanide and wondered if he could be right. 'Some people watch films in an uncritical fashion and one has to exercise caution for that reason alone. I wanted people to think about Fred's self-deception, the nature of his delusion. If people didn't see it clearly, the whole purpose of the movie would be lost. So the clarification, if you like, was re-proving something that had been proved many times before.' He says that the students, looking at the unfinished film, were asking a legitimate question. 'Maybe not politically correct but legitimate.'

Errol says that at the end of the student screening he decided it would be morally indefensible to release a movie like this, where there was any room for doubt. He says, 'The question was legitimate, so I examined it. I am a Jew. Have I ever entertained doubts that poison gas was used at Auschwitz. I am terribly sorry but no, I have not. Yet I put this movie together about this man who doubted the Holocaust and some people thought I was endorsing his view.' He says, with some irony, 'I thought, this is not good.' And he adds, 'I often joked that in my next film I would prove that the earth was round and that there were heavier than air flying machines.'

A Brief History of Time (1992) considers the life and work of the brilliant physicist and writer, Stephen Hawking. It was inevitable that this man and his philosophy would interest Errol, with his scientific background and his fascination with what he describes as a character's internal space, their mental landscape. Hawking contracted motor neuron disease as a young man and has been confined to a wheelchair for many years. He gradually lost the use of his voice and now communicates to the world through a computer. The movie is based on Hawking's best-selling book of the same name.

Errol read the book on the plane, flying over to meet Hawking at his home in England. He was delighted by the book, which he says is not really a pedagogical work, it is a romance novel about Hawking's life and work. He says that he does not like psycho-analytical biography, where you provide some reductionist explan-ation of why people are the way they are. However, he was fascinated by the way Hawking made those connections himself. In the book, Hawking writes about his now famous scientific theory about the black hole. Errol says, 'This region of space/time from which no information can escape, cut off from the rest of the universe, when he writes about this, is he talking about himself?' He says the book is full of reflections and metaphors and illusions that are so much a part of Hawking, the man, that he knew he was going to enjoy playing with them in his film.

The film opens with a starry night sky. Hawking's voice, an almost sci-fi delivery because it is communicated through a computer, asks, 'Which came first, the chicken or the egg? Did the universe have a beginning and, if so, what happened before then? Where did the universe come from and where is it going?' So far, so regular science programme. Except that, in the middle of the voice-over, superimposed on the starry sky is an animated shot of a chicken's head. The film has hardly got going and Morris is already playing. We now see Stephen for the first time. Only his eyes, wearing spectacles, an impossibly young-looking man. He is clicking on a mouse, staring at a computer screen, which is responding to his instructions.

The next sequence features Hawking's mother, an admirably stoical woman with a striking resemblance to her son. She too has one of those 'forever young' faces. She is saying how lucky the family have been; everybody has disasters but they have survived. She goes on to tell how she bought a book at Blackwells in Oxford while waiting for Stephen to be born. It was an astronomical atlas. How prophetic, a sister-in-law said later. She talks about the beauty of the night sky when she was able to ride in a train across one of the London bridges when the bombing had stopped – this was in the middle of the Second World War. She describes lying on the ground at home, looking through a telescope at the night sky. She says, 'Stephen always had a strong sense of wonder and I could see how the stars would draw him – and further than the stars.'

In the middle of the sequence with Stephen's mother, there are two evocative archive photographs: one, right of frame, his father, holding him as a baby; the other, left of frame, the mother in identical pose. Stephen's voice runs over these classic family album shots. 'How real is time? Will it ever come to an end? Where does the difference between the past and the future come from? Why do we remember the past but not the future?' These few opening minutes are brilliantly conceived, combining the personal and the theoretical, the domestic and the scientific, drawing in to the picture even the most resistant of viewers, many of whom would surely never have considered reading a scientific book about the origins of the universe. In my view, it is the decision to foreground the mother which makes this film not only intellectually stimulating – which it was bound to be with a hero like Hawking – but also really accessible to a popular audience. It is not a pure science film, it is also a film about the heroic struggle against terrible odds of a very courageous man. Somehow, it is the philosophical acceptance of his fate and the pride in his achievement by his mother that makes the whole story more moving and altogether more human. At one point, talking about Stephen, she says to camera, 'He does believe intensely in the power of the human mind . . . Why shouldn't you think about the unthinkable? He's a searcher.' Errol says that, after a screening of the film, Stephen said to him, 'Thank you for making my mother a star.'

Of all the Morris documentaries, this is the most highly stylized. This is partly because of the logistical problems, but also because it seems to suit the spirit of scientific challenge that pervades the film. Errol says that when he was discussing the movie with his team before they started he said, 'What if we made a documentary without a single "real" image?' (These are my inverted commas, by the way, not his.) The first decision was how to film Stephen, described by Errol as the first non-talking talking head. It seemed obvious that the task of interviewing him would not be the same as the task of filming him. A very unusual challenge. Errol decided that they needed to create a 'dictionary' of Stephen Hawking shots with different lighting and different angles. The other challenge was writing the text with Stephen for the voice-over. They put together a script from things he had written and interviews Errol had done with him. They already had his voice recorded on a computer in Cambridge, Massachusetts, where Errol lives and works. (Hawking refers to this town as the pseudo-Cambridge, a typically British joke at the expense of the *arriviste* American universities. Hawking is an alumnus of Cambridge, England, having graduated originally from Oxford, of course.)

They recreated Hawking's office in the studio, copying accurately his real space, including the Marilyn Monroe poster, which surprised me. All the other interviews are conducted in sets, made up and built by designers. All the houses, all the offices are studio built. When I heard this it came as rather a relief, because my recollection of scientists' offices is that they look nothing like that. The men are shot in sharp focus with the background visible but not obtrusive. The eye concentrates on the person speaking; just as well since most of the time they are asking for a lot of concentration, at least from the non-scientists in the audience.

Morris plays with imagery, as he always said he would. There are recurring ideas, used metaphorically, to emphasize a point. The map of the solar system, where stars are represented by tiny pearls, first appears in Stephen's mother's introduction and is reprised again at the end. A cup and saucer fall onto a tiled floor, breaking into pieces but are later restored, when the action is reversed. This is history, going forward, then backward. Time itself is represented by a flying wristwatch, which turns and turns and floats through space. Naturally, it is a Rolex. The production designer is once again Ted Bafaloukos and the music by Philip Glass.

At the end of the film, echoing the beginning, Hawking takes the floor. He says:

> *If we do understand a complete theory of the universe, that should, in time, in broad principle, be understandable by everyone, not just a few scientists, then we should all, philosophers, scientists and just ordinary people, be able to take part in the discussion of why it is that we and the universe exist. If we find the answer to that, it would be the ultimate triumph of human reason. For then we would know the mind of God.*

Errol's Academy Award-winning film *The Fog of War* is, on the surface, a simple enough construct. It consists of a long interview with Robert S. McNamara, who was United States Secretary of Defence under Presidents John F. Kennedy and Lyndon B. Johnson. The interview is interspersed with archive film. McNamara had never given an interview before and now, in his old age, he talked frankly and revealingly about some of the major events in recent American history and the pivotal position he held in the US government. As pure history, it is fascinating but, as always with Errol Morris, it is much more complex than that. Through the story of McNamara, Morris is exploring themes that have always fascinated him, big themes, like the nature of good and evil and mankind's endless capacity for self-deception.

Of course, the film was controversial. Morris was taken to task for only interviewing McNamara. He says, 'I always wanted to make a movie with just one person. You're not supposed to make a movie with just one person.' He says that he had been deflected from his original idea, in *Mr Death*, of making a film around a single interviewee. In *The Fog of War*, he achieved that ambition. He tells, with some amusement, about one of the challenges he received after *The Fog of War* was premiered. 'I was asked by a journalist at the New York Film Festival if I was aware that I had only interviewed one person.' He hesitates before repeating his considered answer, 'I said, "Yes. I was aware of that."'

Talking to him about this whole issue, I was reminded of his pleasure in that mischievous Marques quotation: 'I didn't know you were allowed to do that.' He goes on to explain his reasons for deciding 'to do that'. He says of the McNamara film, 'It's not balanced. Not balanced, by choice. In fact, I'm not even sure that I believe in balance. I'm pretty sure I don't. I'm not sure what it means. Is it a way of avoiding controversy, of showing you're open-minded? A way of actually saying nothing, under the guise of saying something?' In my view, the film does, in fact, have a balance, an internal balance which comes from McNamara himself, gently encouraged by the voice-off questioning from Morris. Looking back 'in tranquility', at the age of 85, he talks with great candour about the eventful times he lived through and questions his own role in some of the most momentous events in contemporary history. Like the fire bombing of Tokyo by US forces towards the end of World War II, which killed more people than the atomic bombs dropped later by the western allies. Like the Cuban Missile Crisis of 1961/2, which brought the world to the brink of nuclear war. Finally, the Vietnam War, with its carnage on both sides and the chemical warfare practised by the United States with the use of napalm and Agent Orange.

Errol rarely asks questions on camera in his films, but in this one we hear his voice quite often. The voice has the quality almost of a heckler at a political meeting. Unlike the modulated delivery of the average television journalist, neck-miked and conversational in tone, he sounds as if he is interrupting the flow and being slightly provocative. He says that this was deliberate but a difficult decision to make editorially – how much of his voice to put in. Eventually, the rationale was mostly to do with clarification. He points out that not everybody is familiar with recent American political history. So, when McNamara is talking about the time when the Soviet Union, under Khrushchev, put missiles on Cuban soil, 90 miles from the Florida coast, Errol felt he had to interrupt and ask him, 'But didn't we try to invade Cuba?' and later, 'Didn't we try to assassinate Castro?' He says these questions were there to clarify the situation; in a sense, a reality check for the audience. 'It was important to remind the viewer that the Soviet Union did not put missiles into Cuba for no reason.'

A regular feature of Errol Morris's work from the beginning has been his refusal to conform to the documentary convention of interviewees looking off camera, to right or left, apparently addressing a person the audience never sees and rarely hears. He has even invented a system which he calls the Interrotron, a way in which the interviewee can look directly at the camera while also seeing the image of the person conducting the interview. This has the effect of having the interviewee apparently addressing the audience directly, while the traditional technique appears to exclude the audience in some way from a conversation on which it is merely eavesdropping. At the same time, the Interrotron allows the director to maintain eye contact with the interviewee, and this was particularly important in the conversation with Robert McNamara, a man who appeared, perhaps for the first time, to be examining his conscience and his life's work.

In another significant way, this film is different stylistically than some of the other movies. While in earlier films he often used fades to black – often long enough, I am sure, to cause moments of panic in transmission control rooms when they are shown on television – in this film he regularly uses the jump cut. It is as if he is drawing attention to the form he has chosen, in a sense deliberately interrogating the form itself. Right at the beginning, in the pre-title sequence, McNamara is asking, 'Is this map at the right height, is that alright for the television people?' After the titles he is having a conversation with the offscreen film-maker. He says he knows 'the sentence' can be cut to explain what he means to say. We don't know what he is talking about and we never find out. He asks is that OK. Errol's voice off camera says, 'Go ahead.' Often he is filmed with more headroom than is acceptable in conventional shooting. At other times there is more space on the left or right of frame, giving a sense of imbalance to the picture. These are all deliberate editorial decisions to do the things you are not allowed to do.

Some people questioned Errol's non-judgemental attitude in his interviewing of McNamara and said that he should have been more aggressive. I am quite sure that it would have been a waste of time to do that. McNamara is a brilliant man and highly defended emotionally. Errol's technique paid off. He explains what actually happened, 'Out of nowhere, McNamara makes connections. Self-serving as this may sound, I do not believe these connections would have been made if I had not adopted a non-adversarial point of view.' I do not think that is self-serving and I am sure he is right.

One of the most shocking episodes in the film, for me and the friends with whom I first saw it, was the description of the fire bombing of Tokyo in 1945, at the end of the Second World War. People of my generation, the baby boomers, who grew up after the war into what was hoped would be a permanent peace, are reasonably familiar with the moral arguments about the Vietnam War. Many of us were active at the time, demonstrating, lobbying, helping draft dodgers to escape from the USA. So I am still moved by the powerful emotional punch of hearing the presidential tapes from Johnson's Oval Office, recently declassified, with McNamara trying to be diplomatic in his disagreements with an increasingly bellicose LBJ. Or the fascinating discussions about the escalation of the war, justified by accounts of attacks on US forces, like the events in the Gulf of Tonkin, some of which later turned out to be false. The details of the Vietnam War continue to shock but for me, personally, there is something even more terrible about hearing McNamara's account of what he calls 'The War with Japan'.

I think that this episode incorporates all of the strengths, visual and editorial, of *The Fog of War*. McNamara was a soldier, working under the command of General LeMay. The Second World War was nearly over when this incident happened. McNamara says, 'I was on the Island of Guam in March 1945 and in a single night we burned to death 100,000 Japanese civilians, men women and children, in Tokyo.' A question from the floor – Errol's voice. 'Were you aware that this was going to happen?' 'Well I was part of a mechanism that in a sense recommended it.' McNamara wrote a report analysing bombing operations, particularly the use of the super bomber, the B29, looking at how to make them more efficient. The General in charge decided to use the B29, bring it down low, where it would be more accurate, and fire bomb Tokyo. McNamara says he does not want to absolve himself from blame for what later happened, although he only wrote a report. After the bombing, he attended the debriefing. A pilot complained about the low flying and the loss of his wingman. McNamara describes the General's answer. This was a man of few words. As he describes what the General says, he begins to show emotion. It almost seems as if he will cry. The General said, 'I sent him there. This hurts me as much as it hurts you. But we destroyed Tokyo.' McNamara adds, 'It was a wooden city. We just burned it.' The General argued that American troops would be in danger if Tokyo had not been destroyed.

A feature of the film is the chapter headings, which contain the lessons McNamara has learned from life. This one says, 'Proportionality should be a guideline in war.' The Americans went on to bomb city after city. McNamara says that 67 cities were bombed; each time 50–90 per cent of the population was killed. This was before the nuclear bombs were dropped on Japan. He goes on to speculate about war crimes. He imagines a conversation with his General, 'OK McNamara, how many deaths is proportional?' He says that if America had lost its war in Japan, the two of them might well have been considered to be war criminals. He says you are only a criminal if you lose. This is a moment of extraordinary honesty, coming from a man who some people do believe to be a war criminal.

In many ways the visual elements in this film are fairly standard. None of the impish humour from some of the earlier films is evident here, rightly, given the seriousness of the subject. But as usual with Morris, it is the editing and the graphic work which raises it out of the realm of conventional history films. In the Japanese bombing section, great use is made of contemporary handwritten documents. When McNamara talks about efficiency, close-ups of statistics, lists of meaningless numbers are featured, algebraic calculations, none of them in context, just numbers. Over and over we see archive film of the terrible destruction, the exact place never specified; this is simply edited to increase the emotion level. It is intercut with colour footage from the Japanese campaign of clean-cut American soldiers, pointing at maps of the region and politely chatting to their General. At the end of the chapter, a symbolic sequence, repeated through the film, of dominoes collapsing in tidy lines across a map of Asia reminds members of the audience who are old or educated enough of one of the most pernicious doctrines of the US anti-communist zealots, the 'domino effect'.

Another telling moment in the film is the story of Norman Morrison, a Quaker who burned himself to death under McNamara's window at the Pentagon. McNamara was Secretary for Defence under Lyndon Johnson and the Vietnam War was at its bloodiest. This was a terrible moment for America and especially for McNamara. The story of Norman Morrison, who sacrificed his life as a protest against the war, is deeply moving and McNamara tells it with some feeling. Morrison was holding a baby and he doused himself with petrol. Bystanders begged him to save the child and at the last moment he threw the baby into the crowd and she was saved. His wife issued a statement, McNamara explains. She said that human beings must stop killing each other. Then he says something really surprising. He says he agrees with her. He says, 'How much evil must we do in order to do good?' While he is speaking the picture cuts away to close-ups of three phrases, one after the other: 'Ethical Truths', 'Moral Law', 'Free Will'. McNamara goes on to compare General LeMay to Sherman, who torched Atlanta during the Civil War. They both felt that war was cruel. But LeMay was trying to save the nation and was prepared to do whatever killing was necessary. 'It's a very difficult position for sensitive human beings to be in. Morrison was one of those. I think I was.'

For Errol Morris, this is one of the key moments in the film. Morrison was a pacifist who died in a protest against war, McNamara was running the war from his office at the Pentagon, how could they possibly be alike? But he says he asked himself, 'How can McNamara even say such a thing? Then another thought came. What if he really is like Morrison? What if he really was operating with the best of intentions, in some kind of inner agony? What does that mean? It raises a whole lot of deep questions about the nature of character, about free will, and ethics, ideas at the centre of this story. That is why it engages me in a really powerful way.'

I wondered if Errol felt that the coming of digital technology had affected his work in any significant way. He said it most certainly has. His interviews are different. *The Fog of War* is a good example of this. Every previous interview was on film, but he shot McNamara on 24-frame, high-def. digital video. He says there is a difference:

> *Now an interview that used to be 11 minutes, a 100-foot roll of 35 mm runs 11 minutes, then you have to take the mag off, unload it. Put another roll in. Now interviews can go on forever. I have actually interviewed for 11 hours in one day. The length of the cassette is close to two hours. Although that makes very little difference because you can eject it and put in another one in a matter of seconds, you don't need slates or any of the old apparatus of shooting on film. Also the 24-frame, high-def. Sony system is quite beautiful.*

He also says his films have changed as a result of digital editing. His movie *Fast, Cheap and Out of Control* (1997) tells the parallel stories of a lion tamer, a wildlife expert in search of the African mole rat, a gardener who specializes in topiary and works for a rich and eccentric old lady, and a scientist who designs robots. It is a film which is itself fast, although certainly not cheap, and the central theme for me is the need to control or be controlled. It is a highly entertaining film which nonetheless raises serious questions. It includes many elements pictorially. There is Super8 and standard 8 mm, 16 mm, Super 16, 35 mm. There is material transferred to film from old video cassettes of old movies, also 35 mm filmed off television. It would have been quite impossible to make without digital editing.

In *The Thin Blue Line*, before he used digital editing, he shot the bulk of the film on 16 mm and the reconstructions on 35 mm. There was not a lot of money so, for the edit, they had to do basic reduction onto 16 mm and it looked terrible. It made editing difficult because they were not sure about the quality of the picture. When they saw the final print back on 35 mm, it looked terrific, so it worked out but obviously it was a worrying process. Errol says:

> *The digital editing system gives every form of media an equal vote. It gets down to ones and zeros on the hard drive, so it*

matters not at all where the original material came from – VT, whatever. For the first time you can think about film and VT in a totally different way. You can see them as a kind of artist's palette. I don't believe we will move to all digital, although films will be edited digitally and delivered digitally. You can shoot on Super8 and use it as a kind of texture in a whole range of styles and shapes and forms. Fantastic. It hasn't destroyed film, it has changed the nature of how we use film and film itself has become part of a wider universe of possibilities.

With the exception of *A Brief History of Time*, Errol Morris has produced and raised the funding for all of his films. In that one, he worked, as he puts it, as 'a director for hire' and, although he is proud of the film, he would not want to work that way again. Now he makes commercials in between his major film projects and this helps him to maintain his independence and creative control. This he can do, because he is one of the great stylists of the American cinema and is always in demand. Maintaining creative control is a major issue for all of the film-makers in this book and they have found different ways of dealing with the problem. It can be a real problem, particularly for younger film-makers who do not yet have the status in the industry to help them fight their own corner. Most of the directors interviewed here have discussed the issue and I hope that it will be at least a comfort to rising stars to know that everybody has to find their own way. One way or the other, it will be possible.

FILMOGRAPHY

Gates of Heaven
1978

After reading an article in the *San Francisco Chronicle*, '450 Dead Pets go to Napa', Errol decided to tell the story of two pet cemeteries, one set up by the idealistic Floyd McLure, who placed his venture at the junction of two major highways and the other, set up by the Harbert family, who embrace contemporary market-driven values. McLure's venture fails and the film follows the remains of the dead pets being transported from his cemetery to that of the Harberts.

Vernon, Florida
1982

The film was originally meant to tell the story of people in a small Florida town who cut off their own limbs for insurance money, 'becoming a fraction of themselves to become whole financially' as Errol put it. He had to rethink the project when his life was threatened. The illuminating film he then made reveals the lives of the eccentric residents of a southern swamp town, Vernon, Florida.

The Thin Blue Line
1988

Probably his most controversial film, it was billed as 'the first movie mystery to actually solve a murder'. It is credited with overturning the conviction of Randall Dale Adams for the murder of a Dallas police officer, Robert Wood. It was voted the best film of 1988 in a *Washington Post* survey of over 100 critics. *Premier Magazine*, in a survey of films of the 1980s, described it as one of the most important and influential films of the decade.

A Brief History of Time
1992

A film about the life and work of the brilliant physicist Stephen Hawking, who has spent much of his life in a wheelchair, communicating with the world via a computer. Errol's interviews for the film were published in a book, *A Reader's Companion*, which accompanied the film. It won the Film-maker's Award and the Grand Jury Prize at the Sundance Film Festival. The film appeared on many 'Top Ten' lists for 1992, including *Time*, the *Los Angeles Times* and the *San Francisco Chronicle*.

Fast, Cheap and Out of Control
1997

The film links the fascinating, yet seemingly unrelated, stories of a lion tamer, an expert on the African mole-rat, a topiary gardener who carves giant animals out of hedges and an MIT scientist who designs robots. The film won the Best Documentary Film Award from the National Board of Review, National Society of Critics and Independent Spirit Award. It was also selected as part of the 2000 Biennial at the Whitney Museum.

Stairway to Heaven
1998

The story of Temple Grandin, an autistic woman who designs humane animal slaughterhouses.

Mr Death
(subtitle: The Rise and Fall of Fred A. Leuchter Jr)
2000

The film focuses on Fred A. Leuchter Jr, an engineer from Malden, Massachusetts, who decided to be the 'Florence Nightingale of Death Row' – a humanist whose mission was to design and repair gas chambers, electric chairs, lethal injection systems and gallows. His career and life are ruined after he becomes involved in the world of Holocaust denial. The film appeared on many of the annual Top Ten lists, including *USA Today*, *Entertainment Weekly* and the *Boston Globe*.

First Person
2000
Season One, for the Bravo Network.

First Person
2001
Season Two, for the Independent Film Channel.

The Fog of War
(subtitle: Eleven Lessons from the Life of Robert S. McNamara)
2003

The story of the US Secretary of Defence under Presidents John F. Kennedy and Lyndon B. Johnson. The film includes recently declassified material from the White House, rare archive footage, reconstructions and a score by the Oscar-nominated composer Philip Glass. It has been described as 'a disquietening and powerful essay on war, rationality and human nature'. It won the American Academy Award, 2004, for best documentary feature. It was also best documentary at the US National Board of Review,

Los Angeles Film Critics' Association, the Chicago Film Critics and the Washington DC Film Critics. It was officially selected for the Cannes Film Festival, Toronto Film Festival Tellurdie Film Festival and was the Centerpiece premiere Film of the New York Film Festival.

2   Nicolas Philibert
French sensibility

Nicolas Philibert

Nicolas Philibert says he did not wake up one morning thinking, 'I want to be a documentarist.' It was just that the first film he made happened to be a documentary. He thinks that a lot of things simply happen by chance. He might have gone to film school but, in the days when he was moving into higher education, the emphasis in film school entrance in France was on science subjects and that was not his preferred field. So he went to university, where he studied Philosophy and at the same time started dabbling with film. He worked as an assistant director after graduating, with distinguished directors like René Allio, Alain Tanner and Claude Goretta.

He says:

> *What I like about making documentaries is that I can invent the film, day by day. With a mix of fragility and freedom. It is*

important for me that things are not prepared. The less I know about the subject the better I feel. My point of view is not to teach the viewers something they need to know. I don't want to deliver 'a message'. I want to learn myself, without prejudging. I approach a subject with a certain innocence, naivety.

His first film was co-directed with Gérard Mordillet. Called *His Master's Voice* (1978), a feature-length film shot in black and white, it includes interviews with 12 chief executives of large companies. They talk about the issues that matter to them, like power and self-discipline, the nature of hierarchy and also, of course, this being France, the trade unions and industrial action. This film was shown in the cinemas with no problem but his next project, three hour-long films made for television, got him into trouble. The series was created from material gathered for *His Master's Voice*. The title of the series was *Bosses* and the individual programme titles reveal the nature of the content. 'Confidences sur l'ouvrier' (Secrets About the Worker); 'Un pépin dans la boîte' (A Spanner in the Works); 'La bataille a commencé à Landernau' (The Battle Started at Landernau).

Bosses, too controversial for the contemporary climate, was banned from French state television but, a few weeks after the ban, Philibert got cinema distribution for it. This must have annoyed the 'powers that be'. Thirteen years later, when he had firmly established himself as a major figure in the documentary world, it was finally transmitted on television in France. But in the meantime, he faced a long period – six years – when he did not work in the industry. He says, 'In that period I had many projects. I wrote a book. I wrote a fiction film.' Then with a big smile, he says, 'I had a daughter.' He says it is always easy to say it was other people's fault but he does not blame any one person. However, he tells a funny story about a big producer who liked his screenplay. The movie started as comedy but gradually descended into tragedy. The producer's advice was that he should rewrite the whole thing and make it a complete comedy. This he did. It was all terribly urgent, like most requests from the film industry. He sent in the new script and for three months heard nothing. After four months, he finally saw the producer.

The only comment the man made on the script was, 'Page 142. Why is he riding a bicycle?' The film never got made. Philibert still believes that his first draft was the best. But he says he also learned a lot of important lessons from that period. 'It was a period for introspection. I learned the importance of just being yourself. Stand by your own convictions. Be sincere about what you want to do. Those who want to be cineastes must find their own path.'

In 1985, Nicolas found himself back in the business, this time making sports films and, in particular, mountaineering stories. For the next couple of years, he made films about brave exploits on the mountains, particularly with the great and intrepid climber Christophe Profit. These were beautiful and stirring films, with subtexts dealing with themes like humanity under duress, sheer courage and the extraordinary power of the will. They were popular with the public and won many prizes, but Philibert did not feel that he was fulfilling his potential. Then, in 1990, came one of those chances that he so believes in. He was asked to direct one day's filming at the great Paris museum, the Louvre. The curators wanted to move some huge paintings out of storage to an exhibition room. The paintings, by Charles le Brun, were so big that it took a precise operation involving a number of men. The paintings were wrapped around cylinders and had to be rolled along the corridors, then a special construction had to be built to get them up the stairs.

Philibert wanted to know what happened next. He says, 'So I came the next day and the next. I was fascinated. Behind the scenes at the museum I discovered a universe I didn't imagine. Hundreds of people work there and we never see them. Everybody was busy, beginning the transformation of the Louvre.' They were building the pyramid, building new rooms, transforming the place. He continued to film for three weeks and nobody stopped him. They were all so busy and everyone assumed that he must have permission. After three weeks, he put together some scenes, went to see the director of the museum and confessed that he had been filming all this time. He asked for permission to continue and the director 'with a lot of class', says Nicolas, agreed. He had been able to show what he had already shot and he says, 'It was not like writing a proposal and asking for permission.

We would never have got it. Never.' After that, he shot two days a week for four months.

The film begins slightly mysteriously. The light from a torch is flashing in the dark. Now and then it picks up some detail; it is not obvious what we are looking at. Footsteps echo in an empty corridor. There is the sound of a key, a big, heavy-sounding key, turning a lock. The opening credits begin, intercut with the torch pictures. Now it is obvious that we are seeing fragments of classical statues, eventually detail of a painting, still picked up in the dark. Classical music, violin music, plays on the soundtrack. The music has a vaguely sinister tone, enhancing the drama. Who is holding the torch? Is it a thief? Then, after the title, *La Ville Louvre*, the mystery is solved. Two weary-looking workmen are tramping down a long corridor in the dark, shining their torches to light the way for them. It is dawn and people are starting work at the Louvre museum.

The first scene establishes where the interest of the film will lie. A heavy vehicle is driving into a courtyard at the museum. Workmen are winching up a huge painting, shouting instructions at each other like workmen the world over. The sky is beginning to brighten. The film cuts to an interior shot. A man on roller skates is whizzing down long, empty basement corridors and the camera is chasing behind. There is something surreal about this whole opening few minutes. This theme, the spooky empty corridor with a lone person hurrying down it, recurs from time to time in the film. An evocative image. Corridors have their own place in the history of art and the art of psychoanalysis.

Like all effective documentaries, this one is multi-layered. In one sense, the film could be considered as what used to be called 'a process film', the type of film which follows, for example, a manu-facturing process. We see in some detail the wrapping up and transporting of the large canvases, the number of people involved in the whole procedure, including picture restorers and curators. However, the film is more than that. It has some wonderful human moments and is often very funny. In one scene, a man is trying on a jacket. He is talking to somebody whose voice is off camera. He says he does not want to button up the jacket because it is too baggy. The voice off says, 'What do you mean. It's Yves St Laurent.' Another man has not worn a shirt to work and asks if he can wear his old jumper underneath his coat. He is told, 'We don't want people to think that the staff at the Louvre are badly dressed.' Now the women are trying on their clothes. One of them says she must have lost her trousers, somebody has taken them. The scene is cleverly placed, juxtaposed between more weighty matters as it is. These moments of intimacy constantly bring the film back to the humanity that dwells within the walls of a cultural icon.

Sometimes, the pressure on the staff becomes so obvious that it even seems to descend into something close to farce. Women workers are taken through a fire drill and learn how to use a fire extinguisher, with much laughter and understandable incompetence on display. In another scene, a curator and colleague are labelling and checking exhibits in a vault. This wonderful conversation results.

> She says, 'Haven't you found the Rondini?'
> 'Which one?'
> 'The carrache.'
> 'The carrache is at the marble masons.'
> 'I could have looked for ages.'
> 'And the Bridan? The Titian by Bridan?'
> He stands up, looking puzzled. 'The Titian by Bridan? It must be there.' 'There's one, I don't know.'
> 'The Titian has a beard and a bonnet.'
> 'The one with a beard and a bonnet is marked. The label says Leonardo da Vinci by Moitte . . . the one I mistook for the Titian.'
> 'But we've also got the Moitte. Brought back from Fontainbleau.'
> 'Yes but all these painters look alike.'

In another moment, workers who have been helping to place a huge painting in a gallery, tilting it up against a wall, walk out from behind the picture, left of frame. There seems to be rather a lot of them. Philibert explains that some of the men decided to go round and emerge on the left a second time, knowing that the right side of the picture was out of frame so their little joke would not be spotted, just to test his sense of humour – a test he passed with no problem.

There were four of them in the crew. They never used lights and this gave them a great advantage. So they were mobile and free to go anywhere. I asked Nicolas how he managed to shoot such a good-looking film without lights. He says that they used sensitive film stock and the aperture was often wide open. But perhaps more important, they spent such a long time making the film and got to know the museum very well. He says, 'Little by little you learn. This room has sun in the afternoon but don't shoot there in the morning, it will look ugly.' He says that film-makers often go to the Louvre to make 'didactic films about this artist or that'. They always have lights and a lot of equipment. So they will be accompanied by a curator and guards, in case there is accidental damage to a painting. So they are not so free. He had the freedom to roam at will.

The film took five months to edit. He cut each scene and kept them separate until he had 25, perhaps 30, scenes. Then he assembled the film. He started to shift the scenes around, changing the order. He says it was a bit like working on a puzzle.

It seems that the Louvre is best known to those people with only a vague interest in art for three special pieces. In the latter part of the film, a curator, addressing a crowd of sceptical-looking visitors, explains: 'But the Louvre is like a giant book that you consult more than once, so it is better to have a menu with a wide selection and to come back several times. If the Louvre were only for tourists we'd put Milo's *Venus*, the *Mona Lisa* and *The Regent* alone so as to please everybody. People would be delighted it would be much less of an effort but I think we should show the collections.' Of course, it is a long walk if you want to get around a reasonable amount of the collection in one trip. If any film ever made the case for making the effort, this is it.

La Ville Louvre ends with quick shots of the painting collection and at the end of this sequence we see busts arranged in ranks in a gallery. Then the film cuts to real people, head and shoulders only, the people who have appeared in the film, the staff of the Louvre. They all look into the camera, without expression, like the historic artefacts we have just been looking at, clear-eyed, serious, intelligent faces. It is a telling moment and ends the film as it began, with the people who help to maintain the Louvre as the marvel that it is today. End captions explain the number of people who work there and the tasks they carry out. I am something of a Francophile, so maybe I exaggerate the importance of this closing sequence. But for me, it is very French and represents what I most admire about the French. That is, the public commitment to culture and learning, the easy-going relationships of the featured members of the staff, despite a real mix of racial backgrounds – presumably a result of immigration from 'Greater France' – and the widespread attitude of support and respect for ordinary working people.

The film was well received, enough to facilitate the belated showing of his television series *Bosses* the following year, 13 years after it was banned. Now Philibert was on a roll and he has not looked back since.

His next film, *In the Land of the Deaf*, was released in 1992. Nicolas admits that he had some doubts about tackling this subject. He says:

Like everyone I had prejudice about handicapped people. We look at them with pity and think of them, as it were, through the prism of their handicap. But then I realized that the deaf have their own language and culture. A culture often misunderstood by society, even scoffed at. I made this film to give these people a voice. Making this film made me question everything – my work, my attitudes, my cinema.

The film opens with four people using the deaf sign language to communicate a musical quartet. All four are standing in front of music stands with sheet music in front of them. They interpret the music though hand movements and facial expression. There is complete silence on the soundtrack, which is quite disturbing. Watching the film in the cinema I felt a sense of tension in the audience. When do we ever hear absolute silence? I cannot remember any film in which there is no sound at all for the first few minutes. At first you wonder if there is a fault, then you start to feel a little uncomfortable. Like townspeople visiting the countryside who complain because nature is too noisy, we are having an aural experience which is new. Then the characters clap their hands and we hear sound for the first time.

The next scene shows a young man, talking to camera in sign language, telling how he grew up in a hearing family but everyone communicated perfectly well and he did not feel there was any problem being deaf. His words are translated in subtitles for those of us who do not speak his language. This is another strange experience for an audience accustomed to hearing the words of a foreign language while reading the subtitles in their own. He goes on to say that his mother used to take him to the cinema and he loved it. He decided he wanted to be an actor and went to see a famous director who was a neighbour. The director said to him, 'Impossible, you are deaf. How will you manage with the hearing people?' He says, 'I answered, I can mouth the words, like all the actors in the films. You can see that they are just miming. Somebody else just needs to record the words. But he kept saying no, it's impossible. You have to be hearing to be an actor. That was a terrible disappointment for me.'

Of course, the young man was right. Most movies do post-sync the actors' voices, although they usually record their own words, unless it is a musical, when anything can happen. Personally, I really warmed to the young man when he said that. I find bad post-syncing very irritating in the cinema, often to the point where I cannot enjoy the movie. We discover later in the film that the boy did, after all, grow up to be an actor, so the great director got it wrong.

These two opening scenes are incredibly effective. They catapult the audience into a different world, a different way of thinking. All through the film, new ideas are suggested that makes it an educational experience as well as an entertaining film with some attractive characters. There are a number of scenes in which deaf people are taught to sign and also where children are helped to make sounds so that they can communicate more easily with hearing people. Some of the children are so sweet and one of the teachers, an important character in the film, reminds me of the teacher in *Etre et Avoir*. In an interview that takes place in a café, the only sound a vague background noise, he signs a fascinating fact in a very amusing way. He says that people assume that sign language is universal but in fact it is different in every country. He gives the example of the words 'man' and 'woman', and demonstrates how the French, Germans, Belgians, Americans and Chinese sign these words. He manages to convey cultural stereotypes of those countries' national characteristics at the same time. He says, 'When I go abroad, I meet deaf people in that country. It's a bit difficult at first, but after a couple of days we can be chatting away with Chinese, Africans, Americans. It's easy for us. But for you hearing people, if you go to China,' here he conveys complete confusion just through his facial expression, 'even with a dictionary. A couple of days does for us.'

By this point in the film I am beginning to think that maybe deaf people are better off than hearing people. This seems to me to be a remarkable achievement by Philibert, who has admitted that he had doubts and prejudices when he set out to make the film. However, he has succeeded not only in entering the world of the deaf, but also revealing all kinds of new ideas and attitudes. The film is quite intimate, there are a number of interviews and the director's presence is always felt. He says, 'I don't want to steal images. I am not a thief. My camera is not a surveillance camera, it is more like [this cannot be translated] not *sur*veillance, but *bien*veillance.'

Nicolas worked with a crew in his early years but now shoots by himself. Following the influence which he believes defines his career, of what is best translated into English as 'chance' (*hasard* in French), his whole working pattern was changed overnight. He explains:

> *One day, the cameraman did not come. I had two days to replace him. I had to decide whether to find somebody else or to try and shoot by myself. My assistant cameraman encouraged me. So I tried and liked it very much. I am not a technician and it is important for me to have someone to help with lighting, focus pulling, lenses. To me, framing is very important but I am not interested in the technical detail.*

So he was his own cameraman for the filming of what is probably his favourite film, *Every Little Thing* (1996). This is, he says the story of a film crew and the people who live and work in the psychiatric clinic, La Borde, in the Cour Cheverny region of the Loire Valley. He is very conscious of the dilemmas facing the documentary film-maker working in such a sensitive situation. 'The camera gives you a certain power. The challenge is not to abuse that power.' Dealing with the mentally ill is obviously a difficult task, which worried him in the beginning. He says he was pushed into the film by friends and he was reluctant to do it:

I had scruples about making a film about people who were vulnerable and suffering. What does it mean to go into such a place to film these people? My friends insisted and so finally I went to look. I started to talk to people there and they would ask, 'What are you doing here?' I would explain my scruples and little by little they encouraged me. They told me I had to confront myself also. Some of the inmates there told me, 'Do not be afraid, you cannot manipulate us. We are crazy, not stupid.' And the founding director of the clinic said, 'There is nothing here for you to film but if you want to film the invisible, you are most welcome.'

This was a challenge Philibert could not resist. He makes an important distinction between cinema and television and points out that documentary is often a television form and has journalistic origins. So it has to be 'about something'. He prefers to work for the cinema, where you can get beyond 'the subject' and the film becomes something more 'complex, a metaphor, or a poem, or a philosophy. Then it becomes cinematic.' Filming the invisible was something he had to try.

The film begins with individual shots of people who look in their different ways severely mentally disturbed. Then there is a long scene where a group are rehearsing a theatrical production. Some of them are clearly professionals, others patients in the institution. Now we see workmen, constructing a platform of some sort in the garden. It looks like a stage. Now an interior and Philibert enters the film. Obviously ill patients are talking to the camera, addressing him and we can hear his voice, off mike, replying.

One says, 'Are you filming, Nicolas?' (Voice off, Nicolas replies, 'Oui.')
'Alright, you'll film my papers tomorrow, won't you?' ('If you bring them.')

'Alright Cocolas. I'm being filmed.' The man breaks into a delighted
smile and waves at the camera.
'You're laughing at the things I say, aren't you. *You* are completely
crazy.'

The film cuts between the preparations for the theatrical performance which is about to take place in the grounds of the institution
and the daily life of the patients and staff who live there. As
usual in a Philibert film, there are some funny and even bizarre
moments. In one of my favourite scenes, one of the patients is
working the hospital switchboard and takes a call for 'Severine'.
He explains that he will take a while to find her. The caller is
clearly not understanding what he says. Naturally we assume
that this is because the person on the phone has no faith in the
temporary switchboard operator of a psychiatric hospital. Then it
becomes clear. The caller does not speak French. So the patient
then clearly enunciates in perfect English, 'Do you want to call
back in half an hour? Very good.' It is a classic, reversed roles
comic situation. The obvious question – So who is the clever one
in this conversation?

One scene that certainly challenged my prejudices shows the
inmates helping to prepare lunch. Some of them are working with
knives or sharp instruments. One, chopping up parsley, is rocking
back and forward; later, he bursts into a chirpy song. In charge is
the director, Marie; she is serving up a colourful salad, arranging
it to look attractive. She says, 'It's economical too.' Then, with a
smile, 'Would you like a glass of iced vodka with your starter?'
Another patient is peeling an onion. The camera is close to him;
he turns to it and says, 'I'd like to film things. I'm doing my best.
I pull faces, I can't help it. It's not my fault I pull faces. He's here.
They are taking everything. What's going to be left? There'll be
nothing left for me.' Presumably he is talking about the food. But
maybe not.

Philibert does not go in for explanatory captions of even the
names of his characters in the course of the film itself, so the
story gradually unfolds. We have to work out for ourselves
who does what on the staff. Sometimes it is not clear who is
a patient and who is a worker. So a useful explanatory scene
which follows lunch tells us that the rehearsing that is going on

is leading to a performance of *Operetta* by Witold Gombrowicz on 15 August at 5 p.m. This information is conveyed to staff and patients by somebody they refer to as Doctor. It seems that the people responsible for the funding of the hospital will be invited.

As the film progresses it is obvious that this is an ambitious and complicated costume drama, with everybody being challenged to the limits of their acting and musical abilities. The professional actors and musicians are so bright, talented and generous, not only to the patients but to us, the audience, as well. It was a risk for them to agree to this film being made and that is one of the reasons why I find it very moving. There must have always been a danger that the film could tip over into mawkishness or sentimentality, but it never does. I think that this is partly to do with the observational style of shooting and the lack of artifice in the camerawork and editing. Scenes often run for a long time and there is very little in the way of editorialized cutaways. Philibert, true to form, is not hyping up the emotion or telling the audience what to think.

Tension builds leading up to performance day and, since they are performing in the open air, there is some concern about the weather. The author's wife will be there, a thought that makes people nervous. But the play is a triumph and the audience, including Madame Gombrowicz, is enthusiastic and generous with the applause.

The last word in the film goes to the character who manned the switchboard and cut up the onions. He is the most regularly featured of all the patients and he is interviewed after the successful performance.

He is looking directly at the camera and he says, 'First of all, you are the ones who made me ill.' Pointing directly into the lens, he carries on, 'Society in general, I make no distinctions. And now I'm a little better, thanks also to society. I wanted to give you a word of advice, if I may. Never mention your health to a doctor because he could enslave you. I'm not enslaved here but I am offered up to doctors. My brother deals with it differently. If you mention psychiatry to him he thinks up an excuse to go to the cellar. That's what I wanted to say.'

Nicolas asks him to talk about the performance. It seems that he is reasonably pleased with his own part in it. And he shook the hand of the writer's wife. He was very happy about that. Then he says, 'Marie is on holiday. The director. She deserves it, she worked so hard. Now I'm floating. But I'm at La Borde so I will be alright.' Nicolas asks, 'You feel protected here?' 'Not exactly mothered but we are protected from the outside world. We're here among ourselves. And now you are here among us too.' He is still looking straight at the camera and the unasked question hangs in the air. Who is now among the patients at La Borde? Nicolas and his crew? Or all of us, the audience?

Etre et Avoir (2002) has become one of the most successful documentary films at the box office, worldwide. It has propelled Philibert to international fame. It is, on the surface, a simple enough story of a little country school in a village in the beautiful countryside of the Auvergne. The school has one class only and the village children aged between five and 11 are taught in one room by one teacher, Georges Lopez. Philibert shot the film over a 10-week period. It took a long time to find the right location but, when he did, he started filming as soon as possible, as he always does. He showed the camera and the equipment to the children, talked to them about the filming process and explained to them what he was doing. He says it is important to win their trust, 'I am not here to judge them, especially these children, working so hard learning difficult things, mathematics, grammar, etc., so difficult.' He says he told them, 'We are working here and so are you.' He says it is very important not to overuse the camera. 'If you miss something you wish you had filmed, like an interesting lesson, or maybe you decide against filming because of the light, you know it will happen again in a few days. So just wait.'

Philibert does not expect people to ignore him or his camera and often intervenes directly by asking a question or, occasionally, answering one that has been put to him. He told the children that he was not interested in little ones pulling faces and showing off, but he did not mind if they looked at the camera. In one of the most charming scenes in the film, the children do just that. In the previous scene, the teacher is taking an individual child through a lesson. The film then cuts to a shot of another small child, standing on a chair by a photocopier. The lid is up, he is shouting instructions at another child, out of shot. 'Wait, it is the wrong way round.' The light on the copier flashes. 'It is no good,' says the child on the chair, 'Put it in the bin.' This child is JoJo, who won the hearts of people all over the world when the film was released. The other child – her name is Marie – now comes into shot. She runs towards the camera but cannot get past it. She goes back and they try again. The lid is still open, the light flashes. 'Another failure.' The boy on the chair looks at the camera. 'Let us try to understand.' He is stuffing pages into the copier. The other child urges him to stop now. 'I understand now. It's because there is no more paper.' 'I am doing it upside down.' Now the little girl gets up on the chair and pushes the boy away. 'It's upside down.' He walks away. She says, 'You won't understand either.' She seems to be talking to us, the audience. In my case, she has a point.

This little scene is marvellous and stays in the mind long after the movie has finished. It is impossible not to be touched but also to laugh at the serious way in which these small children try to understand the photocopier. I asked Philibert about the scene. He says it illustrates to some extent the way he works. He does not set anything up but sometimes he might, as he puts it, 'provoke something'. In this case, he had observed the younger children sometimes trying to use the photocopier and not being able to work it, so naturally they would come back in the classroom and ask an older child to help. On this particular day, he saw JoJo and Marie going out of the classroom to the photocopier next door, 'When I saw them, I put the camera in the doorway.' Of course, the children ran into problems straight away. 'But I was in the doorway with my camera so they continued and I had that scene. It was a strategy; I simply provoked a reality. Not invented or re-enacted. A reality.'

Another compelling scene in the film is a different example of Philibert's method of making things happen. The schoolmaster was due to retire soon and Nicolas asked him if he had told the children yet. He said no, not yet. Nicolas asked if he could be there to film that when it happened. The teacher said that was fine, maybe next week. The scene reveals the tact and sympathetic nature of the teacher probably more than any other in the film. He is sitting at a table, surrounded by the older children. The camera roams around, picking up the individual expressions of these children with their so expressive faces. For once they do not look at the camera, their eyes are fixed on the schoolmaster.

He was about to give a dictation lesson but now he says, 'I just realized it's been 35 years since I started giving dictations.' One of the children asks a silly question. 'How many have you given?' 'I don't know, I never counted.' He goes on to say that he will be leaving the school next year. One child makes an 'only in France' threat. 'We will go on strike.' 'No, you won't be here any longer.' These children will have moved on to middle school when he goes. He says that he probably won't be able to stay in the schoolhouse because the next teacher might need it. Perhaps he will live nearby. 'We'll have to wait and see.' It is a poignant moment, the distress of the children obvious, but also the sadness of a man who is clearly a brilliant teacher, reluctant to retire but knowing he must. He has been in the village for 20 years.

This scene is followed by another that seems to have captured the hearts of the most hardened critics and documentarists alike. Starring, once again, is the little boy, JoJo. He has been sent by the teacher to clean crayons off his hands. He claims he is afraid of the wasp in the corridor that is trying to sting him, so he comes back into the classroom with his hands still not clean. He then has to have his forehead and his hands cleaned properly for him by the long-suffering master. The still picture of this lively, mischievous child with his hand up, palms towards the camera, a big grin on his face, is the one that was used to advertise the film all around the world. It has become instantly recognizable, a modern icon, a celebration of hope, youth and education.

Philibert finally joined us in the digital age, after resisting for a long time, when he agreed to try editing *Etre et Avoir* on Avid. He had cut his own films previously on film but now he agreed to listen to the chorus of support for digital editing. He says friends told him it would be easier. He had somewhere between 55 and 60 hours of rushes. He made the first selection at home on VHS, cutting the material to be digitized down to 20 hours. He then started to edit. He had never worked on Avid before and for the first three weeks had an assistant to help him and to teach him how to use the machines. He says that, after a few days, it was quite simple. (Not the experience of many of my students at film school but then, this is Philibert.)

I asked him about the difference between working on film and working on digital. Many people argue that film requires a more disciplined approach. It is expensive so it is not possible to shoot too much and not practical to digitize huge amounts. Film requires discipline. He disagrees, although he acknowledges the argument and its popularity. He says:

> *People tell you that you can save all your different cuts, you can save 200 versions. Some people say you can lose your-self in so many possibilities. I don't think so. You must be strong enough to resist what the machine offers. You can resist. For most scenes I had one version. For some scenes I had two other versions. Just a few. Mostly I had one.*

We discussed the popular argument that digital technology is often responsible for the indecision demonstrated by many documentarists these days, an argument with which I fundamentally disagree. Shooting on DV, I am told, film-makers often shoot in an undisciplined way, with far too much footage. Then in editing, they are indecisive, because they can change their minds as often as they like without damaging the original stock. So, the argument goes, the technology encourages indecisiveness. I asked him, don't you think that the technology is often blamed for the individual film-maker's inability to make a decision. He said, 'Yes, I totally agree with you.' Then, speaking in what sounded like it should be written in capital letters, he said, 'The Technology Is Not Guilty.' I have framed that statement and put it on my office wall.

I also asked him why he made all his films in France. Had he not been tempted, now that he has a worldwide reputation, to stray into exotic foreign locations? He says that there are so many stories around his own house in Paris that he could make a film in the café next door and be happy to do it. He illustrated his point with a story about the French/German channel Arte. They were setting up a series in which they wanted to send recognized film-makers off around the world for each of them to find some new story in some new land. Nicolas said, 'Why? There are so many stories around me. I can make a story about Africa by filming two streets down from my house, where so many African immigrants to France live and trade.' Indeed, he actually has an idea to make a film about an African that he knows in Paris. He is a binman.

If I may allow myself a little luxury here and address directly my many ex-students, who are now living and working all over the world. Please learn this lesson from Nicolas Philibert. Integrity does win out in the end. As he says, 'Know yourself. Never compromise.' He held out, refused to prostitute himself and in the end he is getting the recognition and the rewards he deserves. Let that be an example to you all!

FILMOGRAPHY

Nicolas Philibert was born in 1951 in Nancy. After obtaining a degree in philosophy, he started out as an assistant director, in particular with René Allio, Alain Tanner and Claude Goretta.

His Master's Voice
1978, 100 min, 16 mm, black and white
Co-directed with Gérard Mordillat

Twelve CEOs of large companies face the camera and talk about power, hierarchy, trade unions, strikes and self-management. The image of a future world is gradually sketched out.

With Michel Barba (Richier), Jean-Claude Boussac (Boussac), Guy Brana (Thomson-Brandt), François Dalle (L'Oréal), Bernard Darty (Darty), Jacques de Foucher (Paribas), Alain Gomez (Saint-Gobain Emballages), Francine Gomez (Waterman), Daniel Lebard (Comptoir Lyon Alemand Louyot), Jacques Lemonnier (IBM-France), Raymond Lévy (Elf Aquitaine), Gilbert Trigano (Club Méditerranée).

Produced by INA and Laura productions with the participation of the SERDAV-CNRS and the Centre National de la Cinématographie (CNC). Released in France in February 1979. Distributed by Laura productions.

Bosses
1978, 3 × 60 min, television, 16 mm, black and white
Co-directed with Gérard Mordillat

Three programmes made on the basis of material gathered for *His Master's Voice*: Confidences sur l'ouvrier (Secrets About the Worker); Un pépin dans la boîte (A Spanner in the Works) and La bataille a commencé à Landernau (The Battle Started at Landernau). The three were banned from television but released in cinemas a few weeks later.

Produced by INA and Laura productions with the participation of the SERDAV-CNRS and the Centre National de la Cinématographie. Distributed by Laura productions.

The North Face of the Camembert
1985, 7 min, 35 mm, colour

For the requirements of a scene from the film *Billy Ze Kick*, the young mountaineer Christophe Profit is asked to 'understudy' and 'stand in for' an actor. He has to climb the smooth front of a 200-foot building.

Produced by Les Films d'Ici. Distributed by Hachette/Fox.

Christopher
1985, 28 min, 16 mm, colour

Christophe Profit's '100 per cent solo' climbs (without ropes and without belays) of the west face of Le Dru, a gigantic pyramid 1100 m/3600 ft high, in the heart of the Mont-Blanc massif. Christophe Profit is considered to be one of the greatest contemporary mountaineers.

Image: Laurent Chevallier, Amar Arhab. Sound: Bernard Prud'homme. Montage: Marie H. Quinton. Music: André Giroud. Produced by Maison du Cinéma de Grenoble, with the participation of Antenne 2, Alpa and Sandoz-France.

Grand Prix du Festival international du Film d'Aventure Sportive, La Plagne (France), 1985
Diable d'Or, Festival international du Film Alpin, Les Diablerets (Switzerland), 1986

Prix Cinégramm, Les Diablerets, 1986

Grand Prix et Prix du Public au Festival de Teplice nad Metuji (Czechoslovakia), 1986

3e Prix du Festival International du film de montagne de Grâz (Austria), 1986

Prix du meilleur film d'alpinisme, Festival du film de montagne, Banff (Canada), 1987

Prix du meilleur film d'alpinisme, Festival international du cinéma de montagne de Torello (Spain), 1987

No Problem
1986, 13 min, 16 mm, colour

Clinging to the middle of the mountain like so many spiders, a dozen film-makers and mountain guides busy themselves above the abyss to film Christophe Profit's ascent of Le Dru. Little by little, the director finds himself dreaming of the tranquil seaside holidays he might have had, like so many other nice people.

Image: Laurent Chevallier, Amar Arhab. Sound: Bernard Prud'homme. Montage: Marie H. Quinton. Music: André Giroud. Produced by Maison du Cinéma de Grenoble, with the participation of Antenne 2.

Prix du meilleur reportage de télévision, Festival de la vidéo sportive, Arcachon (France), 1986

Prix de l'Humour, Festival Mondial de l'Image de Montagne, Antibes (France), 1986

Prix de l'Humour aux Journées Internationales du Film d'Aventure Sportive, Annecy (France), 1986

Prix spécial du jury, Festival du film de montagne, Banff (Canada), 1987

Trilogy for One Man
1987, 53 min, 16 mm, colour

The most legendary 'sequence' ever achieved by a mountaineer: on 12 and 13 March 1987, in 40 hours, 26-year-old Christophe Profit managed to climb three of the highest north faces in the Alps, in winter: Grandes Jorasses, Eiger, Matterhorn. But over and above this 'coverage' of the feat, we discover the wings, the story behind the project, the peaks and troughs of the preparations for it, and the personality of the man behind the climbs, a dancer on sheer rock faces, focusing all the energy and reflexes of life itself in his fingertips.

Image: Laurent Chevallier, Denis Ducroz, Olivier Guéneau, Richard Copans. Sound: Olivier Schwob, Bernard Prud'homme, Freddy Loth. Montage: Marie H. Quinton. Music: André Giroud. Produced by Les Films d'Ici, Antenne 2, with the participation of Millet.

Grand Prix des Journées Internationales du Film d'Aventure Sportive, Hakuba (Japan), 1987
Diable d'Or, Festival International du Film Alpin, Les Diablerets (Switzerland), 1987
Grand Prix du Festival Mondial de l'Image de Montagne, Antibes (France), 1987
Prix spécial du jury, Festival international du film d'aventure, La Plagne (France), 1987
Grand Prix du Festival de Teplice Nad Metuji (Czechoslovakia), 1988
Triglav d'argent, Festival international de Kranj (Yugoslavia), 1988

The Measure of the Feat
1987, 23 min, 16 mm, colour

A film arising from *Trilogy for One Man*, about the medical and nutritional monitoring of Christophe Profit during his 'trilogy' and the intensive training period leading up to it.

Produced by Laboratoires Sandoz and Wander, Les Films d'Ici.

Go For It, Lapébie!
1988, 27 min, 16 mm, colour

At the age of 77, Roger Lapébie is the oldest winner of the Tour de France still alive. Half a century has passed since his legendary victory in 1937. Yet Roger still covers more than 200 miles each week by bicycle on the highways and byways of the Landes. The portrait of a great, good-natured cyclist, who declares: 'I love my bike more than I love myself.'

Image: Olivier Guéneau, Frédéric Labourasse. Sound: Freddy Loth, Julien Cloquet. Montage: Nelly Quettier. Produced by MC4, Pathé, Canal+, with the participation of Centre National de la Cinématographie (CNC).

Baquet's Comeback
1988, 24 min, 16 mm, colour

In July 1956, together with the mountaineer Gaston Rebuffat, the actor and cellist Maurice Baquet made the first ascent of the south face of the Aiguille du Midi (3842 m/12,606 ft), a magnificent wall of red granite soaring up like a rampart above the Vallée Blanche (the White Valley) in the Mont Blanc massif.

Thirty-two years later, as if to pay tribute to the memory of his friend Gaston, now deceased, Maurice Baquet once again climbed this mighty crag, suspended between sky and earth, behind Christophe Profit.

Image: Laurent Chevallier, Denis Ducroz. Sound: Olivier Schwob, Bernard Prud'homme. Montage: Marie H. Quinton. Produced by Les Films d'Ici and Antenne 2, with the participation of Sandoz-France.

Grand Prix du Festival Neige et Glace, Autrans (France), 1988
Prix du Public, Festival Mondial de l'Image de Montagne, Antibes (France), 1988
'Best Mountainfilm Spirit', Festival de Telluride (USA), 1989
Prix Spécial du Jury, Festival du film de montagne, Banff (Canada), 1989

Migraine
1989, 6 min, 16 mm, colour

An episode in the '*Et vous, comment ça va?*' (*And How Are Things With You?*) series proposed by Dr Sylvie Quesemand-Zucca.

Produced by La Sept, Les Films d'Ici.

La Ville Louvre (Louvre City)
1990, 85 min, 35 mm, colour

What does the Louvre look like without the public? For the first time, a great museum lets a film crew into its wings: people are hanging paintings, reorganizing rooms and moving works around. Little by little, characters appear and weave together the threads of a narrative. From studios to stacks and reserves containing thousands of pictures, this is the discovery of a city within a city.

Image: Richard Copans, Frédéric Labourasse, Eric Pittard, Eric Millot, Daniel Barrau. Sound: Jean Umansky. Montage: Marie H. Quinton. Music: Philippe Hersant. A co-production with Les Films d'Ici, La Sept, Antenne 2, le Musée du Louvre, with the participation of the CNC and the Ministry of Foreign Affairs.

Prix Europa, 'Best Documentary of the Year', 1990
Prix Intermédia au Cinéma du Réel, Paris, 1990

Released in France in November 1990. Distributed by Cinéclassic. Les Films au Losange have had the distribution rights since summer 2002.

Bosses 78/91
1991, 75 min, video, black and white
Co-directed with Gérard Mordillat

Thirteen years after *Bosses* was cancelled, these images at last appeared on the small screen, in a condensed version.

Produced by INA and Laura productions with the participation of the SERDAV-CNRS and the CNC. Reissued by La Sept.

In the Land of the Deaf
1992, 99 min, 35 mm, colour

What is the world like for the thousands of people who live in silence? Jean-Claude, Abou, Claire, Philo and all the rest, who have been totally deaf since birth or since the early months of their lives, dream, think and communicate through signs. With them we set off to discover that distant land where seeing and touching are of such crucial importance. This film tells their story and gives us a glimpse of the world through their eyes.

Image: Frédéric Labourasse. Sound: Henri Maïkoff. Montage: Guy Lecorne. A co-production with Les Films d'Ici, La Sept Cinéma, Le Centre Européen Cinématographique Rhône-Alpes in association with Canal+, the Rhône-Alpes Region, the CNC, the Ministry of Foreign Affairs, RAI Tre, BBC Television and RTSR.

Sélection officielle au Festival de Locarno, 1992
Sélection au Festival de Yamagata (Japan), 1993
Prix de la Fondation GAN pour le Cinéma, 1992
Grand Prix du Festival de Belfort (France), 1992

Grand Prix du Festival dei Popoli, Florence (Italy), 1992
Grand Prix 'section documentaires', Festival de Vancouver (Canada), 1993
Prix 'Tiempo de Historia', Festival de Valladolid (Spain), 1993
Prix Humanum décerné par l'Association de la Presse Cinématographique de Belgique (Belgium), 1993
Grand Prix du Festival de Bombay (India), 1994
Golden Gate Award, San Francisco International Film Festival (USA), 1994
Prix du meilleur documentaire, Festival de Potsdam (Germany), 1994
'Stephanie Beacham Award', 13th Annual Communication Awards, Washington, DC (USA), 1994
'Peabody Award', USA, April 1998
Prix du Public au Festival du film francophone de Bratislava (Slovakia), March 2004

Released in France in March 1993. Distributed by MKL.
Les Films au Losange have had the distribution rights since summer 2002.

Animals
1994, 59 min, 35 mm, colour

The Zoology Gallery of the National Natural History Museum in Paris was closed to the public for a quarter of a century, leaving hundreds of stuffed animals in a forgotten twilight zone: mammals, fish, reptiles, insects, amphibians (frogs and toads), birds, crustaceans. The film was shot during the renovation work in the gallery (from 1991 to 1994), and describes the resurrection of its strange residents.

Image: Frédéric Labourasse, Nicolas Philibert. Sound: Henri Maïkoff. Montage: Guy Lecorne. Music: Philippe Hersant. A co-production with Les Films d'Ici, France 2, National Natural History Museum (Paris), Mission Interministerielle des Grands Travaux, with the participation of the CNC, the Ministryof Advanced Education and Research, the Ministry of Foreign Affairs, Channel 4, Rai Tre, VPRO and Television Suisse Romande.

Prix du meilleur film de recherche, Festival dei Popoli, Florence (Italy), December 1994
Golden Gate Award, San Francisco International Film Festival (USA), 1995

Released in France in June 1996. Distributed by MKL for Lazennec Diffusion. Les Films au Losange have had the distribution rights since summer 2002.

In a Badger's Skin
1994, 7 min, video, colour

In a workshop in the National Natural History Museum (Paris), a taxidermist undertakes the task of stuffing a badger. This film was earmarked for the renovated Grande Galerie in the NNHM.

Image: Frédéric Labourasse. Sound: Olivier Schwob. Montage: Guy Lecorne. Produced by Les Films d'Ici, National Natural History Museum, Mission Interministerielle des Grands Travaux.

Metamorphosis of a Building
1994, 8 min, video, colour

This film was made for the Grande Galerie in the National Natural History Museum, retracing the major stages of its recent restoration.

Image: Frédéric Labourasse, Nicolas Philibert. Sound: Henri Maïkoff. Montage: Guy Lecorne. Produced by Les Films d'Ici, Muséum National d'Histoire Naturelle, Mission Interministérielle des Grands Travaux.

Family Portraits
1994, 2 min 30, video, colour

Four hundred animal portraits. This film was made for the renovated Grande Galerie in the National Natural History Museum.

Image: Nicolas Philibert. Montage: Guy Lecorne. Music: Pascal Gallois. Produced by Les Films d'Ici, Muséum National d'Histoire Naturelle, Mission Interministérielle des Grands Travaux.

For Catherine
1995, 30 min, video, colour, unreleased

For the 50th birthday of a friend (Catherine), her nearest and dearest, close friends and family file past the camera to wish her a happy birthday.

Every Little Thing
1996, 105 min, 35 mm, colour

During the summer of 1995, faithful to what has now become a tradition, residents and staff at the La Borde psychiatric clinic get together to put on the play that they will perform on 15 August. During rehearsals, the film retraces the ups and downs of this adventure. But over and above the theatre, it describes life at La Borde, everyday life, time passing, trivial goings on, loneliness and tiredness, as well as the moments of merriment, laughter and wit peculiar to certain residents, and the close attention that people pay to one another.

Image: Katell Djian, Nicolas Philibert. Sound: Julien Cloquet. Montage: Nicolas Philibert. Music: André Giroud. Producteur délégué: Serge Lalou. A co-production with Les Films d'Ici and La Sept-Cinéma, with the participation of Canal+ and the CNC, with the backing of the Centre Regional Council, in association with Channel 4, WDR, VPRO, International Film Circuit and Filmcooperative.

Sélection officielle au Festival International de Locarno (Switzerland), August 1996
Grand Prix du Public des Rencontres Internationales de Cinéma à Paris (France), October 1996
Grand Prix du Public au Festival International du Cinéma et des Nouveaux Médias de Montréal (Canada), June 1997
Prix du Meilleur Documentaire au Festival du Film de Potsdam (Germany), June 1997
Prix Spécial du Jury du 11e Festival International du Film anthropologique de Pârnu (Estonia), July 1997
Grand Prix du Festival Amascultura (Lisbon, Portugal), November 1997
Golden spire (Epée d'Or) Festival international de San Francisco (USA), April 1998

Released in France in March 1997. Distributed by MKL for Lazennec Diffusion. Les Films au Losange have had the distribution rights since summer 2002.

Us, France's Illegal Immigrants
1997, 3 min, 35 mm, colour

In support of illegal immigrants, a collective film jointly signed by 200 film-makers and directors, producers, distributors and cinema owners. With Madjiguène Cissé.

Released on 26 March 1997.

Who Knows?
1998, 106 min, 35 mm, colour, fiction

With the students of the 30th class of the Strasbourg National Theatre.

On this particular evening, they decided to gather in their school premises to jointly plan a show project whose theme – or pretext – is the actual city of Strasbourg.

Lighting: Katell Djian. Cadre: Nicolas Philibert. Sound: Julien Cloquet. Montage: Nicolas Philibert, Guy Lecorne. Music: Philippe Hersant. Producteur dèlèguè: Gilles Sandoz. A co-production with AGAT films and Cie, La Sept ARTE, Strasbourg National Theatre.

Programmed on Arte in May 1999. Released in France in September 1999. Distributed by Diaphana.

Etre et Avoir (To Be and To Have)
2002, 104 min, 35 mm, colour

Here, there and everywhere in France there are still 'one class schools' where all the children in one village are taught by the same schoolmaster or mistress, from the very youngest children to pupils in the 'cours moyen 2ème année' (10–11 years). Between introversion and an open-minded attitude to the world, eclectic little bands share their everyday life, for better or for worse. This film was shot in one such school, somewhere in the depths of the Auvergne.

A co-production with Maïa Films, Arte France Cinema, Les Films d'Ici and the CNC, with the participation of Canal+, the CNC, Gimages 4, and the backing of the Ministry of National Education, the Auvergne Regional Council and Procirep.

Sélection officielle, Cannes, 2002 (hors compétition)
Prix Louis Delluc 2002 ('Meilleur film français de l'année')
Prix pour la distribution, Festival de Tübingen (Germany), October
  2002

Prix Tiempo de Historia ('Meilleur documentaire') au Festival de Valladolid (Spain), November 2002

Grand Prix du Festival France Cinéma, Florence (Italy), November 2002

Best Documentary (Prix ARTE), European Film Awards, Rome (Italy), November 2002

Prix 'Humanum' 2002, décerné par la Presse Cinématographique de Belgique (Belgium), December 2002

Prix Méliès ('Meilleur film français de l'année') décerné par le Syndicat français de la Critique de Cinéma, January 2003

Prix des auditeurs du 'Masque et la Plume', France Inter, January 2003

Nominations aux César 2002, 'Meilleur montage', 'Meilleur réalisateur' and 'Meilleur film'. César du 'Meilleur montage', 2002

Prix de l'Association Cubaine de la Presse Cinématographique (Fipresci), 11e Festival du Cinéma français à Cuba, March 2003

Etoile d'Or ('Meilleur film français de l'année') décerné par la presse

Prix du public au 4e Festival du film français à Athènes (Greece), April 2003

Grand Prix et Prix du public du Festival du Film francophone de Bratislava (Slovakia), April 2003

Released in France on 28 August 2002. Distributed by Les Films du Losange.

The Invisible
2002, 45 min, video, colour

Interview with Jean Oury, director of the La Borde psychiatric clinic. Complementary to the DVD edition of *Every Little Thing* (autumn 2002).

Produced by Les Editions Montparnasse.

Emmanuelle Laborit, Sign Shards
2002, 7 min, video, colour

Interview with Emmanuelle Laborit, actress. Complementary to the DVD edition of *In the Land of the Deaf* (autumn 2002).

Produced by Les Editions Montparnasse.

What Drives the Taxidermist
2002, 18 min, video, colour

Interview with Jack Thiney, taxidermist at the National Museum of Natural History, Paris. Complementary to the DVD edition of *Animals* (autumn 2002).

Produced by Les Editions Montparnasse.

3 Paul Watson
Influential innovator

Paul Watson

It is almost a cliché in British television circles to say that Paul Watson is 'the father of reality television'. He rejects the description in a typically robust way. 'How can I be a father to those little bastards?' He is, all the same, an immensely influential figure in the documentary world and I would argue that while he cannot be blamed for 'reality', he is – to continue the analogy – 'father' to the genre known as 'docusoap'. The series he invented and executive produced for the BBC in 1993, *Sylvania Waters*, has been followed up and imitated countless times. (This series is discussed in some detail in the chapter of this book about Brian Hill, who directed it, together with Kate Woods.)

Sylvania Waters is pure documentary in the sense that it is a portrait of real people living their normal lives – a middle class family with a home in a suburb of Sydney, Australia – in spite of the constant presence of a film crew. However, it is edited like a drama serial, with each episode having multiple storylines, some of which are left unresolved at the end of each programme so the audience has to tune in next week to find out what happens. Incidental music is used to enhance atmosphere and the programmes are narrated, not by a professional voice-over expert but by a member of the family. Although the whole series is real, nothing staged, it still feels like we are watching a drama or, more specifically, a 'soap opera'.

'Reality television' is a totally different genre. Programmes like *Big Brother* place real people in unreal situations, where they are then manipulated by the production team in some spurious, pseudo-scientific attempt to find out how they will behave when faced with unlikely challenges. It is light entertainment, relying to a large extent on the fact that the participants will make fools of themselves. As a genre it owes more to those Japanese game shows, in which people are deliberately humiliated so the audience can laugh at them. Documentary it is not. And Paul Watson is right to argue strongly that it has nothing to do with him.

Nonetheless, he always was and remains a controversial filmmaker who many people accuse of being unfair to his subjects, because his films are always searingly honest and people reveal so much about themselves, often long-held secrets. I put it to him that he achieves relationships with people which have more in common with good psychiatrists or, for some people, sympathetic priests. He did not like the word priest. But he agrees that people feel that they have to tell him everything, however damaging the revelations might be. He said, 'I'd love to have my own chat show.' He laughs, 'Well maybe my films *are* chat shows.' He is selling himself short in that quote. While he is without doubt a brilliant interviewer, he is also a great craftsman, particularly in his use of sound, his pictorial sense and his skill in directing a complex edit.

This chapter will concentrate on the later films, those made in the digital age, when he decided that he no longer wanted to work with film crews and preferred to do his own shooting on DV. However, because I think these films have to be read in the context of a whole long and distinguished career, I will first briefly sketch in his background and talk in general about the early work.

Watson was something of a tearaway as a child and could, he says, have taken a very different road in life if he had not been lucky enough to go to Altrincham Grammar School in the north of England, which turned him around. He went on to art school in Manchester then, after an adventurous time in Mexico and the USA, came back to the UK to the Royal College of Art, where Iris Murdoch was his tutor and David Hockney his contemporary. His conversation is spattered with references to art. When talking to young film-makers he says:

> *You need to be in control of your craft. To artists I say, 'When you can draw a face with the eyes, the mouth and the muscles in the right place, then draw me a face with three eyes.' I say the same to young film-makers. Show me you can make an informational film before you break the rules, before you start to experiment.*

Making a Paul Watson documentary is like portrait painting, he says.

> *I'm not Annigoni, painting the Queen. I'm more Graham Sutherland painting Churchill – a nasty, venal, bad-tempered bugger of an old man who he caught brilliantly. Churchill's wife took the painting, paid for it and then burned it. I suppose that's a compliment to Graham Sutherland. If you are going to make documentaries, you must expect to lose friends. You are making a portrait of a subject which may not be the way people want to see themselves in the mirror when they shave.*

Paul first attracted national press attention in 1974, when his series *The Family* was transmitted by the BBC. It followed over the course of 10 weeks the life of the Wilkins family of Reading. It was watched by huge audiences and, as the weeks went by, attracted a great deal of attention from the press. He says that it was a breakthrough for the BBC in the sense that, before that time, BBC production was dominated by middle-class producers with middle-class values, which they expressed in rather patronizing tones in commentary or pieces to camera. He wanted to give a free, unrestricted opportunity to this ordinary working-class family to express themselves honestly, in public.

If his criticism of the BBC in those days is legitimate, they were clearly behind the times. Throughout the 1960s, on independent (commercial) television, 'fly-on-the-wall' programmes were being made, often with working-class people as their subjects. Granada Television, which took pride in its northern English base in Manchester, advertised itself as 'From the North'. Granada had a particularly distinguished record in this field. At the same time, in the United States and France, similar subject matter was being explored by distinguished film-makers like Fred Wiseman, the Maysles Brothers and Jean Rouch. I would also argue that making films about working people was very much in the tradition of the British Documentary Movement, starting in 1929 with Grierson's *Drifters*, a film about an ordinary Scottish fishing community.

The Family was a breakthrough, in my view, for an altogether different reason. It was filmed, edited and transmitted on a weekly basis. A location director, Franc Roddam, supervised the shooting and three cutting rooms edited the footage as it came in, supervised by the series director, Watson. I commissioned and co-executive produced a series myself in 1992 – *Real Life* – which followed the lives of four Scottish families. It was also filmed and transmitted in the week of filming. However, living in the digital age, we had the advantage of being able to shoot on lightweight video and edit on Avid. Even so, it meant many late nights and a large degree of genuine stress for the production team and the broadcaster. (See Chapter 12 for details about this project.)

Real Life was made almost 20 years after *The Family*. Watson's series was on film, involving all the problems of shooting film: picture and separate sound, in low light, and processing, editing on Steenbecks, neg cutting and printing, and post-production sound. Not to mention the fact that the production team would have to go through the laborious approval procedures by television executives that continues to this day at the BBC. Until we made *Real Life* in Scotland, *The Family* stood alone as an extraordinary experiment in documentary, creating as it did a bang up-to-date observational documentary serial. To a large extent, I think, this is because the technology was not available until the 1990s to easily make such a series, without a huge production team and budget. But I also think that the will was not there, particularly at the BBC, which continued until quite recently to perpetuate the middle-class values that Watson has always kicked against.

After *The Family*, Watson made a number of successful films for the BBC and picked up numerous awards in the process. However, one film stands out in this period. It is called *The Fishing Party* (1987) and in many ways is the best example of his early work. He sees this film as part of a pattern in his productions, because it is, on the surface, about a relatively innocuous subject (four wealthy young men from the south of England go fishing in Scotland), but it is really about 'the times we live in'. The film was criticized internally at the BBC for being a blatant attack on the Thatcher government. Watson accepts this description, with some pride.

The Fishing Party is quintessentially a Watson film and all of the praise which he rightly routinely receives and all of the criticism he also regularly suffers can be demonstrated in the reactions of the industry to this film, even today. The film follows the friends as they enjoy their holiday. They fish and shoot – one actually shoots at an endangered species of bird, on camera – and as they carry on with the trip they eat fancy food and drink a great deal of alcohol. In one telling image, a boatman eats his sandwich as the four gorge themselves on luxury fare. Watson always says the cutaways are what matter. They provide 'the commentary'.

The trip itself is edited with background scenes of the individual men at home, at their clubs, at work. They are all wealthy and obviously politically to the right. Some of their statements are quite shocking to a liberal audience. One says the only reasons for getting married are to have children and to have someone to drive you home when you are drunk. He also says, in voice-over, that he thinks capital punishment is a good idea. Ninety-something per cent of people who were hanged were guilty and the ones who were not, who cares?

The film is regularly counterpointed with extracts from the radio news, recorded contemporaneously with the filming. So, in one scene, the aristocratic figure with the stately home walks across his land with a gun under his arm. The radio voice-over tells of riots in a desperately poor, mostly black, suburb of London. All through the film, the political and economic context is spelt out in this way. There is no doubt as to where the film-maker's sympathies lie. He says of the radio commentaries: 'These are markers for history. Otherwise the film will not be readable, it will have no context in 50 years' time. It will just be a film about four amiable buffoons.'

When it was transmitted, many people accused Watson of 'setting up' the subjects, not being straight with them, making them look callous and cruel. In fact, the four saw the film before transmission and approved it. Watson explains, 'I don't usually show films in advance but this one I did. They were making a lot of money. They were able to go to law . . . or pull the film at any moment.' He says he had a pleasant evening with the men and they made no complaints, beyond joking among themselves as to who had been the least discreet. Then the film was shown on television and friends complained to them that the film-maker had taken advantage of them, they had been made to look ridiculous. There was a great deal of debate about the film and much criticism. Even the Prime Minister joined in.

The Fishing Party is usually the film which comes up when the question of being honest with your contributors is raised. But Watson says he only makes films about people he likes and he did like the people in that film. 'They make you laugh, even when you know you shouldn't . . . The people I make films about know that the film is them. Even if they want to sue me. If they want to hit me. I get them to be who they are. If they start performing, I stop filming.' He tells people in advance, in long conversations, what the film is about but – importantly – he does not tell them 'the subtext'. He says, 'Partly because sometimes I don't know. I am working it out in the cutting room.' He agrees that he does manipulate but not while filming, only in the cutting room. Another artist's analogy serves to explain what he means. 'Cezanne paints orange that sits back in the landscape. All art students will tell you that orange sits in the foreground. But it depends on what you put next to it. I do that with editing.'

After a period of executive producing at the BBC, accompanied as usual by numerous fallings out with the people he calls 'the suits', Watson left and went to work for the ITV company, Granada. This began a partnership with documentary executive John Willis, himself a distinguished film-maker, now one of the most respected and principled executives working in television, anywhere in the world. For purposes of this story, it is important to add that Willis is brilliant at handling 'difficult talent' and he is one of the few bosses for whom Watson has a genuine respect and affection. The two of them have worked together, through various take-overs and restructuring in British television, first at Granada, then at Anglia/Meridian, then Granada again, after it acquired the afore-mentioned companies. Later, after a period when John went to the United States to work for WGBH Boston, Paul worked for a while for Channel 4. When John came back to the UK to work, he invited his old friend and colleague to come and executive produce a series with young film-makers at the BBC. So for the moment at least, he is back where he started, at 'the Beeb', his own television Alma Mater.

While *The Fishing Party*, made during the first phase of Watson's career for the Documentary Department at the BBC, represents his finest achievement of that period, the later work, when he began to shoot for himself, is equally impressive. In the early years, he worked with the Corporation's finest technicians achieving, with the winning combination of their expertise and his artist's eye, some memorable images, excellent storytelling and finely tuned editing. But in the 1990s, the technology was changing fast and making it possible for documentary film-makers to become true auteurs, in the full sense of the word, able to take complete control of their own visual material, without the mediation of a crew of technicians. Watson has said that he would never consider working without film editors, even in this liberating age of portable electronic editing. But he was happy to dispense with film crews, however much he liked and respected them and however brilliant they may have been. His transition to shooting his own films came gradually and it is interesting to examine the reasons why he did it.

In 1997 he was in South Africa, working on two programmes called *White Lives*, commissioned by Granada for transmission on Channel 4. He was working with a very experienced crew with whom he had worked before. He began to feel that they thought they could anticipate his ideas, what would interest him. But Watson says he is always looking for funny, quirky images or pictures which somehow carry a subtext and which, used as cutaways, will illuminate his message. Sometimes he wanted to direct very precisely, 'Shoot it from here. Now, from there,' explaining exactly how he wants shots to be covered. This quirkiness set up a certain amount of tension because experienced camera people naturally want to have a degree of artistic freedom themselves. In my own experience as a director, I found that cameramen and women always say that they like to work with directors who know exactly what they want, but in reality they prefer to make the important artistic decisions themselves. You can look after the story but they want to control the pictures. So Watson's experience on this particular shoot is not that unusual, in my opinion. Eventually the cameraman lost his temper and shouted at him, 'Look, who is photographing this?'

During this time, with tension building, Paul had been experimenting with a DV camera, the VX1000, and shooting some material himself. (The crew were, naturally, shooting on film.) He was enjoying the freedom of working alone, without having to explain himself to a team, capturing exactly the image that he required. He also felt that the crew were unhappy about working in potentially dangerous situations, where a group of technicians with lots of gear are obvious targets. One man, alone with a tiny camera that could belong to a tourist, was much less conspicuous. So he went off to shoot the gangsters and criminals on his own. He had been making the point to his sceptical crew for some time that portable digital technology, sound, picture and editing is the technology of the future. He insisted on taking his DV camera with him on most shoots.

He remembers one morning which he says was a turning point for him. His crew were loading their transport van with the usual number of boxes and lights and the rest of the gear that a film crew on the road has to carry. The sound man turned to him, voice dripping with sarcasm, and said, 'Shall we be taking "the future" with us today, sir?' Watson replied, 'Yes we shall, and all the old baggage from the past as well, unfortunately.' He says that that was the moment of truth for him. That was when he said to himself, 'It's all over now. Life's difficult enough without unpleasantness in the workplace.' He decided to shoot his own films from that moment. Nowadays he works on PD150 and as far as possible also records his own sound. Of course, these small cameras do not have the technical sophistication of the Aarton or Arriflex, the lenses are not yet versatile enough. But there are so many advantages in using the DV cameras that Watson says, 'If I have to sacrifice something in picture or sound quality, so be it.'

White Lives is a mixture of film and digital video. It was shot in 1997 and deals with the preoccupations and fears of the white South African communities in Cape Town and Johannesburg. Most of the characters are irrational bigots and there is only one white person, a journalist, married to a black man, who supports the new black government. Her story punctuates the two films, intercut with a group of characters who appear from time to time, usually in close-up, looking at the camera. She is investigating South Africa's role in the death of Mozambique president Samora Machel. She is the enlightened white, a character who represents hope for the future. A drag queen comedian also appears from time to time, his role in the films to underline the contradictions in South African society. He is coloured, although he could easily be white. He appears as himself, an articulate man, at the beginning of the film; later we see him in drag and assume it is someone else. At the end he walks into his dressing room and takes off his wig. He looks at the camera, a surprised look on his face, and says, 'Oh, the film people are here.' He is not what he had seemed to be. So the films end on a note of ambiguity.

The second film contains a chilling interview with a desperate character, a black man who freely admits to his violent lifestyle. He is held in close-up throughout and the film-maker's voice from behind the camera is almost conversational in tone, matter of fact, unshockable. This interview is vintage Watson.

Paul:	How much did you pay for your gun?
Interviewee:	I get it free.
Paul:	Where did you get it from?
Int.:	The police.
Paul:	The police gave you the gun? Why?
Int.:	They want to give criminals the guns to kill innocent people, I don't know why. They give us the gun and say, go and kill the kaffirs. But I don't kill the kaffirs. I only shoot the person if I want money.

This whole scene is intercut with a boxing match in which a black man is fighting a white. A coloured man sits in the audience of the fight. He tells a terrible story, deadpan, in voice-over.

He owns a 357 Magnum and a 9mm Luger. Some gangsters had approached intending to rob him. He says, 'I shot three of them. Two of them died. I was fortunate that I could shoot before they did.'

The boxing match continues. The black is in the corner being hammered by the white boxer.

Cut back to the interview with the gangster. Still head and shoulder shot.

> **Paul:** So policemen give you the guns and ask you to go and shoot other black people. Why would they do that?
> **Int.:**   I don't know.
> **Paul:** Is there still a racist war going on?
> **Int.:**   Yeah. Racism is our life in South Africa.

The film now cuts to the drag queen comedian. He says, 'We don't need a crystal ball to predict the future of South Africa. The future is certain. It is just the past that is unpredictable.' The black audience laughs appreciatively.

This sequence reflects well some of the regular features of Watson's later work. It is an angry film but it has its moments of humour. Even the title is a joke. When it first comes up on screen, the graphics read, *White Lies*. Then after a second, the letter V drops down into place, *White Lives*, almost as if the original text had a spelling mistake. The very last word in the film goes to the drag queen just as he emerges from another successful show. He says, 'Only in South Africa can a person who does not exist appear live.' Then he winks and walks away from the camera. End credits.

Watson is much more of a presence in his later films than he had been in the past. This film probably marks that turning point. While all the documentaries are strongly authored, in this one we hear his voice and feel his presence more strongly. This is, to some extent, a result of the more relaxed atmosphere in commercial television, where individualism is more likely to be encouraged than it was at the BBC in the 1970s and 1980s. At that time many executives still clung to the notion that there was something called 'objectivity'. This had caused a lot of problems for Watson, particularly over *The Fishing Party*, which had been seen by some BBC executives as an anti-Tory propaganda film.

He had even more trouble with the next film he made at that time, *Convictions*. It was actually banned, considered unsuitable for broadcast, because it did not challenge sufficiently robustly the violent criminal behaviour of the young men who were the subjects of the film. Watson had made it in response to a challenge from the men who appeared in the fishing film. Responding to the way their own performances had been received, they had said to him, 'Bet you wouldn't treat your precious working class the way you treated us.' But one of the central tenets of Watson's work is that they have to reflect the times we live in and at the same time stand as a record for future generations to understand the way we live now. *Convictions* is an illuminating companion piece to *The Fishing Party*, working as counterpoint to the philosophies of the rich men in the first film. The BBC was cowardly in its refusal to transmit it. Unfortunately, not for the first, or last, time.

Perhaps as a reaction to his often stormy past, when he joined Granada Television, he decided to make a film that he describes as a love story. *Malcolm and Barbara* is probably the most universally popular of all his films. In a rare and courageous act by the scheduler, it was shown on ITV (commercial television) in peak time and was two hours long. It achieved an audience of eight million viewers, unprecedented in that slot for a documentary in those days. It also attracted huge amounts of press attention, political debate and audience response. It obviously struck a cord with the nation. The film follows the gradual disintegration of a loving relationship as Barbara, the wife, has to cope with the ever-increasing early onset of Alzheimer's disease in her husband Malcolm. He shot it himself. He explains his reasons:

The films I have made in recent years, I would not want to make with a film crew. Take Malcolm and Barbara. *Man dying. I do not want to take a different person each time to this very intimate situation. We called it a love story. It was her and him and me. Like a* ménage à trois. *It was very close and I did not want strangers walking in and out.*

There is no doubt that the presence of the film-maker became important in the life of these two suffering people. He came regularly to see them over a period of years, until the time when Malcolm had to be taken away to a hospital. He acted as a sounding board for both of them although, sadly, Malcolm became less rational as the filming progressed and therefore inevitably Barbara appeared to find some relief in having a sympathetic observer of her painful plight in regular attendance. Unusually for Watson, the editing of the film is quite straightforward, telling the story through the medium of a clear, linear time-frame narrative. Watson shot and recorded sound himself and much of the film is in close-up, very intimate, appropriate for the human tragedy which is unfolding.

A series of three scenes in the film encapsulate the collapse of the couple's old life.

Barbara is talking to camera and powdering her nose at the same time. She says:

> *A few days ago Malcolm came into the kitchen and he said, 'Who are you?' I said, 'I'm your rotten old wife. Who are you?' And he said a man with a green nose was telling him what to do. He walked away and then a few minutes later he came back and put his arms around me and said, 'You won't leave me will you?'*

Later Paul says to Malcolm, 'You weren't very nice to her. Does she mother you too much?' Answer, 'No.' Then,

> 'Are you angry with Barbara?'
> 'Yes, it's over me, not anyone else. I'll take the blame.'
> 'What for?'
> 'Don't know what it is.'

In the next scene she is trying to get Malcolm ready for bed. He is resisting, holding her hands in a tight grip. She cries out that she is hurting, he does not know his own strength. Half dressed, he walks in and out of the bathroom, mischievous, disorientated, like a baby.

It is a heartbreaking sequence that must have resonated in many homes as the film was transmitted.

While many people consider *Malcolm and Barbara* to be the best film by Watson for many years, he prefers his 'portrait of late twentieth century manners', *A Wedding in the Family*. This is another film which created great controversy when it was first shown. It is the most highly orchestrated of his films, featuring constant parallel editing, with no scene allowed to continue to its natural end without interruption. The film relies on one basic conceit. The wedding ceremony of a young couple, Stuart and Anna, forms the spine of the film, which cuts back and forth to the church service. Much of the other material is interview, with the film-maker's voice regularly heard, asking lots of frank questions. Four cameras covered the wedding itself and Watson shot the rest of the film himself.

He appears to have a fairly dim view of contemporary attitudes to marriage in Britain in the 1990s and this is made obvious as the film progresses. He says, 'You'd be mad to make a film about a wedding because we all know the questions, we all know the answers. They never change. Two people marry, their families are supposed to get on and they will all live happily ever after. It's doomed to failure.' At the beginning of the film, the bride's stepmother is foregrounded. Close-ups of the happy bride and her proud father are intercut with shots of her, a sour-looking woman in a big hat. Interviews with her are cut across the ceremony shots. She does not want to be at the wedding. She feels sure she is unwelcome. It is clear that the father's second marriage is unhappy, at least according to his wife. In the regularly used Watson style she is filmed in close-up, at home, sitting still, apparently looking into the camera. She is brutally frank.

Stepmum:	If you are hitting each other and arguing and all the crap that goes with unhappiness then you don't stay together, you do something about it. If you can live like adults and there is no emotion or physical contact or whatever and everyone appears to be happy then I think, why not?
Paul:	But you are quite obviously not happy.
Stepmum:	It's shit, isn't it? I'm not. But there you are.
Paul:	Why do you have to be here? There are a lot of single parents these days.
Stepmum:	This is what the men were frightened about you know. You wheedling things out of them.

There is shot of Watson with his camera, reflected in a window. His voice-over says, 'This is a film about relationships at the end of the twentieth century, about people going into a marriage and there are these . . .' She finishes the sentence for him, 'Things falling apart.'

This conversation happens early in the film. It is clear that the story will be a lot more complex than the opening shots suggest – a chocolate box sentimental picture of two good-looking young people, in love, on the happiest day of their lives. This will be a film about the pain and sacrifice of people living in a loveless marriage. The stars of the film will not be the young people, their marriage is merely a device to tell a tragic, though not uncommon, story. The real stars of the film are the father, the stepmother and, it soon emerges, the father's ex-wife, the mother of the bride. As the tale unfolds it becomes clear that the wedding itself is only a subplot.

A number of other characters appear in the film – the parents of the groom, best friends, grandparents, children. In the first part, the father of the bride features only peripherally. Other people talk about him but he does not speak for himself. His ex-mother-in-law, ex-wife and present wife are all scathing about him. His daughter, the bride, says she knows he loves her but she wishes he would show it. His ex-mother-in-law is particularly critical. When he was married to her daughter she says he 'did a lot of night duty'. Watson says, 'That's a naughty joke.' She claims, unconvincingly, that it was not intended that way. She describes how her daughter was desperate to hold on to him. 'She asked me to sit in while she tried to persuade him not to go. And I was silently praying that he would. Because you can't get over things like that.' In commentary, Watson explains that her children's marriages all ended in divorce, but hers was a faithful and happy marriage. Briefly, we see her husband, who she looks after because he has had a stroke. Somewhat bizarrely, he explains that he 'used to spend a lot of time in the shed'. The recipe for a happy marriage, perhaps?

Who, then, is this unlikely heartbreaker, the twice married father of the bride? Everyone admits that he is good at his job, he is a dedicated doctor, popular with staff at work. We see him at the scene of an accident; the police like and respect him. His patients in his surgery are indebted to him. He always puts work first. But he has had affairs, one of which led to the breakup of his first marriage and his remarriage to his present wife, stepmother to the bride. Eventually, he speaks for himself.

Watson had been filming for three months when the doctor decided to talk. He describes the moment:

We were standing under a light in his study, where he sleeps. By going in there he was admitting that he was not sleeping with his wife but dossing down in his study. We talked for about four minutes. I had the camera with me. I said, 'Would it help if I filmed this?' He agreed. I'd had a long day, I'd been up since seven o'clock. I fell to the floor with the camera, grabbed a lamp, a flick of light in his eye. I put it on automatic, locked it off and sat there on the floor for 44 minutes. The only reason why I changed the shot was muscle fatigue; the camera was shaking.

In the film, this interview is not allowed to run as recorded but cut up into small segments, often run in voice-over pictures of the doctor working and further interrupted by scenes from the church as the wedding ceremony continues. For me, this discontinuity reduces the natural sympathy that an audience might feel for a man who, as it emerges, lost his mother when he was three and as a child was never allowed to show emotion. Also, the interview appears towards the end of the film after the womenfolk have had their disapproving say. It is a very tight close-up, shot against a venetian blind.

Asked how he feels about his decision to leave his first wife he says, 'The grass is always greener.' Paul says, 'And the truth is you're not really sure if you love your first wife more than your second wife.' The doctor replies, 'I'm not sure if what I left behind is any worse or any better than what I have now.'

The interview is incorporated in a particularly complicated sequence which seems to carry a strong message, a warning for the young couple now about to start their married life together. It is worth looking at in detail.

First, we see the doctor at the scene of an accident, directing the paramedics as they rescue a young woman. Cut to a quick shot of the bride's flowers and the priest's voice, 'Have given their consent and marriage vows to each other . . . ' Cut to interview with the first mother-in-law, sitting at a lunch table, 'We never ever wanted them to marry. My son said, "They'll never marry, no." But they did. Because he needed a mother.' Cut to the doctor in the church. Cut to ex-wife interview: 'I don't think you can ever get over losing your mum at three as Steve did. I think that was a frightful thing.'

Now the doctor speaks (close-up from his interview). 'If Heather and I had been able to forgive each other.' Picture cut with his voice over a photograph of him with his second wife, probably a registry office photograph, 'and forget many of the things that were overwhelming considerations at the time that I changed horses'. Picture cut of a hand dealing playing cards, 'then life for me would have been a lot easier'.

Cut to close-up of teenage son shouting, 'Play the game woman.' Reverse shot of his partner at cards, the second wife, looking pained. 'Play the card game' shouts the boy.

Back to close-up of the doctor. Paul's voice off camera. 'Those reasons for changing being sex and ephemeral things like that?' 'Absolutely.' Cut to wife at card table, kid still shouting. Close-up of doctor. 'And I see people all the time in my surgery who are changing relationships for one reason or another.' Picture cut, cards being slammed down one after the other, shot of wife looking pleased, cut back to close-up of doctor: 'And when they talk to me about the reasons for wanting to leave their partner . . . ' Back to close-up of doctor: 'I think to myself, why don't you just stick with it.' Shot of table with cards and a glass of sparkling wine in the foreground. Back to priest in church, couple kneeling at his feet, 'I now pronounce you man and wife.'

Watson says that he has a rule about commentary. 'Never write more than 30 words, that's 10 seconds. Only write to clarify a point so people will not lose the plot by asking each other what is going on. The real commentary in this film is in the cutaways.' Given this advice from the film-maker, I have to assume that the device of cutting away to a card game must be the point I am supposed to ponder on. I am therefore assuming that this highly complex piece of editing is emphasizing the point that marriage is a game of chance. Gamblers will go ahead in spite of best advice to the contrary. So what hope is there for the naive young couple who have just been pronounced man and wife? Will they too make mistakes but decide to stick with it? Or will they change partners? And will Stuart enjoy the fate of being married to a self-pitying second wife who will not sleep with him and a teenage son who acts in a highly aggressive manner while wearing lipstick and eyeliner? I am only guessing. However bravura a piece of editing this sequence is, I think the lack of clarity in the message is probably deliberate, particularly as the film is nearing its end.

In the last section of interview with the bride's father, Watson asks if being a successful doctor is enough. No, he says, but it is a compensation. Watson says, 'Really? But separate bedrooms, what a price to pay.' The doctor agrees, it is a high price. 'Yes it is a price.' The film ends as it began, with the stepmother getting the last word. As it cuts in and out of the ceremony she says how she wishes she could be happy like Stuart and Anna. The congregation are singing *Jerusalem* and the soundtrack is clear for us all to take in the irony of the famous line, 'In England's green and pleasant land.' Stepmom says, 'What is the point of being affluent and having plenty of money if you are not happy?' On this cheerful note, the procession leaves the church to line up for the wedding photographs. The film has ended.

A Wedding in the Family is technically brilliant and, like all Watson films, gives real insight into the lives of the people he features. He is a skilled interviewer and establishes rapport with all kinds of people from many walks of life. His editing is always complex, showing great attention to detail, especially with sound, which many excellent film-makers neglect, particularly when covering the real-life scenarios that Watson specializes in. But personally I have a problem with this particular film, which is that I fail to respond to the emotional subtext. I do not accept the proposition that the 'wicked stepmother' is actually a brave, wronged woman, which I know is Watson's view.

This could be a gender issue, or it might just be personal prejudice on my part. For me, she represents the classic double standard of the woman who has no problem having an affair with another woman's husband, resulting in the breakup of the family, then feels hurt and aggrieved when he goes on to cheat on her. However, she will not leave him because of the children. Watson asks the question himself – why not? She was working as a nurse when she met him. The country is desperate for nurses. But she stays in the comfortable marital home, refuses her husband sex and makes his life a misery. Meanwhile, all the female characters give the father of the bride a hard time when, so far as I can see, he is the only person in the film who spends his life helping others. He has genuine job satisfaction and that is a comfort to him. Watson seems surprised that anyone could feel that way.

He has made two other productions since *A Wedding in the Family*. One is, in theory, a companion piece, *The Queens' Wedding*, about a group of gay men in Manchester preparing for the wedding of two of their gay friends. It uses many of the techniques of the previous film: frank and intimate interviews, fast and sometimes disorientating cutting, a lot of affection and a lot of humour. His latest production was a serial about a group of British couples on an adventure holiday in Namibia, run by a tough Falklands War veteran ex-SAS man. More conventional in its approach and editing than the previous films, it is, as usual with a Watson production, more about the emotions and relationships of the people than whether they were going to achieve their goal. Good popular television. Once again, he shot the films himself.

Watson has finally returned to the BBC to work again alongside his friend and long-time supporter, John Willis, to work with some young people there. He has always been a generous giver of his time, advising and mentoring new film-makers, teaching at film schools, chairing award-giving juries, travelling and presenting his work at international film festivals. In his 30 years in the industry, he has been tremendously influential and always controversial. Even those people who criticize him and claim that he intrudes unfairly into the private lives of ordinary people have to concede that he is a brilliant film-maker and a constant innovator, always investigating the possibilities created by the new technology.

FILMOGRAPHY

1967–8

Whicker's World
4 × 50 min
SFTA nomination
ARCA – First Class Honours
Silver medal, Royal College of Art
Represented in the National art collection

1968–9

A Year in the Life
SFTA Best Documentary Series

1969

A Fine and Private Place
Writer and director
EMI feature, producer Bryan Forbes – a disastrous production!

1970–74

The Block
BAFTA nomination
Press Critics Prize

Lost in Space
Inside NASA during a mission.

War in the Middle East
Jordan.

Race of the Power Bikes
The dangerous TT Isle of Man race.

1974

The Family
12 × 30 min
First 'fly-on-the-wall' documentary serial.
Press Critics Prize – National Archive

1975–80

Runaway Girls
4 × 50 min drama docs
Writer and director

Nothing Doing
Youth unemployment.

Nobody Asked Us
1980
A working-class family during the Corby steel strike.

Diary of a Search
Archaeologists search for treasure in Egypt.

The Rothko Conspiracy
Directed for 'Masterpiece Theatre', USA.

1981–3

Vox Pop
Weekly documentary serial about the public and private concerns
of the people of Darwen, a small Lancashire town.

1984–6

Single documentaries, including:

House of Hope
An alternative way to treat addiction.

The Fishing Party
1985
BAFTA nomination
Press Critics Prize – National Archive

Convictions
Three brothers 'duck and dive' in criminal West London.

1987–8

Left UK to work with WNPB, USA

Revelations
US prizes – *LA Times/Washington Post*

1988–92

One Day
Portraits of models, rock managers, surgeons, etc.

Present Imperfect
20 × 60 min
Editor
Britain through a year.
BAFTA nomination – Director, 'Loveless in Letchworth'

In Solidarity
4 × 50 min

Total access to members of the Polish democratic movement as they created the new government.

Wimps to Warriors
6 × 45 min
Frank look at male sexuality.
Press Critics Prize

States of Mind
Co-production with PBS
Lifestyles across the USA.
Winner, Emmy Award

BBC Documentaries 1992–3

Sylvania Waters
12 × 30 min, co-production with ABC, Sydney and BBC1
Documentary soap about an Australian family.

Sarajevo – A Street under Siege
90 × 2 min films, BBC2
Shot and transmitted every day.

Trick on Two
BBC2
Close-up magic.

40 Minutes
BBC2
Editor of 39 transmissions

Granada Television 1994–9

The Factory
1994, five-part series
Winner RTS Award
Press Critics Prize – Best Documentary Series

The Home
1995
BAFTA nomination
Press Critics Prize
Winner RTS

The Dinner Party
1997
Broadcasting Press Guild Award

White Lives
1998, Channel 4
Nominated for Grierson Award 1999

Malcolm and Barbara
(subtitle: A Love Story)
1999, 90 min, film, first for ITV

Winner of three RTS awards, including Best Single Documentary 1999
Bafta nomination

United Productions, May 1999–January 2001

Jungle Janes
4 May 1999
Executive producer

Twelve women bored with life and their controlling husbands set out to prove that they can survive in the jungle.

A Wedding in the Family
2000, 90 min, film, Channel 4, transmitted 28 March

January 2002–present

Set up own production company, Priory Pictures.

Desert Darlings
3 × 60 min, Channel 4

About six couples resolving who they are as they trek across the Namibian deserts.

The Queens' Wedding
90 min, Channel 4

A group of gay drag queens work in a bar in Canal Street, Manchester. Two of the men in the group fall in love and marry each other.

4 Pawel Pawlikowski
Eastern European analysis

Pawel Pawlikowski

When I asked Pawel Pawlikowski if I could interview him for this book, he readily agreed but felt he had to point out that he was 'not very digital'. That is putting it mildly. He is a convinced supporter of the idea that film is the only medium for producing wonderful pictures and even carries his pro-celluloid convictions into the cutting room. He was still editing on Steenbecks long after his contemporaries had embraced the new technology and started to work on Avid. He argues even today that the only advantage of cutting on Avid is that it saves money on the budget. He has recently made the transition to fiction and has been working on 35 mm film, which he loves.

Pawel was born in Poland during the dark days of the Soviet Union. His mother lectured in English at Warsaw University.

At the age of 14 he was, as he puts it, suddenly and unpleasantly uprooted and taken by his mother to England. He lived there for a year, unable to speak the language and attending a school for expatriots, which was paid for by the Polish government in exile. He was very unhappy at the school and eventually, he says, they kicked him out, so he went to live with his father in Germany and stayed there for three years. In 1977, he went back to England to study, first at London University, then at Oxford.

During those restless teenage years, he felt that he could not speak the languages of his adopted countries well enough and he could not return to Poland. So it is hardly surprising that he turned to a different kind of communication, the visual language of film-making. At Oxford, he started writing for a film magazine and then joined a film-makers' workshop, where he was introduced to the technology and started working on his own projects. He says:

Film-making suited me temperamentally in some way because I was always a bit of a starer, an explorer of new spaces, always looking. Looking at life without fully understanding what was going on. The fact that I came from a different culture meant that I empathized and understood more than was healthy for me. I was always surprised by how the locals, whoever they were, misconstrued 'the others'. So I developed this kind of obsession, how inexplicable 'the others' are and felt we should try to explain them, enter into their perspective. So for me film-making is a kind of exploration of the world, and in a way, an exploration of who I am.

This theme of 'otherness' runs through all of Pawlikowski's films. The suggestion is always there: the film-maker is an outsider, looking in. He also favours characters who are themselves outsiders. The films are highly constructed and edited more like drama than conventional documentary. Music is important and usually serves the function of enhancing mood or leading the film into an emotional gear-change. Unusually for a documentary film-maker, he does not get close to his subjects. In fact, in the case of two of his subjects, Vladimir Zhirinovsky and Radovan Karadjic, he actively disliked them and felt very uncomfortable in their presence. Pawlikowski's films are about ideas and the characters

79

serve his dramatic purpose, almost like actors, living out their personal drama in front of his 'staring' camera.

The films are always thought provoking, often disturbing but also, somewhat paradoxically, very entertaining. I cannot imagine this body of work being made by any other film-maker, nor could I imagine them being made by anyone who was not Eastern European. Despite his long exile, Pawel is steeped in the literature and culture of that part of the world. And his culture influences everything he makes. A sense of humour pervades the films, but it is the black humour of occupied Eastern Europe during the Cold War.

I have, myself, felt a great affinity for the people of Poland ever since I first went there as a researcher for the BBC in the early 1970s. An ability to distance themselves and laugh at their own trials seemed to me to be the most effective weapon the people I met in Warsaw had to help them maintain their dignity and pride. I remember one day asking my minder what he thought about the Russian soldiers who were always in and out of my rather elegant hotel. He said, 'What soldiers?' I pointed out that a Russian in uniform had just opened the door for me. My Polish colleague smiled and said, 'Ah, you mean "our brothers"?' Why 'brothers' I asked. 'I thought the Russians referred to you as "our friends".' 'That's right, they do. But we prefer the word "brother". You can choose your friends.' It seemed to me, then, that these people could never really be defeated, however powerful the enemy, because they were so well protected, psychologically, by their belief in their own history and culture, and by their sense of the absurd. I see this quality still in the work of Pawel Pawlikowski.

Three of his four award-winning documentaries are set in Russia. The first in the group follows the election campaign of an extreme right-wing Russian politician, running for president in the first free elections after the fall of the Soviet Union. As the film begins, a man walks into the picture from left of frame. He is carrying two Russian flags. He is on the bank of a huge river. As he tries to set up the flags he drops one of them. Voice-over begins as he struggles. The picture cuts and we see the man who is talking. He is pacing along the river bank, speaking into a megaphone. 'Today at 11 o'clock, the leader of the Liberal Democratic Party will sail in and speak to you from this stage, Vladimir Zhirinovsky.' The flags are finally fixed, although rather lop-sidedly. A dirty campaign bus is parked by the river, tinny music emerging from it. Now the music changes; it is a marching tune played by a brass band. The picture shows the prow of a boat, cleaving through the water. On deck some well-dressed men are having a group photograph taken. As the boat clears frame, leaving only the disturbed water with a red buoy bobbing around in it, up comes the title, *Tripping with Zhirinovsky*. The title, with its play on the word 'tripping', the shot of the red buoy, the accompaniment of the jaunty military music, all combine to create a slightly surreal mood. This is classic Pawlikowski. From the very first moments of the documentary, the tone is established. It is clear that this will be a detached, ironic and often very funny film, entertaining to watch, beautifully shot, but also raising some very worrying questions about the political climate of the newly democratic Russian nation.

It emerges that the river is the Volga and the boat, a luxury affair, complete with its own disco, is the campaign headquarters of the presidential campaign. Throughout the film the boat is photographed sailing down the Volga, light changing, stunningly beautiful scenes recorded while the distinctly unlovely Zhirinovsky and his campaign team live the life of Riley on board, stopping every now and then to address the local populace and ask for their votes. In one bizarre scene, Zhirinovsky gives a lecture on the moving boat to his respectful supporters. Pointing with a stick at a map of the world, he delivers his surreal message, warning them first that geopolitics is important.

'Our country is once more faced with a historical mission. To save humanity, to save western Europe. This is how I see world history developing.' Pointing at Africa, he says, 'This continent is dying little by little, it has been sucked dry. Wars, terrible diseases, it's no threat to us. Black Africa is going to die of its own diseases. It will never represent an element of civilization. When I was in Europe I told the German foreign secretary and everyone else, "Take Africa, its yours, try and save it from AIDS. You'll catch AIDS and die too. Here you are, its yours. Russia is giving you the entire continent as a gift." ' Now pointing at South America he says, 'And when I was in America I told them, "This is yours, here you are." ' The stick now traces a line from top to bottom in all the main land masses on the map. 'Let's reorganize the world along the axis north–south, north–south. We'll have safe neighbours – India and the Arabs. China we will move south and here in the west we will give them some leftover bones . . . We will get more than anyone.'

A mini-organ is played on board by a man who later became the Russian Minister of Culture. The old tune, known in the west as 'A hundred miles' and repeated as a regular motif throughout the film, emphasizes the constant movement of the campaign boat. In between, popular Russian political songs are woven in and out of the soundtrack. One talks about having tried the left and how now seems the moment to try the right.

> *Zhirinovsky is a regular Russian bloke*
> *Even though he doesn't drink or smoke.*

However, in spite of his abstinence, Zhirinovsky has no qualms of conscience about selling his own-brand vodka, a profitable sideline which he happily explains to Pawlikowski.

His campaign speech, delivered to hundreds as he progresses along the river, embodies the kind of unrealistic promises that only a no-hoper could get away with. Everyone will have a job. Tourism will be more successful. Living conditions will improve and everyone will be given credit to buy a home. Pay it back when you can. Pawel says that Zhirinovsky was rather fond of Yeltsin, the President after Gorbachev, who did so much to liberalize Russia but fell badly from grace in spite of that. He says:

> *Yeltsin realized in the eighties that democracy was the next big thing. Zhirinovsky thought that the big thing after that would be fascist/soviet populism. He developed a confused ideology with some fascist overtones but also with a love of the free market. Basically, he was a spiv.*

At the end of the film Zhirinovsky goes to America, where he is interviewed on television, surprising even the cynical US journalists with his extreme views. Not included in the film, there was a telling moment which Pawel tells about with wry amusement. He was asked what he thought of American democracy. That very week there had been a referendum in California asking if basic civil rights should be given to the illegal immigrants who had come in from Mexico and settled there. The Californians voted against allowing them civil rights; Zhirinovsky thought that was wonderful. 'If only we had that kind of democratic freedom in Russia,' he said. Pawel defines this as 'the confused hybrid ideology of the taxi driver'. In a hotel suite in America, lavish in its décor, huge amounts of food are brought in by his aides. Zhirinovsky is enjoying himself, living the high life, being taken seriously, making money. He explains to the camera, 'My son found me Russian dumplings in the middle of New York.' Over shots of him exercising by the hotel pool, he says that he has shot to fame and fortune in five years. Everybody is talking about him.

The penultimate sequence of the film introduces an abrupt change in style. Suddenly, we are in pop video territory. As he dives into the hotel pool, the image of disturbed water mixes through to interference on a television screen, followed by a rocket taking off. Electronic music begins as a visual montage, cut very fast, seems to explode across the screen. A rap song begins. The images, breathtakingly fast, show Zhirinovsky in action man mode, intercut with military action footage, people rioting and the talking heads of international politicians. The words of the song are chilling:

> *The third world war*
> *I'm famous in Poland*
> *I'm famous in Finland*
> *They fear me*

Twice and very briefly, we return to the poolside, where Zhirinovsky is still talking to the audience, boasting about his success.

Back in the montage, again very fast cutting to the rhythm of the song. Increasingly, the images become more violent:

> *I dream of the Indian Ocean*
> *I dream of the Indian Ocean*
> *They fear me*

This is an extraordinary piece of editing. At the beginning of the sequence, Zhirinovsky looks posturing and ridiculous, a would-be demagogue with delusions of grandeur. By the time it has reached the third part of the sequence it has ceased to be funny and we read the whole piece differently. It has a nightmarish quality. This is a dangerous man, with dangerous, extreme right wing views. There is nothing funny about him. As the film comes to an end, the deranged music stops and the film slips back into a more convention documentary form. A group of Zhirinovsky fans are gathered on a quayside, literally singing his praises. The point of view of the camera is that of a boat sailing by. The closing shots remind us of the fatal attraction that many people feel for dangerous demagogues. The faces of his deluded but devoted followers tell their own story.

Pawlikowski says of the film, 'I love that landscape. The Volga. The contrast with this petty crook going through this magnificent landscape, it was quite eloquent. The *nouveaux riches* on the boat, his wife dripping in gold, all those people with nothing at the quayside, all those babushkas, those poor crowds, it was all so eloquent on a visual plane.' Zhirinovsky polled about 30 per cent of the vote in the presidential election. He is still active in politics, a member of Parliament, but now concentrates on making money out of his position. Nevertheless, his party still poll 10–11 per cent of the popular vote. He has not gone away.

While Zhirinovsky is a demagogue with no real power, the dominant character in the next documentary made by Pawlikowski was, for a time, very powerful indeed. Radovan Karadjic was the leader of the Bosnian Serbs, who started a terrible war resulting in untold misery for his country and eventually dragging in the United Nations and the forces of NATO. Today, he is universally recognized as a war criminal, indicted by the International Court of Criminal Justice, and he remains a fugitive, still in hiding, still on the run.

Pawlikowski and his crew filmed him while the war was raging around them. *Serbian Epics* is, in Pawlikowski's words, 'a very disturbing film'. The Bosnian Serbs were fighting for territory, claiming that they were merely trying to regain their lost homeland. Pawel says the film is, in one sense, 'A study of myth-making, myths being the basis for a nation state. It looked at these Serbian, would-be intellectuals and poets with their romantic, nineteenth century nationalist ideas, which is what they were.

It tried to show how these ideas seemed normal and familiar and at the same time also sinister and monstrous.'

The film was shot in 1992 after the death of Tito, the Communist leader of the former Yugoslavia and the fall of the Soviet Union. Pawel was granted extraordinary access to Karadjic and other Serb leaders which most current affairs journalists would, in the popular parlance of Fleet Street, have killed for. In my view, the insights the film gives into the character of Karadjic are incredibly revealing. Pawel rather underplays the power of the scenes with the Serb leader when he talks about them. He says, 'To call him a character in the film is an overstatement. I didn't spend much time with him, just grabbed moments. It is impossible to develop deeper insights if you don't spend much time with them.' Those grabbed moments, however, speak volumes. Pawel says, 'I totally disagreed with his view of the world, which was archaic and absurd. But it fitted the thesis of my film or, rather, the theme.' Asked why he did not challenge Karadjic, as any journalist would, he says, 'I did not engage with him on a political, rhetorical level. If I had attacked him like a journalist attacks, he would have defended himself in the usual way. There would have been a lot of pointless exchanges of words.'

No pointless exchanges of words then. But, in spite of that – or maybe even because of that – an illuminating portrait of a mass murderer and his bloody cohorts. No amount of descriptive journalism could make me shiver like some of the scenes in this extraordinary, skilfully crafted film. The film begins with a man shaking a tree; children are picking up the fruit as it drops. One of the children has a rifle and hands it to a man in uniform. A caption comes up, white on black:

BOSNIA 1992

A big gun is moving from left to right, pointing into the valley, where there is a large city. A soldier in combat gear raises a flag: red, blue and white. A man in military uniform is singing a patriotic song, surrounded by farming people and soldiers.

In the next scene, an archbishop baptizes people in a river, many of them small children. He calls on the patron saints, saying that his people have not been able to receive baptism for 50 years, a reference to the fact that the minority Serb population have been oppressed, first by the Communists and now by the Bosnian Muslims.

Over shots of cute children being passed from hand to hand to reach the archbishop, who pours water over their heads, a choir sings:

> *The eternal heavenly Serbia*
> *Will shine like a flock of stars*
> *Before God's face*
> *We pray to you Christ*
> *Lead our entire nation*
> *To holy paradise*

The final shot in the scene is a wide one. A huge crowd is gathered around the holy lake. A church bell rings, one single peal. The picture cuts to an arm resting on the window of an aeroplane, beautiful lush countryside visible through the window. The camera pans left. At first the picture is practically dark, the contrast between the bright exterior and the inside of the plane so great that the camera has to adjust. A technical problem, used here to advantage, to raise expectation, heighten our awareness. Who is this person? Out of the darkness, the face comes into focus. He is already world famous from television and newspapers. He is gazing with a look of serious concentration out of the window, the plane now flying high through beautiful mountain scenery.

The shooting in this scene and some others, where the singing soldiers appear, has echoes of Leni Riefenstahl, most notably her infamously brilliant homage to Hitler and the Nazi Party, *Triumph of the Will*. At the beginning of her film, Riefenstahl called on the mystical imagery of the traditional German mountain films to reinforce the suggestion that the Fuhrer had, surely, been chosen by the gods to lead The Fatherland back to its former glory. In *Serbian Epics*, another war leader in another era is also flying above the clouds, encouraged by the prayers of the archbishop, backed by the farmers/soldiers, even supported, it seems, by the children, some of whom are carrying guns. It is a clever and subversive way of introducing a character. The man gazing out of the window knows that he has a divine mission.

The screen cuts to black with two lines of text, in white:

Doctor Radovan Karadjic,
Poet and psychiatrist.

Then, on a new card, almost like it is an afterthought, one more line:

Leader of the Bosnian Serbs.

Now, in what, for me, is a totally unexpected appearance, Radovan Karadjic is talking to camera. He is in a house belonging to his family. He lights a candle under an icon of St Michael the Archangel and talks about his ancestor Wolf, who, he says, reinvented Serbian culture after it had been suppressed for centuries by the Turks. Then, astonishingly, he begins to sing. He is playing the same traditional instrument we saw at the beginning of the film.

There were 30 chieftains drinking wine
Among the vast crags of the Romanja mountain
In some freezing cavern
Among them was Chief Mitar.

Outside, he is walking towards the camera, rather like a presenter in a television history programme, talking about his favourite painting, *The Last Supper*. Can this be real? In the middle of a bitter war, the rebel leader is singing us a song, talking about his family and discussing his favourite painting? Later in the film he will recite one of his own poems, again walking towards camera in a highly professional way. And later again, he introduces a song which his supporters begin to sing. Everybody claps in tune. Karadjic claps on the off beat. Perhaps that should not have surprised me.

These scenes, of course, support Pawlikovski's theme, that sentimental nationalism is one of the great threats to stability and peace in the world, and national culture can be subverted to support cynical political ambition. He says that Karadjic has to be seen in a Balkan context, post Communist, at a time of 'cynical power grabbing'. Certainly, at the time of the Bosnian War, the whole of former Yugoslavia was in turmoil and regions which had lived in an uneasy peace during the supremacy of Tito were now jostling to establish more favourable positions. (The political background to this period is also discussed in the section on *The Death of Yugoslavia*, in Chapter 6, about producer Norma Percy.)

After the leader's cultural contribution, we see another musical interlude, with the troops being urged on to 'defend' their country by their traditional warrior minstrel. After a shot which seems to show an out-of-focus burning city, we are back with religion. This time in a beautiful, ornately decorated church with clergymen in richly embroidered vestments and a magnificent choir. The picture cuts to a black and white archive sequence. A military parade. A caption tells us that this is the coronation of King Peter I. 'After 500 years the Serbian nation is born again.' The archive is run at the wrong speed, contrary to contemporary practice. (It is now possible to run silent film at the speed at which it was actually shot – usually anything from 16 to 20 frames a second. The cameramen in the early years of cinema were hand cranking and had to estimate the speed as best they could. Nowadays, we can correctly run at the right speed for projection, thanks to new technology.) At the same time, a scratchy record of martial music is playing. This cannot possibly be the original music, since the film was clearly shot without sound. Apart from the captions on the archive film, no further information is given. The decision to run silent film at sound speed is surely a deliberate one. It certainly helps to add to the bizarre mood of the film.

Then we meet a new character, Prince Tomislav. The grandson of Peter I, he explains how some of the artefacts in the church were made from the weapons of previous Balkan wars. Before introducing us to his own family portraits, he makes a preposterous claim. 'This is a national monarchy, a monarchy of the people for the people and with the people.' Watching this film with increasing incredulity, I found it difficult to believe that I had not accidentally dropped off and woken watching some savage satire about hypocrisy and greed and imperialism gone mad. A product perhaps of the imagination of Stanley Kubrick or Joseph Heller. But no, this is a documentary. It is all true, but orchestrated with the ironic detachment, wit and intellect of Pawel Pawlikowski.

Just when the film seems to be settling down into the slightly less grotesque – a tour of the portraits of the new royals, a demo demanding the return of the king, a bemused child being danced around by people who want their nation to be free again – another wonderfully cool caption tells us:

The leader of the Bosnian Serbs visits his mother

Here is Karadjic, explaining his plans to his tough old mother, who chain smokes throughout the discussion. He seems to be seeking her approval.

Mother:	What is happening in your republic?
RK:	There's still a lot of fighting. With the Croats we could come to terms immediately and end hostilities. That would cut the war by half. But the Muslims don't want to negotiate.
Male voice off:	Why not?
RK:	They count on military intervention or for some-body to send them more arms to continue the war.
Voice off:	Who would want to die for a Muslim state in the Balkans?
	What mother would send her son to die here?
Mother:	No-one asks mothers.

Karadjic shows her a newly minted republican bank note. She looks at it and says, 'Lovely, but will it buy anything?'

His mother does not seem very impressed and later in the film an even more surprising scene reveals that his War Cabinet are not too happy about his plans either. This is a scene which, had it been filmed by news or current affairs journalists, would have been headlined, constantly repeated and no doubt the film-makers would have received bravery awards. Except, of course, that it is highly unlikely that any other crew would have got the access that Pawlikowski managed to get. Three men are sitting at a table, although at first we see only two of them. The camera is at the right-hand side, filming them in profile. Karadjic is in the middle, explaining his tactics. He is drawing lines in black felt tip on a map as he talks. Circling Sarajevo, he says:

> *We must prove to international opinion that we are not besieging Sarajevo but defending our own territory. This map clearly shows that Sarajevo is built on Serb land.*
>
> *We'll only discuss the areas where the population overlaps, like the Neretva and Sava valleys.*

Now the third man interrupts and the camera moves to include him. He is Mladic, the general, and, Pawlikowski believes, the man who really makes most of the important decisions. His voice is cold, almost bored, not argumentative, just uncompromising.

Mladic: No. Sava will not be discussed.
RK: Well, they could claim . . .
Mladic: They can claim but it's ours.
RK: Well we could make some concessions in the Kupres area.
Mladic: No we can't.
RK: In a political sense we are open to discussion.

Mladic has a cynical look on his face. The camera pans down and we see his fingers, tapping impatiently.

They go on to discuss access to the sea, avoiding war with Croatia and telling the United Nations when their planes are flying. The body language is so revealing. The others are not interested in diplomacy or, for that matter, telling the UN the truth. A woman says, 'Why don't we just tell them our planes are not flying?' Karadjic is starting to lose his cool by this point. 'How can we tell them that when we obviously are flying, like crazy?'

During the latter half of this discussion, the light keeps coming and going. A dull thudding noise constantly sounds in the background. It seems that a war is going on, even as they meet.

The meeting was being held prior to discussions in Geneva with the UN, which came to nothing. There is no real political context in this film, a deliberate decision, and the talks in Geneva are cut very quickly. News bulletins are quoted but not long enough to help us work out what exactly is going on. There is no commentary and the text captions tell only basic information. For example, the archive film of Peter I's coronation is not dated. People who know that sound came to the movies in 1929 will be able to make a fair guess as to when this event took place, but a guess is all it is. The lack of factual context in the film is deliberate. It is not about events, history as told in the conventional way, in the manner described by one dismissive writer as 'one damn thing after another'. This is a film with a theme, the dangers of romantic nationalism.

Pawel says:

> I think you get the idea even now when you watch the film – without context – it's a very disturbing film. In the War Cabinet scene you get the idea that Karadjic wasn't exactly in charge of the war, even though he may have started it. Mladic was really calling the shots, overriding his attempts to look like a diplomat. The camera angle was really useful there. We see all three faces. The body language of Karadjic was all over the place, he was humming and hawing. Whereas Mladic was like a man of stone, his face was hard, his views were sharp, he knew what he wanted, no messing around. Suddenly the power relations became obvious. It is great in films when one shot becomes so dramatically eloquent. The whole banality of that situation was quite striking, the amateurishness and haphazardness of some of these decisions, a war largely improvised. Except for Mladic, a general in the style of Patton. The kind of man Americans love in their movies. Except he was Serbian.

Towards the end of the film there is a scene which seems to support this point. It starts with soldiers in full battle dress, singing in the strange harmonies of traditional Serbian folk music, 'Our mountain will win.' They are on a hill above Sarajevo; the big gun is aimed at the city. Karadjic is with them. He is on the field telephone, trying to get through to his wife at home. The scene cuts from soldiers firing machine guns at the city below and an increasingly confused conversation between the leader and Camp

Command. There is a wrong number. A dog is playing around at the leader's feet. The soldiers are still firing on the city. Finally, an important message comes through from 'Eagle' at headquarters. The leader's wife is not at home. Another moment, watching this film, when you wonder if you have suddenly slipped into a black comedy, maybe written by Kurt Vonnegut. The terrifying fact, though, is that it is all true.

Pawel says:

> There was a slightly pitying look about the whole film. Everyone was referring to the Serbian War Machine as if they were the German SS. Most Serbs involved in that war were local farmers who knew how to use guns because they had been conscripts in the past. They were like Dad's Army with heavy artillery. My basic hypothesis about the war was that they had no chance of winning. Maybe in the days of the Soviet Union, but never in the world as it is today.

In *Dostoevsky's Travels*, Pawlikowski wanted to explore this idea, how the world has changed, notably the relationship between east and west, since the removal of the Berlin Wall. He was researching in St Petersburg when he met a man who was the only living descendant of Fyodor Dostoevsky, the great Russian novelist. The man explained that he was just on his way to Germany to make a speech at the Dostoevsky Society and he also hoped to buy a car. Pawel says, 'He had grown a beard to look more like Dostoevsky and I thought, great face, great character, he could be a good key to the east/west situation today.' So he phoned his friend Nigel Williams at the BBC. Williams was running *Bookmark*, a series that dealt with literary subjects, and Pawel told him that he had found this character who was descended from Dostoevsky, although he had no literary pretensions himself. In fact, he was a tram driver. Apparently Williams said, 'If he's Dostoevsky's great-grandson, that's literary enough for me.' So the film was commissioned. Those were the days!

Pawel hired equipment and started shooting, with no idea where the film was going to take him. 'One of those scary leaps into the dark,' he says. 'Normally when you make a film for television you have a kind of safety net, you can interview a lot of people, you can come up with some kind of 50-minute construct. I didn't have that so it had to work as a kind of drama.' Pawel went with Dmitri Dostoevsky to Germany. 'There were some poignant situations. The mismatch between his aims and the German people's expectations propelled the story forward.' Pawel was looking for some other theme to give the story more complexity, but nothing emerged. 'My hero's motivation was just to make some money and buy a car, and he was rather obsessed by that to the exclusion of everything else. So the film became a constant escalation of the same joke.'

It is undoubtedly a funny, thoroughly enjoyable film, which plays well with cinema audiences. The theme of 'otherness', and Pawlikowski's abiding interest in the way strangers so often misunderstand each other, is explored here in a light-hearted way, but it makes its point all the same. The film is shot and edited like drama.

In one key scene, the German Dostoevsky Society are meeting. It begins with a shot through a window, looking in at a room full of people. A woman's voice from the meeting runs over this picture. 'Dostoevsky is a true prophet.' The picture cuts to the beautifully lit interior. 'He depicts the fragility of the human condition.' Close-up of a serious-looking man with a beard. 'In all its sinfulness.' Shot of another serious chap with glasses. Dmitri enters the room and sits down. 'But then he always shows that little flame in the dark.' 'Jesus the light of the world.' Dmitri is sitting rather uneasily next to a middle-aged woman. The disembodied voice now says that most people know about Dostoevsky because of the film, *Anna Karenina*. A wide shot of the group. They are speaking in German and their voices begin to overlap. There is no translation for the audience, or for Dmitri. Three close-ups of him follow. He nods, he covers his mouth, looking thoughtful, he clasps his hands. No cutaways, mixes or fade to black, which would be the normal grammar in a sequence like this. The effect is to portray a man completely out of his depth, understanding nothing.

The film cuts abruptly to a high-angle shot of a lavatory; the sound is of a toilet flushing. Dmitri sits down on the closed seat, picks up a can of beer, drinks from it and lights a cigarette. Rock music in the background, voice-over in Russian begins – his voice, we assume. Immediately the sound of the original track is lowered and an English translation is heard. Dmitri picks up a book and some paper. The translation is:

> *Will I get a Mercedes out of it? I decide not to waste time. I dig up a few German language books about Dostoevsky, there's some more or less relevant passages, and compile a lecture. Quite a good one too.*

The camera angle has now dropped to ground level, profile. First a pan from his handwriting to his face. Then a close shot of him hunched over, writing.

This is dangerous territory, formally speaking, for many documentarists. The scene is clearly directed, that is obvious from the camera positions. And who wrote the commentary – is it an interview or a construction? Is it true? Is this man really Dmitri Dostoevsky or an actor? Is the whole thing made up? What are we to believe? OK, I am satirizing what I consider to be the rather po-faced, puritanical view of many film-makers, usually 'old-school observational'. I have to say, as far as I am concerned, all that matters is the short question – is it true? Film school students can have lots of fun dealing even with that discussion. But, short of disappearing into the Pontius Pilate territory of 'What is truth?' (we might never get out alive), I am happy to accept that this is a real character, in a real situation, taking direction from a documentary film-maker because he was enjoying himself and because he needed the publicity.

Dmitri manages to buy himself the car he really wants – a Mercedes – from a scrapyard, having turned down the offer of a perfectly good Audi from a scary-looking second-hand salesman. 'The Russian wants a Mercedes, the idiot,' the salesman tells a colleague. As he happily drives along, singing to himself, the car breaks down and he is forced to abandon it. There he is, hitch-hiking as the sun goes down. This is another sequence, cut very quickly, beautifully shot, looking like drama. Pawel says that lots of people asked him if he had set up the whole scene, if only because it is so funny. He says it all happened as they filmed it. Sometimes you just get lucky.

The film continues to follow the great-grandson's tour as he is feted in Baden Baden and eventually in London, where Dostoevsky is introduced to Count Tolstoy, along with the high society with which the count regularly mingles. Eventually, he gets back to Germany with enough money to buy the car he always wanted. A caption at the end tells us that he was attacked by bandits on his way home, escaped because the car had so much speed but then, sadly, drove the car into a ditch when he fell asleep. The car was a write-off.

From Moscow to Pietushki, the last in the group of documentaries about Russia, traces the life, work and friendships of Benedict Yerofeyev, a man who had achieved fame as a writer but who had remained a mysteriously elusive figure until Pawlikowski came to find him in Moscow, just before he died. The film quotes constantly from the work of the writer, whose most famous work, the title from which the film takes its name, uses as a conceit the train journey from Moscow to Pietushki. Around this simple idea, he weaves his fantasies, philosophy, stories about his crazy friends and sometimes, vividly described, his dark, terrifying, drink-induced paranoia. His book had struck a cord with many people and had been been sold to many countries, even adapted for the stage, by the time this film was made. But still he remained elusive.

Pawlikowski explains why he was so interested in this man and his gang of friends:

> *His outlook and personality, the mixture of comedy and wit, the lyrical self-destructive streak, is something I just love about Russia. He and his disciples would not be feasible in any other country. As for soviet society, he opted out of it, wanted no truck with it. He just dropped out, through drunkenness and living on the fringes, not even having papers, which was unthinkable at the time. He embodied something very Russian. His friends, brilliant characters, they just ingested literature. For them literature was an anarchic liberating thing, a protest against reality. They didn't need books, a bit like* Fahrenheit 451, *they were walking literature.*

Pawlikowski tracks down Yerofeyev at an apartment block in Moscow. He first encounters a woman, sweeping the steps.

He asks if the famous writer lives there. She gives him the apartment number but says he is not, by Moscow standards, a writer. Why not, Pawel asks. 'Because he is drinking all the time, even as we speak.' We now meet Yerofeyev's wife. She tells about how he was left on the stairs, like a kitten, after a party and she invited him in. He stayed. A photograph shows Benny as he was then, a stunningly good-looking young man, movie star material. The film then cuts to Benny today, bloated, ill and needing to speak with the help of a special microphone pressed to his throat. He has cancer. He is asked 'Do you regret the way your life turned out?' 'No,' he says. 'It turned out as it turned out, to hell with it.'

Benny has a group of loyal friends who talk about his past. After he was thrown out of university for upsetting the military, his life took some strange turns. They say that, like them, he spent eight years living on the Moscow train. Sometimes they stayed with a friend in a one-room apartment, sleeping under the piano, but mostly they lived on the train. They bribed the conductor and travelled back and forth. They played a game, the one that Pawlikowski likens to *Fahrenheit 451*, when everyone had to quote accurately and extensively from a work of literature. The first person to make a mistake had to go and buy the wine, because, however wide-ranging the literary quotation, the others always knew it.

In a brilliantly crafted and desperately sad sequence towards the end of the film, the section of the book *From Omutishche to Leonovo* is quoted. A darkened train runs across the screen. The voice-over, quoting from the book, says:

> And then everything went hazy. If you were to say that there was a fog, I think I'd agree with you. But if you were to say there was no fog, just flames and ice, I might agree with that too. It's cold, ever colder and then it started boiling and then it froze again. I started trembling and shuddering too.

Then we cut to a brightly lit psychiatric hospital where a patient is being unceremoniously stripped. From this point, the film cuts between the night shots of the train and dramatic reconstructions of a psychiatric patient being restrained, hosed down with water and physically humiliated. The dramatic reading from the book continues, stopping occasionally for shocking 'natural' sound from the hospital.

> *The sunset glowed red, horses tossed their manes.*
> *I kept running through the blizzard in the darkness tearing the doors off their hinges.*
> *The Moscow Pietushki train was about to be derailed.*
> *Were these the spasms I desired of you Pietushki? You have slaughtered all your birds and trampled down your jasmine.*
> *This is not Pietushki. If he who has left the earth forever and sees everyone and everything, I am certain he has never looked in this direction.*
> *Footsteps behind me were getting nearer. I did not have enough breath to run any further. I just staggered to the Kremlin wall and collapsed.*
> *They didn't even stop or breathe, they leapt at me and started to strangle me with five or six hands at once.*
> *I never knew such pain could exist. I writhed and a thick word 'why?' spread over my eye. Trembling, I lost consciousness.*
> *I have not come round since and I never shall.*

In a last interview with Yerofeyev, Pawel asks him why all of his works seem to end in horror. Benny is looking rather smartly turned out and quite cheerful or, perhaps more accurately, mischievous. He says that *Titus Andronicus* and *The Spanish Tragedy* both end in the massacre of all of the living characters. He leaves some alive. Then he adds that in his next work he will make sure that he corrects that. Everyone will die. Then he smiles.

As a last comment on his classic work, he says, 'I wrote that book . . . for a small circle of friends, in order to cheer them up and to sadden them a little too. Eighty pages of cheering up and 10 pages to let them forget all cheerfulness.' Shortly after that interview, he died.

Pawlikowski's next film, though made for the Documentary Department at the BBC, was a work of fiction. It was based to a large extent on documentary research and the actors were all ordinary people who lived in the Yorkshire location he chose. The documentary influence is so strong in the film that the BBC

Pawel Pawlikowski directing *The Last Resort*

kept it on ice for a year before showing it. They were worried about a controversy, raging in the press at the time (and many times before and since, in my experience), that the film-makers had been encouraging young people to indulge in criminal activity for the sake of the cameras (*plus ça change*). Eventually, *Twockers* was shown, received well critically, and was the start of what now looks like a new and exciting career in fiction for Pawlikowski.

He has made two well-received fiction films since then. The first, *The Last Resort*, is inspired by an incident in his own life – when he was brought to England as a teenager, unable to speak the language. The second, *My Summer of Love*, is a love story about two young women in the north of England. Both have been successful with critics and at the box office. He has plans for more fiction and is in some demand in the industry, having already turned down a major Hollywood project. But I doubt that docu- mentary has lost him altogether. I feel sure that, sooner or later, he will be back. He won't be able to stay away.

FILMOGRAPHY

Lucifer Over Lancashire
1987
Documentary.

Extraordinary Adventures
1988
Short film.

Vaclav Havel
1989
Documentary.

UN Media Peace Prize
RTS nomination

From Moscow to Pietushki
1991, BBC TV
Emmy International
Prix Italia
Canadian Rocky at Banff
Royal Television Society Award, Best Documentary

Serbian Epics
1992, BBC TV

Gran Prix, Documentary Film Festival Marseilles
Gran Prix, Festival dei Popoli, Florence

Dostoevsky's Travels
1992, BBC TV
Documentary.

Royal Television Award, Best Documentary
Felix – European Film Academy
Canadian Rocky at Banff
Prix Italia nomination

Tripping with Zhirinovsky
1995, BBC TV
Documentary.

Grierson Award, Best British Documentary, 1995
Golden Gate Award, San Francisco International Film Festival, 1995

Charlie Chaplin and the Cossack Gold
1998, BBC TV, Odessa Films/FR3/TSR
Nominated, Prix Italia

The Stringer
1998, BBC/British Screen
Feature film.

Directors' Fortnight, Cannes Film Festival, 1998
Montreal Film Festival, 1998

Twockers
1999, BBC2
Medium-length feature.

Screened at London Film Festival, 1998
Screened at Sheffield Documentary Film Festival, 1998
Screened at San Francisco Film Festival, 1999
Screened at Input, 1999
Screened at Krakow Film Festival, 1999

The Last Resort
2000, BBC Films
Wrote and directed

Feature film starring Dina Korzun, Paddy Considine, Artiom Strelnikov.

European Film of the Year – awarded by German Ministry of Culture
Michael Powell Award for Best British Film, Edinburgh Festival,
    2000
Best Picture at Thessalonika International Film Festival (TIFF), 2000
Paddy Considine, Best Actor at TIFF, 2000
Dina Korzun, Best Actress at TIFF, 2000
International Critics' Prize at TIFF, 2000
Best Film at Motovun Film Festival, 2000
Best Film at Gijon Film Festival, 2000
Dina Korzun, Best Actress at Gijon Film Festival, 2000
Screened at Toronto Film Festival, 2000
Screened at Venice Film Festival, 2000
Nominated for Best Film and Director at Bratislava Film Festival
Dina Korzun, Best Actress at Bratislava
Special Mention at London Film Festival, 2000

Nominated for Best Director at South Bank Awards, 2001
BAFTA Best Newcomer, 2001
Nominated for BAFTA, Best British Film, 2001
Nominated for Best British Independent Film at British Independent Film Awards (BIFA)
Nominated for Best Screenplay at BIFA
Nominated for Best Director at BIFA
Dina Korzun, nominated for Best Newcomer at BIFA
Screened at Sundance Film Festival, 2001

My Summer of Love
2004, Apocalypso/BBC Films
Wrote and directed

Feature film starring Paddy Considine, Nathalie Press, Emily Blunt.

Winner of the Michael Powell Award for Best British Film, Edinburgh Film Festival, 2004
Screened at Toronto Film Festival, 2004
Nominated for Best Director at The British Independent Film Awards, 2004
Nominated for six London Critics' Circle Awards, 2005, including Best Director and Best British Film
Winner, Outstanding British Film of the Year, BAFTA Film Awards, 2005
Winner, Best Screenplay at the Evening Standard Awards, 2005
Winner, Most Promising Newcomer for Nathalie Press at the Evening Standard Awards, 2005
Screened at Berlin Film Festival, 2005
Joint winner of the UK Prize at the Directors' Guild of Great Britain Awards, 2005

5 Kevin Macdonald
Oscar-winning polymath

Kevin Macdonald

Since leaving university, Kevin Macdonald has made nine major documentaries, seven for network television, two for the cinema – one an Oscar winner. He has also written a classic documentary textbook, *Imaging Reality*, and a much admired biography of his grandfather, the feature-film writer and producer, Emeric Pressburger. He somehow managed to fit in teaching assignments at a number of film schools and universities, including the Cuban School, where he impressed the students with his fluent Spanish and his boyish good looks. He is now working on his first fact-based drama for the cinema and in gaps in production is expecting to make a documentary for Channel 4. Still only 37 and with a track record like that, wouldn't you think you would just hate him?

Actually, Kevin is modest and easygoing, and though he is also formidably clever, he combines in my opinion just the right mix of ambition and self-doubt to stop him from being unbearable.

Unlike the other documentarists featured in this book, Kevin has not developed a distinctive style which is recognizably his. There is no obvious way of spotting a Kevin Macdonald film. This was a deliberate decision on his part. He says, 'Writing *Imagining Reality* interested me in experimenting with different techniques. I don't want to be classified as having only one way of making films.'

I first met Kevin when I commissioned him to co-direct and sometimes shoot or record sound on a series of half-hour films about Scotland. He worked with his brother Andrew, now a world-class movie producer (*Trainspotting*, *The Beach*, among others). The films were shot in the observational style and from time to time the brothers would also appear on camera. Apart from a short insert, made for BBC Scotland's Edinburgh Festival coverage, this was their first commission. It was also mine. It was 1991 and I had just arrived at Scottish Television and wanted to try and shake things up a bit and commission programmes that would appeal to a young audience. Kevin was 23 and Andrew 24, and although they were working with an experienced independent producer, giving these young men a series of their own still looked like a bit of a gamble, as many people warned me at the time.

The series was called *Shadowing* and, fortunately for me, was a huge success with the audience and more importantly – from the point of view of my bosses at Scottish Television – it was a hit with the advertisers. Fifty per cent of the viewers were young males and that is what the advertising industry was looking for.

There were six programmes. My favourite was the first to be transmitted. It was about a bubbly young woman with a great sense of humour who was a kissogram girl. The brothers preferred their film about a stalker, a man who works with people who want to go hunting deer in the Highlands and need his experience to guide them to their prey. Another of the films dealt with a Royal visit (Princess Anne). The Macdonalds' irreverent attitudes contrasted starkly with much of the sycophancy from the people they were filming and made, as far as I was concerned, a very funny film.

I am not going to go into detail about these early programmes, partly because I no longer have a copy of the series – and doubt that anyone else does – but also because the brothers are, to put it mildly, not exactly proud of it. Andrew says he finds it embarrassing; Kevin describes it as 'sub-Broomfield', his way of explaining that they used the techniques which Nick Broomfield has perfected but did not do it as well as Nick. This is hardly surprising since it was their first effort. In any case, I think they are being hard on themselves. The series was entertaining and threw interesting new light on the various aspects of Scottish culture that they examined. The stalker film gave them the calling card they needed to get their next documentary commission, at Channel 4.

The new film was made for the influential commissioning editor, Nick Fraser, who has since moved to the BBC, where he runs the international documentary series, *Storyville*. Nick liked the idea of a film made by the grandsons of the great Emeric Pressburger, telling his eventful life story and relating his experiences to his writing and his films. Andrew produced and Kevin directed, narrated and appeared in the film. It took the form of a journey, when Kevin researched back into family history in an attempt to understand the grandfather he had only known briefly as a boy.

His role in the film is, stylistically speaking, that of the conventional investigating reporter, going from place to place, interviewing witnesses and being seen on camera from time to time. But there is an additional ingredient in this film. At times, he appears to be taking the role of his subject, almost like an actor. One very quick cutaway, in an apartment in Berlin where Pressburger lived, shows Kevin standing alone, staring at the camera. In another shot, he sits at a pavement café table, pouring sugar into a glass of milk. Pressburger, sitting in this place in the early 1930s, would order warm milk and pour the whole container of sugar from the table into it, for sustenance, because he was so poor. In another scene, near the end of the film, we see Kevin enter a customs and immigration area; in close-up we see the passport he presents. Again in a very quick cut, almost subliminal, we see that it cannot be his own British passport, it is that of a another country, probably European, possibly Hungary. The air of ambiguity is effective. Sometimes Kevin appears to be going one step beyond the role of investigator and beginning to try to reconstruct the emotional life of his grandfather, not in the conventional way, with props and costumes, not literally but metaphorically.

The Making of an Englishman is a heart-warming tale of a brilliant talent who suffered great personal tragedy, mitigated to some extent by the kind of lucky breaks that sometimes seem to be too good to be true, ending when he found success and personal contentment in permanent exile from his homeland. The film starts with home-movie footage of a lovely old English country house with a friendly old man waving from the window. 'This is how I remember my grandfather' says the voice-over. Here he is, in Shoemaker's Cottage in Suffolk. Cut to archive film of Pressburger as a young man, playing cards. He was a Hungarian Jew, born in the last days of the Hapsburg Empire. Cut back to home movie in colour. A man and a woman are pushing a pram, past a red telephone box. He was always more English than the English, we are told. In some ways a lot like many Eastern European refugees. The difference was that he became one of the most successful film-makers ever in the British Isles, together with his partner, Michael Powell, seen in the archive walking towards camera with a big smile. After the Powell–Pressburger logo comes a clip from their classic movie, *The Red Shoes*.

This is the start of a sequence which cuts in and out of very short clips from the partners' films, punctuated by equally short extracts from an interview with Martin Scorsese. So we know what weight we are punching at. Scorsese says that he was drawn to the films because he liked the style, which is 'more florid . . . surprising'. He points out that the main characters are, unusually, anti-heroes, and the films deal with darker, psychological, emotional states. They were not afraid of emotion. They embraced it.

The film cuts to a shot of a 35 mm Steenbeck. The screen shows the closing title, 'Written, produced and directed by Michael Powell and Emeric Pressburger'. Kevin is sitting at the Steenbeck. He says in commentary that the films of his grandfather seem to be littered with cryptic autobiographical references. He wants to find out more about him and maybe, selfishly, that will help him find out more about himself.

The opening of the film is a skilful and articulate use of classic documentary techniques for gripping the attention of an audience. It draws us in with a cosy set of archive images, then hints at a touch of mystery in the past, gives quick tasters from the movies, mysterious and tantalizing in their brevity, introduces the gravitas and authority of the great Martin Scorsese to underline the importance of the film's subject, and then brings us back to where we started the sequence – a young man wants to understand his dead grandfather, not only because he is interested in his work and curious about his past, but for another equally important reason. He wants to understand himself as well.

In commentary, Kevin says he is 'bursting with images' from his grandfather's films. The picture cuts from a close-up of Kevin at the Steenbeck where he is watching the movie, *The Life and Death of Colonel Blimp*, to a clip from the picture itself. Two men are fighting in a swimming pool. One is saying:

> *You laugh at my big belly but you don't know how I got it. You laugh at my big moustache but you don't know why I do it. How do you know what sort of a fellow I was when I was as young as you are. Forty years ago.*

'Forty years ago' is echoing, repeated. A shot of railway lines as a train thunders over. The film music continues. An old map shows the Austrian–Hungarian Empire, then a close-up, the word 'Miskolc'. The music stops. We are out of the Pressburger movie and into Macdonald's again. New filming shows the streets of Miskolc, the town where Pressburger was born. There Kevin finds the old house where his grandfather once lived and tracks down an old school friend and one of the early girlfriends. She says, 'A real gentleman like that only comes along once every hundred years.' Now the quest is under way. The film will follow Kevin's journey as he travels thousands of miles by train, following in the footsteps of Emeric Pressburger.

The technique of cutting back and forth into the films of Powell and Pressburger is used throughout the film, often for the purpose of emphasizing a point, sometimes to illustrate the fact that Pressburger's life experiences informed all of his work. Sometimes, the clips are short and the films not identified. It is the context in which they are used that is important.

In some ways, the story is, in microcosm, that of so many talented Jewish intellectuals, forced to flee from the tyranny of European fascism. The part of Hungary where he lived was absorbed by Romania after the First World War and, eventually, Emeric was called up to serve in the army. Refusing to fight for Romania, he fled the country and went to Berlin, then the capital of the left-wing Weimar Republic. Berlin was a haven for many exiles, foreign artists and writers, drawn by the excitement and creativity of Weimar Berlin. A brilliantly compelling witness, Curt Siodmak, brother of the German film director Robert Siodmak, takes up the story. Emeric was desperately poor, the economy was in turmoil and there was little work available. Emeric started to write short stories and sent them to publishers, but was constantly rejected. Then, one day, came the breakthrough. Soon he was working as a writer at the UFA studios, the place where *The Cabinet of Dr Caligari*, *Metropolis* and many other classic German films of that great period in the country's cinema had been made.

It was a heady, wonderfully stimulating period for Emeric, but of course it would not last. Hitler was elected as Chancellor in 1932. Soon, Emeric was summoned to his boss's office and told that the studio had been instructed not to employ Jews. His name was on an arrest list. He left the country that night, boarding a late train to Paris, where once again he struggled at first but broke through to write movies for the French cinema. But somehow he never felt at home in France and he was having more financial problems, so he decided to move on again. Many of his friends were going to America but he decided on England.

Part 3 begins with a deliberate cliché shot of the White Cliffs of Dover. Music from an unidentified movie, 1940s vintage, plays over it and it is followed by shots of a boat, a customs hall, and Kevin arriving and showing a passport. Not British. The picture now cuts to the movie, reprising the idea from the beginning of the documentary. It is the Powell–Pressburger classic, *The Life and Death of Colonel Blimp*. An immigration officer is looking at a foreign national's passport. He asks the man when he arrived in this country. The man came from Paris France on 16 June 1935. He had arrived in Paris on 15 January 1934. From Germany? Yes, from Germany. Most refugees, says the officer, left Germany earlier than that, in 1933, when Hitler came to power, why not him? Because he had not at first seen Hitler as a threat. Eight months is a long time, says the officer. The reply is delivered politely but very firmly. 'Please, I mean no offence, but you in England took five years.' It is a dramatic moment and a brave one, because this film was released in 1942, right in the middle of the war with Germany. The biographical reference is unmissable.

All of the interviewees in *The Making of an Englishman* are people who have crossed Pressburger's path in some way, except for one, who is used as an analyst, an expert witness. Bernard Tavernier, the French movie director, makes the point that Pressburger was unlike other British film-makers. He was outward looking, open-minded, he liked to confront difficult issues. He was also not afraid of emotion. He says the point in *Colonel Blimp* when the immigrant tells the authorities that he wanted to come back to his wife's homeland, to serve the country himself, is one of the most moving moments in any British film. It is, he says, 'audacious'. Clearly, Tavernier thinks that the British are inhibited and insular, and this is reflected in their films. He could be right, but still this analysis raises a contradiction. The whole thrust of the documentary shows how Pressburger, perhaps inevitably, because of the times he lived in, was drawn towards England, its people and its culture. Another interviewee, the cinematographer Christopher Challis, tells how Pressburger once said to him that he felt more English than Challis was, 'because you were born British, I chose to be British'.

Kevin says that, looking back, he is not too happy with the film. He says he would like to recut it, perhaps with new material if that were possible. He says that what he is saying in the film is a bit oblique, 'something I do a lot'. He adds, 'I am interested in the idea of how history or memory can still be present in a place after the people have gone. You can understand a person better if you go to the place where they used to live.' That is why he wanted to return to the place where his grandfather grew up. For me, one of the last sequences in the film reveals exactly what Kevin says he wants to do, a gut-wrenchingly moving moment. There is nothing oblique about it.

We see a monument, a war memorial, in the small town in Hungary where the story began. It reveals that 14,000 Jewish people from this place were killed in the holocaust, 90 per cent of the Jewish population. Emeric's 72-year-old mother and all of his family living in the area died in concentration camps.

The Man Who Listened To Britain, the story of Humphrey Jennings, was also produced by Figment Films, the company Kevin founded with his brother Andrew. Stylistically, it is quite a conventional television documentary, cutting in and out of extracts from Jennings movies to contemporary footage of the actual locations today and peppered with interviews with a number of key figures – experts, friends and family, as well as some prominent film directors who would probably not object to the description 'Jennings fans'. The interviews are all shot in close-up with neutral backgrounds. Jennings was a film-maker's film-maker and the film pays homage to his huge talent. He was, it says, 'the only poet of the British cinema. He had a painter's eye for the striking and resonant image and an ability to capture spontaneous and truthful moments.'

It is always problematic making documentaries about people who are dead, particularly if there are no archive interviews with them. This film uses a clever technique, right at the beginning. After a montage which cuts from contemporary London shots to scenes from Jennings's masterpiece, *Listen to Britain*, combined with testimonies to his greatness by Mike Leigh, Richard Attenborough and Jeffrey Richards, a host of interviewees have obviously been asked to describe his character. They are rapidly intercut, sometimes saying only one or two words: 'He was a person who stood out, a figure in the landscape' – 'very thin' – 'green teeth' – 'big nose' – 'rather nice hair'. It is an original and ingenious way of dealing with the perennial problem of making the (dead) central character live. At the end of the sequence, we feel we know the man. We are not sure how much we like him, but we know him.

The theme of patriotism, strong in the Pressburger films, is also prominent in the wartime work of Humphrey Jennings. Kevin says, 'I am interested in patriotism; like many of my generation I am suspicious of it. All those émigrés in my grandfather's generation had a love of the country and a great pride in being British. That's what fascinates me about Humphrey Jennings. He is very intellectual, cynical about many aspects of British life and yet he is a great patriot. An avant-garde artist, a rebel outsider but also now known as the Poet Laureate of Britain at war.' People today read the wartime Jennings films differently from the audiences in the 1940s. Still we find them moving. 'You feel a sense of loss that the communities he portrayed do not exist any more. Like Powell and Pressburger, Lauder and Gilliat, David Lean, they were all creating a myth of British unity, real at the time but no longer. We are all a bit dissociated from society these days.'

One of the early Jennings films quoted in the documentary contains a scene which has become famous and illustrates the point that Kevin is making. It is called *Heart of Britain*, made in 1941 when, in Churchill's words, the country 'stood alone' in its war with Germany. It features a northern English choir singing robustly the *Hallelujah Chorus*. Commentary comes over towards the end of the scene, a strong, male voice. 'People who sing like this in times like these cannot be beaten.' The choir sings, 'Hallelujah, Hallelujah'. The picture cuts to an aircraft manufacturer, a war plane being built. 'The Nazis will learn, once and for all, that no-one, with impunity, troubles the Heart of Britain.'

The documentary also features Jennings's most admired film, *Listen to Britain*. This is one of the most influential short films of all time, one that many directors and many more film editors know almost frame by frame. A film with no commentary, only the sounds of life in wartime Britain, it is superbly crafted, almost choreographed like the most intricate of ballets. An interviewee tells us that Jennings and his legendary editor Stuart McAllister would sometimes stay up all night, arguing about one frame.

In 1943, Jennings made *The Silent Village*, a drama-documentary, hailed by the film-makers/fans who act as guides and critics throughout as 'groundbreaking'. It tells the story of a village in Czechoslovakia where the Nazis invaded, murdered all the adult population and marched off the children to work for them in concentration camps. Kevin filmed in the Welsh mining village where Jennings lived for six months when making the film with a cast of ordinary people whose lives mirrored the lives of the tragic villagers of Lidice. Some of the actors are still alive and they are interviewed, talking about the experience of making the film and about their huge respect and admiration for Jennings.

In a sense *The Silent Village* represents a turning point in British documentary history. Until the young film-makers who worked on the documentaries which were sponsored by the state in the 1940s, the working class was rarely seen on the big screen. As Jeffrey Richards points out, they were usually comic characters with bit parts. Jennings took working people, taught them to act and made them into stars. In doing so, as Richard Attenborough claims in Kevin's film, he helped to establish the method of screen acting which continues to dominate in British fiction cinema – the 'realist' tradition. *The Silent Village* and the film which followed it, *Fires Were Started*, continue to be massively influential as they are studied by film school students and aspiring film-makers to this day. This is the thesis of Kevin's film and I, for one, think he is absolutely right.

Production on *Fires Were Started*, according to Jennings's assistant, interviewed by Kevin, had a one-page script. The War Office were demanding a proper outline before he started shooting, but he simply refused. This, again, was one of the influential moments from the point of view of British cinema. The actors were all real, front-line fire-fighters, and Jennings worked with them, developing the story and improvising their lines. The acting is extraordinarily impressive, particularly in the fire-fighting scenes, where the men are replicating their normal, nightly, desperately dangerous jobs, trying to contain the mayhem caused by the *Luftwaffe*'s blanket bombing.

One of the most moving aspects of *Fires Were Started* is the way it captures the humour of the people for whom the London Blitz was 'all in a day's work'. Kevin introduces this section of his film with an interview with one of the surviving actors/firemen, who adopts a fake-posh accent and matter-of-fact demeanour and tells how, after an air raid, BBC radio would issue a news bulletin the next day. 'Last night, enemy aircraft raided towns in the southeast of England. Fires were started and casualties have been reported.' He smiles and adds, 'That was after 1500 people had been killed and half of London had been burned down. That was where the title came from.'

The documentary finishes with a tribute to another great Jennings work made at the end of the war, *A Diary for Timothy*. Another much imitated film, it uses the device of a man writing a diary for his new baby, telling him about the world he has been born into and expressing his hopes for the baby's future. Unusually for Jennings, it is driven by narration, this time written by the great E. M. Forster. Mike Leigh, who appears throughout Kevin's film, talking about the influence that Jennings had on him and so many British film-makers, asks the question that most of them would want to ask. Whatever happened to the baby in the film? He was about Leigh's age. He says, 'He could have been a hippy in the sixties. Is he in prison? Or is he dead? It's fascinating.' Leigh says he wants the film to go on, to project into the future, to tell us what is going to happen. But the film simply asks the question, 'What is going to happen to you, Timothy? You and all the other babies?' A series of captions at the end of Kevin's documentary tell us:

> Timothy Jenkins left school after O levels. He joined a band called the Dolphins in the 1960s.
> He moved to Brighton, bought a lambretta and became a mod in 1971.
> He went to teacher training college. He now teaches in a comprehensive school in Sussex.

As for 'all the other babies', Mike Leigh has answered that question himself, along with all the other British film-makers working in the realist tradition, a tradition that owes so much to Humphrey Jennings.

Kevin's biopic about the fiction film director Donald Cammell, who co-directed the cult fiction film *Performance* (1970) with Nicholas Roeg, was released in 1998. The movie was very much of its time and some people still admire it. Cammell was dead by the time Kevin made his film and it relies to a large extent on an interview filmed with him in the 1990s. The documentary included as interviewees many of the glitterati from the 1960s/1970s period, like Anita Pallenberg, Mick Jagger and Keith Richards.

The Cammell biography was made for television, but Scottish Screen gave Kevin the money to strike a print which meant it could be shown in cinemas and film festivals. It did well on the festival circuit. It was around the time that *When We Were Kings* was released and *Hoop Dreams* had come out a year or so before. Kevin says:

This set me thinking. If you are going to spend a year and a half making something it is nice to see it on the big screen. Also you get more feedback. You tend to have longer schedules. It is a different approach than making something for television. You can spend longer editing and longer making sure that everything is as slick as you can possibly make it. In craft terms that is very satisfying.

His next film was a 90-minute picture for the cinema and it won the Oscar for best feature-length documentary in 2000. The film was *One Day in September*. It tells the story of the massacre of members of the Israeli athletics team by Palestinian terrorists in 1972. Kevin worked with producer John Battsek.

Our original idea was quite intellectual really. We wanted to make a thriller out of a real event, to take a story you would normally tell in a current-affairsy way and tell it more like a non-fiction novel. Like Truman Capote's In Cold Blood. *The two films that influenced us were not documentaries really. One was* JFK, *the Oliver Stone film. The other was Costa-Gavras's* Z. *I wanted that kind of complexity, where you are never quite sure what is going on and there is all the time a sort of hum of chaos all around you. The through line is quite simple but there is so much action, so much dialogue, the complex sense of a conspiracy.*

Pre-title, there is a rather corny commercial for the city of Munich, 'a German paradise', now about to play host to the 20th Olympic Games. Then we see shots of lights shining out of the darkness, what sounds like police tapes, an unidentified voice saying, 'Nobody could have foreseen it.' The credits run over this mysterious opening. Two main witnesses will see us through the film. The first is introduced. She sits in a plain background, a conventional interview shot. She is Ankie Spitzer, widow of one of the Israeli team. There is home video of her wedding and pictures of her husband with their baby. They were only married for just over a year.

The second witness is in disguise. He is Jamal Al Gashey and is the only one of the Palestinian terrorists to survive. He tells how his family were thrown out of their homeland by the Zionists in 1948, how he was brought up in refugee camps and how, when he joined the revolution, he was given a sense of purpose and dignity. Throughout the film Al Gashey gives his eyewitness account of the story from the point of view of the Palestinians. Ankie Spritzer describes the worry and confusion of the families of the team as the tragic drama unfolds. Most of the time the events are described by eyewitnesses, members of the team who survived, German officials, police and journalists. There is a commentary which is purely factual and unemotive. It is read by Michael Douglas, the A-List Hollywood actor.

Various techniques are used to heighten the cinematic effect of the film. When Al Gashey is describing how he met with the leader of the group in Munich and was given his orders, proud to be able to confront the enemy, he is in voice-over and the picture shows fast-motion street scenes of the city at night, with urgent sounding music raising the tension. The classic movie device of a clock, this time digital, recording the time but emphasizing that it is running out for the victims is used throughout the last part of the film. At the end, the disastrous airport shoot-out, where all of the surviving athlete prisoners and five of the terrorists were killed, is reconstructed with 3D animation. Throughout, incidental music emphasizes tone and mood. *One Day in September* is a skilfully constructed film with a strong narrative, but it would have been unlikely to achieve the notoriety which followed its release without the participation of Al Gashey, the Palestinian. It required a great deal of patience and a certain amount of luck to track him down.

Only three of the terrorists survived the carnage at the airport and they later escaped to safety on a hijacked plane, with the permission of the German authorities. The Israelis hunted for them, found two and assassinated them. They also killed 12 others that they suspected of being involved. Kevin had found archive film in the ITN library showing the terrorists giving a press conference when they arrived in Libya, which had given them a safe haven. He discovered that the youngest of the three men in the film, a fresh-faced, good-looking young man, was still alive. He set about finding him and after months of research, first in Germany, then in Lebanon, then Palestine and lengthy negotiations which kept breaking down, eventually, with the help of an influential go-between, he got his interview.

He says that it could never happen today. At the time, the dove-ish Barak had come to power in Israel, Arafat had returned to Palestine and there was great hope in diplomatic circles that peace could, at last, come to the Middle East. In this context, people were prepared to look again at history, try to clear the air about the past. After the film was finished, Kevin sent a copy to the Palestinian Liberation Organization and at first they seemed to like it. Then the recriminations began. Edward Said, an academic who was the self-appointed spokesman for Palestine in the United States, wrote a front page article for the *Guardian* newspaper, attacking the film as being pro-Zionist and for failing to remind the world of the wrongs which had been heaped on the Palestinian people by Israel. There is, in fact, context at the beginning of the film, when the Palestinian terrorist explains what happened to his family, how they were driven from their home and the terrible hardships they had suffered. Sadly, it is likely that no amount of context would be enough to satisfy the determined propagandist.

After the Arabs came the Israelis. Kevin was castigated by the families of the dead athletes for allowing the Palestinian terrorist to explain himself. They said the film 'humanized' him and this was unacceptable. Meanwhile, the German authorities were unhappy at the way their people had been portrayed in the film. In fact, Kevin says, the Germen secret police had tried to lean on some of the participants to prevent them co-operating with the film. This was not a story that they wanted the world to remember. So all three sides objected to the film. When I was a young television journalist I was always told that if you make an investigative film and all the opposing interested parties attack you after transmission, you have probably got it right. But Kevin does not come from a current affairs background and found the response from the various interest groups very difficult to handle. However, in spite of the furore, the film was widely shown and critically praised. And it won an Oscar.

Kevin says he learned an important lesson from the film. 'As a film-maker, don't go near the Middle East unless you are looking for trouble.' He decided his next film should not be controversial, 'nothing about death and destruction or anything that really matters'. He agreed to make a film about Mick Jagger – 'just a bit of frivolous fun'. He shot the film himself, on DV, something he had not done professionally since he worked with me in Scotland. He followed Jagger around for six months and enjoyed the experience. The edit was a different matter. It is always difficult to make a film about somebody as famous as Jagger, particularly if his company is financing it. Jagger had been very guarded during the shoot and now he wanted to control the final product. Kevin gives just one example. 'We were in the cutting room and Mick said he just wanted to have a word with Justine [the editor] about a few little things, why didn't I go and have some lunch? So I went out and came back an hour and a half later and he was still there, going through the film shot by shot and saying, "I look ugly in that shot, and that one . . .".' The finished film, *Being Mick*, is not one of Kevin's favourites but it was at least a respite from the heavy politics of the Middle East.

Touching the Void (2004), a true adventure story about a mountaineering expedition that went horribly wrong, was made for the cinema and had a television screening plus video and DVD. It has proved to be very popular with audiences. Unusually for a documentary, it has won a number of Best Picture awards, beating off the competition from star-studded, flashy fiction films. The one that has given Kevin the most pleasure so far was presented to him by Ken Loach. For a cinéaste and historian of British cinema, this was about as good as it gets. The film broke all box office records in the UK for a documentary film, at the time of its release. It is based on a book by Joe Simpson and tells the story of a climb he did with his friend Simon Yates in the Andes in 1985. The two of them climbed alone with only one other team member, who stayed at base camp. During the climb, Joe falls and is held only by his rope, which is attached to Simon, above him on the mountain. Simon does not know if his friend is alive or dead and is faced with the agonizing decision: should he cut the rope and save his own life? He decides to cut the rope. Joe, who is not dead but has badly damaged his leg, then begins an agonizing journey down the mountain alone. His survival is near miraculous.

The film is a combination of drama and documentary and breaks new ground in its creative decisions about both. The two climbers were happy to appear in the film, the story in itself is 'a good yarn', the locations are spectacular, so the film could have been made using conventional documentary form. Kevin did not want to do that. There is no library film of the climb so it seemed inevitable that there would have to be some reconstruction.

The challenge in making Touching the Void *was how to make the reconstruction and the documentary elements gel together and each bounce off the other, each to have the same weight. I have never liked reconstruction. There are very few documentaries where it is integrated into the film and doesn't feel like an excuse to have something visual because you can't think of anything else.*

The first important decision was how to film the two main characters, Joe and Simon. Since they were the storytellers, he decided that in visual terms he would present them as minimally as possible. He would avoid the usual clichés, filming them at home, or having them walk around the mountain, pointing out the location of the story. Kevin had made a short profile of the American documentarist Errol Morris and been convinced by Errol's argument that the long-established documentary style of filming interviewees looking off camera does not make any sense, unless the film-maker is also a character in the film. Although audiences have got used to it, it is not logical and it can be distracting. What is the interviewee looking at, you think. Or, who are they talking to? In the case of director/performers like Michael Moore or Nick Broomfield, we do know who the interviewee is looking at, but that is unusual, even today.

Kevin decided to use the Errol Morris technique of having the interviewee look directly into the camera. He thinks this contributed to the film working. These men are like camp-fire storytellers, looking you in the eye, and he feels that this helped the audience to suspend their disbelief and engage with the story. There are two frames used in filming Joe: one very close, just showing his head, and the other head and shoulders so we can see his hand movements when he is illustrating some technical point. Simon has only one frame: just the head. Both are animated storytellers and the decision to film them that way was vindicated.

The next big problem was how to film the reconstruction? Kevin decided that, rather than try to find look-alike actors, he would not pretend that these people are not actors but be honest about it and film the reconstruction in an uncompromisingly dramatic way. He says:

> I thought that if we do the two things as full-on as possible, like the documentary is just them sitting there talking and the drama is as full-on as possible, because they are both so different. You are not trying to have one kind of ooze into the other because it won't work. I don't know why I thought that but I did.

The film depends to a large extent on the articulate accounts of the two climbers. The story itself is so dramatic – and combined with brilliant acting and stunning photography, plus the carefully judged use of music to enhance mood – that the matter-of-fact recital by both men actually increases the sense of drama. When we see the actor playing Simon holding the rope, agonizing over his decision, or we see Joe crawling along the ice, fearing that the others will have left base camp before he can drag himself there, then the film cuts to the real people, calmly describing how they felt, the tension in the audience in the cinema when I first saw the film was palpable.

As we left the theatre, all around us people were asking each other how come it was such a scary film when all the time we knew the guys didn't die because there they are on the screen, fit and well? Kevin's decision to use the two contrasting styles of filming has been thoroughly vindicated.

The diversity of themes and styles in Kevin's work so far is quite unusual. Looking at his work again has made me think again about the Pressburger legacy and how much it might have influenced his grandson, however subliminally. Themes which run through the Pressburger films are echoed in Kevin's films. Emeric's first film when he started working in England was called *The Challenge*.

It was about mountaineering in the Alps, exploring the idea of good sportsmanship. Years later, Kevin was to make *Touching the Void*, much of which was also shot in the Alps, exploring, in his case, the very opposite of good sportsmanship. *The Life and Death of Colonel Blimp* examines, in a moving way, loyalty, patriotism and courage under attack. Kevin made a film about Humphrey Jennings, a documentarist who also explored these themes. Pressburger's whole life was marked by the fight against Nazism, the repression of the Jews, and the treachery shown by many of the German people in the 1930s and 1940s towards him and his race. *One Day in September* raises the same issues, however obliquely.

It is perhaps a little neat, too literal, to make such a precise corre-lation. I put this idea to Kevin when I interviewed him and he said that it is always difficult to see your own work in terms of themes. That is for others to judge. But he agrees that steeping oneself in documentary film history as he did when writing *Imagining Reality* and his book about his grandfather, *The Life and Death of a Screenwriter*, is bound to have had some profound effect on his thinking and his technique. Of course, it could also be something in the genes.

FILMOGRAPHY

Kevin Macdonald's first feature, *One Day in September*, won an Oscar for Best Documentary in 2000.

His second feature, *Touching the Void*, premiered at Telluride 2003, was released in the UK in December 2003 and in the USA in January 2004. Awards include a BAFTA for Best British Film and the Evening Standard Award for Best British Film, and it is the highest grossing British documentary in UK box office history.

Kevin co-edited *The Faber Book of Documentary* (1997), and wrote *Emeric Pressburger: The Life and Death of a Screenwriter* (Faber, 1994, winner of BFI film book of the year and shortlisted for the NCR non-fiction prize). His journalism has appeared in numer-ous publications, including *The Guardian*, *The Observer* and *Daily Telegraph*.

Directing credits

Witness: The Making of an Englishman
1995, 51 min, 16 mm, Figment Films/Channel 4/Hungarian TV (MTV)

Chaplin's Goliath
1996, 50 min, 16 mm, Figment Films/STV

Documentary about the actor who played the villain in Chaplin films.

Howard Hanks: American Artist
1997, 60 min, 16 mm, BFI/BBC/Bravo/Canal+/ Star, etc.

Donald Cammell: The Ultimate Performance
1997–8, 75 min, S 35 mm, BBC/Arts Council
Feature documentary.

Winner of Silver Hugo, Chicago Film Festival

The Moving World of George Rickey
1997–8, 56 min, S 16 mm, BBC
Documentary about the renowned kinetic sculptor.

One Day in September
1998–2000, 93 min, 35 mm, Arthur Cohn/BBC/British Screen
Feature documentary.

Winner of Academy Award for Best Documentary, 2000
Best New Director, British Independent Film Awards, 2000
Emmy, Best Documentary (Historical), 2000
Golden Camera Best Documentary (Germany), 2000

The Man Who Listened To Britain
2000, broadcast in December, Channel 4

A portrait of the surrealist painter, anthropologist and film-maker, Humphrey Jennings.

Being Mick
2001, transmitted 22 November, 9 p.m., Channel 4, Jagged Films/ Channel 4

Authorized feature-length documentary on Mick Jagger.

Touching the Void
2003, UK release 12 December 2003, US release 23 January 2004, Darlow Smithson/Film Council/FilmFour/Pathe, US Distribution: IFC Films

Dramatized documentary based on the book by Joe Simpson.

Winner, Best Film, Evening Standard British Film Awards
Winner, BAFTA Alexander Korda Award for the Outstanding British
  Film of the Year
Winner, Best Feature, Banff, 2003
Festivals 2003: Telluride, Toronto, London, Kendal, Banff
Winner, Best Documentary, British Independent Film Awards
Winner, Best Technical Achievement: Cinematography – Mike Eley,
  British Independent Film Awards
Nominated, Best Director, British Independent Film Awards
Nominated, Best British Independent Film, British Independent
  Film Awards

As executive producer

Shoot Out in Swansea: The Making of Twin Town
1997, 70 min, video, BBC

Kindertransport
1998, 30 min, DigiBeta, BBC
Documentary about Jewish child refugees coming to Britain.

In development

Bobby Fisher Goes to War
Company Pictures/Working Title
Producer: Robyn Slovo.

Angola
Company Pictures/BBC Films
Producer: Robyn Slovo.

Last King of Scotland
Slate/FilmFour/DNA

Producer: Andrea Calderwood. Writer: Peter Morgan. Based on the book by Giles Foden.

Mr Wilson
Film Four Lab
Producer: Robin Gutch. Writer: John Preston.

6 Norma Percy
Popular television history

Norma Percy

Norma Percy's track record of producing gripping political history series is, in my view, unrivalled by anyone, anywhere in the world. She is a brilliant storyteller, an indefatigable researcher, an incisive interviewer who is afraid of no-one. Her list of interviewees includes not only most of the world's most powerful heads of state, but also blood-stained dictators, leaders of revolutions, terrorists and hitmen. But she is also interested in the ordinary people, the bit players in some major international drama. 'You have to show respect,' she says and this rule applies to all the players, regardless of position or status.

She works with a close-knit team at Brook Lapping Productions and insists that the long-term partnerships she has developed over the years are fundamental to her work. In particular, her long-term collaboration with executive producer Brian Lapping has helped to mould the very individual style and form of the work she does. She is a producer who has no interest in directing but is always the driving force on any production. She now works with researchers – originally she did her own research – but she is very much hands on and does all the important interviews herself.

She is an American who, after growing up and graduating from university in the United States, went to London to study for a postgraduate degree. She stayed on after graduation and worked as a researcher in the House of Commons. Brian Lapping hired her from there to work for him at Granada Television, where he was then producing the seminal and long-running investigative current affairs series, *World in Action*. This working partnership has lasted for over 20 years. They have won numerous awards in the UK and the USA. Last year, when picking up a prize at the British Academy for Film and Television Arts (popularly known as BAFTA) for special contribution to television, Norma told the star-studded audience: 'I want to thank television for allowing me to exercise my prurient curiosity in public – and for paying me to do it.' Without that sense of curiosity it would be impossible for the formidable list of Percy–Lapping investigations to have even got started.

Their first collaboration came in 1972 when, after two years of stonewalling from government sources, they were able to make a programme about the legislative process in the UK Parliament. They chose to follow the progress of one clause in a bill which, when it had passed through Parliament, would allow the setting up of the Office of Fair Trading. With the co-operation of the responsible Conservative government minister, Sir Geoffrey Howe, they filmed for 50 hours and from this footage made a two-hour programme. This was not exactly popular television, but it certainly threw light on the workings of Parliament. The co-operation they received illustrates, for Percy, the advantages of the television historian over writers and academics. 'Politicians know that they need television,' she says. 'They would never give that much time to an academic.'

Looking back over the career to date of the Percy–Lapping team, it is possible to find a pattern emerging. At first it is hard to see why the people who made the gripping series *The Death of Yugoslavia*, which told a dramatic story of truly Shakespearean proportions, would have previously wanted to spend two years following the progress of a parliamentary committee. But in my view, this attention to detail and fascination with every dot and comma in the paperwork is the key to Norma Percy's main pre-occupations. It is the political process itself which fascinates her. 'I want to know how decisions are made,' she says. Every manoeuvre, every manipulation is forensically dissected. So for her, a political debate in the House of Commons can be just as interesting and worthy of study as the murderous machinations of ex-President of Serbia, Slobodan Milosevic. The challenge is to find out exactly how it all happened. Who won what and how did they manage it?

After the Fair Trading show, Percy and Lapping made two more British political exposés. The Commons Committee programme had been shot on film in the observational style. This time they opted for studio-based reconstruction. The first programme examined the Cabinet decision in 1976 to go to the International Monetary Fund and ask for a loan to prop up the disastrous British economy. It was a seminal moment for the Callaghan government and is still a matter of great sensitivity for the Labour Party today. In many ways, recollections of the humiliations of 1976 have influenced the current government's financial strategy since their election victory in 1997. So there was absolutely no chance of getting the Labour Cabinet members to take part in the programme.

How to tell the story without the co-operation of the protagonists was the real problem for the team. Then they came up with a brilliant idea. They invited political journalists who were close to the leading players involved in the decision and asked them to role-play and reconstruct the discussions on which they had all been fully briefed at the time. The journalists were well cast and surprised their colleagues not only with their detailed grasp of the subject and the vigour with which they put the arguments on behalf of the characters they played, but also because, as Percy explains, 'We found they could act, too. Which was a real bonus.'

The second programme, *Mrs Thatcher's Billions*, reconstructed the heated exchanges at a European summit meeting where the newly elected Thatcher went to demand a rebate for Britain in its contribution to central funds. 'Give me back my money,' she famously shouted, to the astonishment of the massed ranks of European heads of state, most of whom were not accustomed to quite such a brutal style of negotiating. In this programme, journalists from the different European countries represented at the talks spoke on behalf of their ministers. Journalist Sarah Hogg gave a memorable performance as the British Prime Minister, managing to terrify the people around her almost as much as the redoubtable Thatcher herself, in full flow.

The logical next step after journalist reconstructions is one many documentarists have taken – make a full-scale drama-documentary with all the characters played by actors. Percy and Lapping only made the one, *Breakthrough at Reykjavik*. Directed by Patrick Lau and starring look-alike actors playing Presidents Reagan and Gorbachev, it told the story of the failed attempt to agree a nuclear arms limitation treaty at a meeting in Iceland. While Percy found it an interesting experience and as usual enjoyed the process of researching it, she decided then and there that drama-documentaries do not convince an audience. 'Nobody believes them,' she says. Nothing since *Reykjavik* has changed her mind about that. While Lapping has continued to executive produce a varied slate of factual programmes, including a successful run of 'hypotheticals' – role-played imaginary situations where ethical dilemmas are examined and resolved – Percy has stuck, with great success, to recent political history.

Although I had known Norma and admired her work for a long time, I only got to know her really well when we worked together on the Granada series *End of Empire* in 1984. Lapping was executive producer and there were 12 programmes in the series, which told the story of the dismantling of the British Empire between

1947 and 1985. There was a big team of producers, researchers and directors, and I was one of them. Norma produced two programmes and so did I. My films looked at The Gold Coast (now Ghana) and the Central African Federation (now Zambia, Malawi and Zimbabwe). One of Norma's films was about the war of liberation in Southern Rhodesia, starting with UDI, so her film followed on directly in time from the end of my Federation story.

Like all Lapping's history projects since then, we had a long research period, a comfortable time to shoot and a decent amount of time for editing. So Norma and I kept crossing paths on location in Africa, co-operating on research and sharing a crew. Later we were editing on the same corridor at Granada in Manchester. So I was able to see at first hand how she worked. I am generally considered to be a very thorough researcher myself, but I was amazed at the depth of knowledge that Norma amassed and the hours she put in. Every single possible source, on paper or in person, is followed up, the minutiae studied, absorbed and classified.

I have strict rules for how to behave on location – always eat regularly and get enough sleep. Norma and I were in Lusaka at the same time on a research trip and later filming in Harare. I cannot remember ever managing to persuade her to join me and my colleagues and crew for dinner. She never stopped working. I was worried that she would not be able to keep up the pace, but I was wrong. The research was meticulous and the resulting programme justified the time spent on it.

Lapping expected of us producers that we would get all the major players, all the big decision-makers in our stories, to agree to interviews and I managed to get everybody I wanted with one exception, Robert Mugabe, President of Zimbabwe. He kept saying that he would give me a research interview but somehow he was always too busy. I even got one of his chief allies, President Kenneth Kaunda of Zambia, to intervene on my behalf. He did so and believed that he had organized it for me. But still Mugabe was not available. I gradually conceded that I was not going to get my interview. However, much to my chagrin at the time, Norma got Mugabe. That was when I realized that there is persistence and then there is persistence, Percy style. She defines it as a complete refusal to take no for an answer. Because we were co-operating so closely, we came to a pragmatic decision – she would include in her interview with Mugabe questions that I wanted answered if I would share the interview time I had negotiated with Joshua Nkomo, a hero of the independence struggle and Mugabe's great rival.

The *End of Empire* series became the training ground for many of the people who went on to join Brian Lapping when he set up an independent production company in 1989.

After *Empire*, the first major documentary history series produced by Norma Percy and executive produced by Brian Lapping was *The Second Russian Revolution*. They recruited Angus Roxburgh, who worked for the *Sunday Times* as their Moscow correspondent, to open doors and provide up-to-date context. They also brought in the much respected director, Angus MacQueen, another expert on Russia. A lot of the people who were familiar with Russian politics were cynical about the chances of getting the co-operation from top politicians that *Empire* had achieved. The politburo had never been known to leak, so why start now? But Percy had honed her techniques on the Granada series and was confident that somehow the silence would be broken. All that was needed was for some people to talk off the record, so she could then go back to those interviewees who had previously refused to talk and explain that she already had the story that she needed, even without their evidence. As she explains, 'Off the record then becomes on the record, as people are anxious to tell their side of the story.' She has an interesting theory about politicians. She says that they all believe that they are honest people and are normally keen to convince the rest of us cynics of their fundamental decency. That is why, sooner or later, they usually agree to appear on television.

The series charts the history of the Soviet Union up to the moment of liberalization. Like *Empire*, it is narrated by Robin Ellis, who is the regular voice of choice for the Lapping–Percy team. Lapping had chosen Robin to narrate the first series after listening to tapes of at least 16 actors, as I recall. Famous names were rejected as being 'too actory'. Others, like Granada's team of experienced voices, were 'too journalistic'. Lapping wanted what he described as 'a flat delivery'. It had to be authoritative but not dogmatic.

It had to sound 'objective'. I was quietly sceptical that Lapping would ever find his perfect narrator, but thanks to the sterling work of Granada's casting department, he was introduced to Robin, who had been something of a heartthrob after his performance in a bodice-ripping series for the BBC – *Poldark*. He had been a national theatre player and was a serious actor, not a voice-over specialist. But the two men met, liked each other and the audition was a success. Robin has worked regularly with the team now for 20 years.

My favourite programme is called 'Enter Gorbachev'. It starts, in typical Percy fashion, with an apparently obscure little event and some good political gossip. The commentary says, 'A scarcely noticed meeting . . . one of those small events which change history.' Archive film shows a crowd on a station platform. Local dignitaries are waiting, the red flags flutter in the wind and a band plays. Leonid Brezhnev steps down from the train to be greeted by local Communist Party chiefs. The commentary explains that this is Baku and the President is here to present the city with a prestigious award, the Order of Lenin. We are told that the man with the white hair in the picture is Chernenko. Cut to the contemporary interview. Gridon Aliev is Head of the Communist Party of Azerbaijan. He is scathing about Chernenko, who became president after Brezhnev died. 'He never made a single speech,' he says. 'He just went round with Brezhnev all the time.'

The implication is clear – Chernenko is cultivating the President because he wants his job. But another ambitious man is also determined to use this rare visit to further his own ambition and this is the real point of the story. We are told that the presidential train had stopped en route to Baku at the train station in Mineral Nyvody. Andropov, another presidential favourite, has arranged a short meeting so he can introduce a young local party official to Brezhnev. This is Gorbachev. So this short historical meeting takes place where Brezhnev and the three men who will follow him as President of the Soviet Union have a casual chat about nothing in particular on a station platform.

Two months later, Gorbachev is summoned to Moscow. He so impressed the President during the short discussion that he is to be awarded the Order of the October Revolution which, the commentary explains, is 'for people on the way up'. He is made Agriculture Secretary – his rise to power has begun. 'The meeting at the station had paid off,' we are told. And the course of history would change as a result.

This little story is typical of the Percy principle of finding the turning point in any politician's career.

The series told in fine detail one of the epic tales of the twentieth century, the collapse of the Soviet Union. After that, it was probably inevitable that Percy would want to turn her attention to her native land, the USA. With Lapping, she decided to make a series about the great scandal that led to the resignation of the President in 1974. The series was called, simply, *Watergate*, and told the story of how the Republican incumbent President Richard Nixon had been found guilty of covering up his knowledge of a break-in at the opposition Democratic Party headquarters by Republican Party employees. When Lapping and Percy announced their new project, many people thought it was a strange decision. After all, the story was well known. Would she find anything that had not already been revealed by the investigative journalists Woodward and Bernstein or the Senate Committee which investigated the whole affair? Watergate had even been the subject of a hugely successful feature film, starring Robert Redford and Dustin Hoffman. Why Watergate?

A new book, *Silent Coup*, published in 1991, had stirred Percy's interest and Lapping had got some development money from the BBC to investigate further. The book suggested that President Nixon knew nothing of the break-in at the Watergate building and implied that the true villain of the piece was the young counsel to the President, John Dean. Percy ran with this story for some time, but as usual checked it out with detailed, laborious and time-consuming research.

On the first research trip to Washington, she went with the veteran America-watcher, journalist Fred Emery, who was a consultant on the programme, and the director Paul Mitchell. They worked their way through many in-depth discussions with the Senate Watergate committee members and between them accumulated 60 research interviews. Most people working on history projects start with the paper archives then follow up with interviews with the protagonists. While Percy does both, she tends to prioritize the other way round. So the interviews with the people who were there at the time are massively important and, she says, it is their recollections which often lead to new revelations and a paper trail, which is then followed up in the libraries and archives.

There are, according to Percy, 238 books which deal to some extent with Watergate and the team worked their way through all of them. They discovered that President Nixons's personal audio tapes and papers were stored not in the National Archive as one would expect, but in a warehouse in deepest Virginia. Naturally, this put off most researchers – presumably the reason why they had been put there in the first place. In an article written in 1994, just before the series was first broadcast, Percy describes her feelings when she listened to the ex-President's tapes for the first time.

Anyone who made it out to the archive and slipped on a pair of headphones could hear this, recorded on the hidden taping system Nixon himself had installed in the Oval Office:

President: *How much money do you need?*
Dean: *I would say these people are going to cost a million dollars over the next two years.*
President: *You'd better damn well get that done, but fast.*

For me, listening in on a president of the United States urging his aide to find the hush money to pay off the Watergate burglars was a thrill that equalled anything I'd come across in 20 years of journalism – and certainly convinced me that this man had something to hide.

The series is full of colourful characters, many of whom were already household names as a result of the movie *All the Presidents's Men*, as well as the many books and newspaper articles devoted to the story. Suddenly, here they all are on our television screens, telling their side of the story. The apparent lack of remorse from most of the guilty men is quite shocking. The fact that the impeccably researched series provides convincing evidence that the ex-President was guilty of more than the Senate investigation had been able to uncover was a *tour de force* in journalistic history. But it is the characters themselves, good storytellers to a man – and they were all men – who make it so fascinating to watch.

It was not easy to get all these people on camera, but one by one they agreed to do it. One of the interviewees, Jeb Magruder, had become a clergyman after serving his jail sentence. Naturally, he had built a new life and was reluctant to relive his dodgy past on camera. Percy convinced him by playing to him extracts from the interview they had already conducted with Gordon Liddy, a natural showman who is now a radio chat show host. Liddy's testimony so annoyed Magruder that he had to agree to appear.

In programme one, the story of how Nixon and his team came to make such a catastrophic mistake unfolds. A feature of the Percy storytelling style can be illustrated well by the following passage from the film. These recollections by three Nixon aides are inter-cut so skilfully that they appear to be sharing in one seamless narrative. Each one adds little colourful details which add to the credibility of an absolutely extraordinary story.

In this episode, Gordon Liddy, Chief of Intelligence for the Committee to Re-elect the President (known as CREEP), is recalling how he presented his plans for destabilizing the rival Democratic Party's election campaign to the Attorney General, the Counsel to the President and the deputy director of CREEP:

Magruder:	Liddy showed us these charts; I think there were seven of them with ideas for how we could harass the Democrats.
Liddy:	Each operation was given the name of a precious jewel and there were so many operations that we ran out of precious jewels and semi-precious jewels and pretty soon we were down to coal and brick.
Dean:	He said that the big problem would be demonstrations . . . but he said he had retained the services of some very tough men and he would direct these men to kidnap the campaign leaders, drug them and take them below the Mexican border so they would be out of commission.

Liddy: Mr Mitchell said, 'Where do you get such people' and I said it's my understanding that they are from organized crime. Mitchell said, 'What is that going to cost us?'

Just when we have to accept that this unbelievable exchange really took place – if only because it is a fact that all of these men went to jail as a result of their machinations – the conversation spirals off into the almost surreal:

Dean: Liddy said, 'I have hired a Chinese motifed houseboat, we will park it by the convention centre in Miami, it will have two-way cameras and we will use prostitutes to seduce high Democratic campaign officials and get them onto the houseboat.'

Liddy: They were to linger about and attract the attention of middle-range Democratic staffers who would want to impress them with their importance by saying, 'Watch tomorrow, this is going to happen.'

Dean: I said you've got to be kidding. Liddy was quite offended by my interruption. He said, 'I want to assure the general that these are the finest girls from Baltimore.' Then Mitchell took a puff on his pipe and said, 'Gordon, I don't think this is quite what we had in mind.'

Nevertheless, Mitchell did authorize the burglary of the Democratic Party headquarters in the Watergate building, described with relish by Liddy and one of the Miami Cuban burglars in a later episode. Nixon himself and John Mitchell, the Attorney General, are the only characters in this great twentieth century drama who are not interviewed, because they were both dead when the series was made. Percy instead uses an interview which Nixon gave to David Frost to put his excuses for his actions. The contrast between the clearly accurate, and generally apparently unrepentant, accounts of the rest of the conspirators and the refusal of Nixon to accept any responsibility for his own downfall is quite remarkable.

Only one of the plotters expresses remorse and this provides, as Percy says, one of those rare moments that can only be captured on film. Fred Larue, Mitchell's political adviser, says in his interview:

> *I've reflected on this many times – had I gone to Mitchell and said, 'John, this is crazy, this is a hare-brained scheme, it's not going to do a damn thing but get us into trouble. Let's put a stop to it.' Had I done that, and done it forcefully, John would have listened to me and this whole mess could have been avoided. It's one of the real regrets that I have about Watergate.*

Watergate was a tremendous achievement which rightly won the production team many plaudits and was shown all over the world. However, their next production, transmitted in 1995, topped all that. *The Death of Yugoslavia* won 15 international awards and is still reckoned by many to be the best investigative television history series ever made. This is contemporary political history as grippingly told as any best-selling fictional international thriller. The methodology of the the programme team would repay some study, being, for me, a model of how to make serious investigative documentary.

The series had a very big budget – £500,000 per episode, the same price as a major television drama and well over the money normally paid for the average documentary. The money was made up of a number of co-producers – the biggest stake was from the BBC, then Discovery USA and a number of smaller European companies. The production team was small, as is always the case with Lapping–Percy productions. The main expense is time. At the time of the Canal Plus transmission in October 1995, three members of the team – Norma Percy, director Paul Mitchell and associate producer/researcher, Michael Sinkin – explained their methodology to members of the French press.

There were five hour-long programmes and the project took two years to complete. They edited for 40 weeks, taking 26 for the first episode alone. They started by recording 500 hours of research interviews, off the record, without the camera. This period also required in-depth research in newspaper libraries, film and television archives; they monitored radio broadcasts in Yugoslavia and spoke to journalists and academics who were expert in the field.

This research is necessary, says Percy, so they can work out what questions have to be asked on the record and narrow down this complicated story to the key events that they will cover in detail.

Key informants are crucial in these projects and Percy found hers in Borisav Jovic, the Serb representative of the Presidential College. At first he was defensive, but when she was able to prove to him that she was speaking to his adversaries and asking everybody the same questions, he quickly decided that he should put his own case to the world. Although what he was telling the team was disputed by other Serbian politicians, Paul Mitchell's research in Croatia confirmed a lot of the detail of what he was saying. This is how the team began to piece together the truth and, one by one, the big hitters agreed to be interviewed.

Eventually, they got Slobodan Milosevic himself. Norma Percy has a standard method of landing the big fish for her programmes. First she writes a polite letter, not an e-mail or a phone message, but a good old-fashioned letter, in the post, explaining the idea and asking for an interview. 'They always say no the first time,' she says, 'You get used to it.' A second letter is then dispatched. Now that the team has such an impressive track record she is able to enclose reviews of previous programmes, which definitely helps the case. But inevitably, with people who are very powerful, it is necessary to be persistent. Percy befriended Mrs Milosevic, a university professor with a great deal of influence over her husband. She got them a preliminary interview, but the on-film interview took longer. Mrs Milosevic told them he was putting it off, like a visit to the dentist. They phoned the President's house once a week until eventually he answered the phone himself and the Serbia-based researcher, Laura Silber, had minutes in which to convince him. They got the interview. One hour only, but worth all the trouble.

A Percy programme invariably starts with a dramatic story. This is the television tradition of documentary. While a cinema film can gradually lead us into a slow-paced complex tale, television has to grab the viewer quickly before they decide to turn to another channel. *The Death of Yugoslavia* starts with an extraordinary story, one which was very much disputed by Serbs who reckoned themselves to be 'in the know' and who could not believe that a team of English documentarists could find out something so shocking when they knew nothing about it. But the evidence is overwhelming. This is a scoop.

At the beginning of the film, Ivan Stambolic, the President of Yugoslavia when the crisis began, explains that he had been asked to go to Kosovo, part of the Federation, because there was trouble brewing there. He asked Milosevic, the party chairman, to go instead. As history now tells, this was a catastrophic mistake. Archive film shows Milosevic arriving to meet a demonstration of angry Serbs. 'The Communist Party has done nothing for us,' one shouts. Their grievance was that Kosovan Albanians were driving them out of the country they considered to be home. 'We want dialogue' they say. Milosevic says he will meet them the following Friday.

The programme then goes to a classic three-people-intercut set of interviews, describing the same meeting. First, an executive from Serb Television, who will later be credited with creating the Milosevic myth. Then the wife, Mira Markovic, who says of her husband, 'He consulted me, how far should he go?' Then the scoop interview, Milosevic himself. Speaking of the Kosovo Serbs, he says with all sincerity, 'Deprived of rights, who would think that our country could be capable of such discrimination?'

As the film later reveals, Milosevic had already decided that he could use the ethnic tensions in Kosovo to advance his own bid for total power. He was about to take a major gamble which, if it paid off, would eventually help him to achieve his ambition. In the days before the scheduled meeting he sent his 'dirty tricks' man down to Kosovo, the local party man testifies in an interview. Milosevic's representative talked with the dissident Serbs. And a plan was made.

When Milosevic arrived on the Friday as promised, a huge crowd was waiting, recorded by local television. As the meeting was going on, disturbances began outside. A Serb leader, Miroslav Solovic, explains in a detailed and self-incriminating interview how party members provoked the police, who were supposed to control the demonstration, by throwing stones at them. They then demanded that Milosevic should leave the hall where his meeting was taking place and surrounded him, telling him, 'The police are beating our people.' Solovic describes the scene. 'He walked outside, obviously afraid. He knew he was playing for high stakes.' Looking at the angry crowd, Milosevic hestitated for a while 'in his characteristic pose', as the Kosovan party boss put it. Then the archive tells the story. 'Comrades, speak up,' says Milosevic. 'The police attacked us, they hit women and children . . . ' shout the crowd. A dramatic pause, then Milosevic says slowly and firmly, 'You will not be beaten again.' This footage, played over and again on Yugoslav television, had a massive impact on Serb public opinion. The commentary failed to point out that the police had been attacked first. The Serbs were portrayed as victims of racial oppression. The television chief who had attended the meeting at the party chairman's house had done his bit. The Milosevic myth was created. 'With a lie', as the *Death of Yugoslavia* commentary explains.

All the Lapping–Percy series depend to a large extent on eyewitness accounts, with a minimum of commentary or explanation and not a great deal of visual illustration. So the 'talking heads', as they are known in television, tend to drive the story. In the case of *Yugoslavia*, there is another massively important element. This is the archive film, recorded at the time by local television in the component parts of the Federation, which is surprisingly dramatic and very well shot. But even more important is the film shot by the Yugoslav Army. As Percy points out, making programmes about countries with a well-established film industry, excellent technicians and good archiving policies can give you a great advantage in telling any story. Countries in what used to be called the Eastern Bloc almost all match this description. But their archives are not easy to penetrate. Getting access to all this footage took time and patience, and was a tremendous achievement by the series' associate producer, Michael Simkin.

Programme two has a sequence in which the archive is fundamentally important. It deals with the crisis in Croatia after the people elected Tujman as their leader, a man described by the federal police as a 'Fascist/Nationalist'. After battles for power with the police, Tujman decided that Croatia needed its own defence force. The Federal authorities would never agree to that, so Tujman's supporters started to smuggle in arms from abroad. The Yugoslav government found out about the smuggling and concluded that

Croatia was planning to secede from the Federation. This is the background to an extraordinary piece of television which would be meaningless without the contemporary archive footage.

The sequence begins with a Macedonian, Vasil Tuporkovsky, telling us in a present-day interview about the time in 1981 when Jovic, Chair of the Yugoslav state council, interrupted a television programme late at night to make an urgent announcement. This was an instruction to members of the council (the highest body in the government of Yugoslavia) to attend a meeting the next day at four o'clock in Belgrade. Stipe Mesic of Croatia takes up the story. He says that when the delegates, from all over the Federation, arrived at the usual meeting place they were ordered onto a bus and taken to Army Headquarters. 'The Army was trying to scare us,' he says. The remarkable archive shows delegates arriving and meeting with Jovic and General Kadijevic, Minister of Defence. The army sits down on one side of the table, with Jovic on their side, in the chair. The delegates sit opposite. Tuporkovsky explains, 'It was very cold, maybe 14 degrees. There was the presidency (the state council), we were trembling before the military. The camera was on. Never before had we seen cameras.'

In close-up, the General delivers in portentous tones his short speech. 'An insidious plan has been drawn up to destroy Yugoslavia. Step One is civil war. Step Two, foreign intervention. Step Three, puppet regimes will be set up throughout Yugoslavia.' He calls for a State of Emergency. Stipe Mesic, the Croat, also in close-up, angrily intervenes. 'Using the army is just your way to enlarge Serbia. That means war.' Back to the General, this time in a group shot showing the high command in profile, 'If you don't order action, you will destroy the Federation. It's up to you,' he says and throws his papers down. The camera stays for a few seconds on the soldiers, one of them tapping his pencil on the table, the tapping sound like the ticking of a clock in the tense silence. The camera then tracks around the room, while the commentary explains that there are nine voters from the different states of the Federation and Jovic needs five votes to get his state of emergency agreed.

Each delegate votes, the camera cutting between the worried delegates and Jovic and his army comrades. It is four votes to four when the camera comes to the Bosnian representative. He is a Serb, Bogic Bogicevic, and is thought to lean towards Yugoslavia, Tuporkovsky tells us. 'The pressure on him was tremendous.' 'I am willing to discuss it further,' Bogic says. Cut to an angry Jovic. 'You are not making any sense.' Cut to a present-day interview, filmed for the programme. 'Everybody thought I would vote with Serbia,' Bogic explains. Back to the archive and Bogic says 'At this stage any move would be counter-productive.' Cut to a stunned General Kadijevic. The army has lost the vote. Then we see Jovic, stony faced, picking up his papers and pushing back his chair. 'I declare the session closed.' There is nothing more to say. Democracy has triumphed, but not for long.

The army had filmed the session for their archives. There were a number of cameras running simultaneously. One cameraman is handholding, moving around the table. We see him in shot at one point, which is helpful to the audience because the whole sequence is so well shot, the situation so dramatic and the expressions on the faces of the participants so intense that it looks like fiction. At the time, the military archivists had no idea that this and other extraordinary footage shot by them – interrogations of prisoners, demonstrations, secret filming – would one day be used to the army's discredit by a British television series. The army footage was simply rushes and the cutting of the sequence was done by the programme's film editor. The editing, cutting as it does between present-day eyewitness accounts and remarkable archive, maximizes the tension that is already there in the material. It is beautifully done.

In another impressive archive sequence, the real-life drama that brought about the virtual collapse of the Communist Party of Yugoslavia is featured. Milosevic and his cohorts are scheming to defeat procedural moves by dissident elements in the Federation. The Slovenes and Croats, it emerges, have a game plan which will allow them to walk out of the Yugoslav party congress with honour. The apparent moment of drama arrives and, as usual, every action, every facial expression of the leading players is recorded by the cameras. The sequence ends with the only part of Percy's interview with Milosevic when he shows any animation. He explains that the Slovenes had planned the provocation and knew that they would storm out in the afternoon. He knew this because they had checked out of their hotels that morning. 'They left their bags at reception,' he says contemptuously. 'Those stingy Slovenes didn't want to have to pay for another night.'

In 2003, BBC television transmitted another three programmes by Percy and her team. She says that *The Death of Yugoslavia* is, in effect, the rise of Milosevic. 'When Kosovo blew up in 1999, we just had to go back and finish the story.' *The Fall of Milosevic* is in three parts, 90 minutes each. All the big players are there, as is to be expected from this production team: Clinton, Blair, Putin, Yeltsin, Chirac. Not Milosevic this time, he was in jail in The Hague.

At 90 minutes the programmes have a more leisurely pace and take time to tell the stories of some of the ordinary people who featured in the drama. A Kosovan Albanian family's story is told at some length. The man was separated from his family and was desperately looking for them among the carnage left in his home village by the Serb Army. He had a mini-DV camera and his footage shows the personal tragedies of this terrible war more poignantly than any professional news crew could hope to do. On the soundtrack we hear his neighbours urging him to film every-thing so there will be evidence.

In the final programme, Milosevic is finally defeated, not by NATO, who had been waging a war against Serbia, but by his own people. Again, the archive film documents the public events as they happened but the programme also highlights two ordinary people who emerged as popular heroes on the day the Parliament building was stormed by demonstrators while Milosevic retreated to his well-guarded house. One character, a rock musician who played the drums, kept the crowd stirred up and determined with his upbeat music. Filmed in a present-day interview, he emerges as an unlikely hero but an effective one.

The other character is a working man, a construction worker who drives in one of the convoys heading for the demo in Belgrade with his friend, the local baker. He is now famous, known as the Digger Man because of two crucial interventions he made on that historic day. The army had tried to stop the demonstrators from getting to Belgrade by putting obstructions on the road. The Digger Man cleared a sand-filled tunnel so the demonstrators could get through. When he and the baker arrived at the Parliament building, they found that the demonstrators could not get in because the doors and lower windows had been secured. So the Digger Man drove up to the building, young men climbed into the shovel at the front and he raised the crane so they were lifted up to a top-floor window. The boys broke in and opened the building up to the people. History was made and the cameras were there to record it.

Both these series received critical acclaim, worldwide screenings and many awards. But Lapping and Percy have some regrets. Four of the characters featured in the series have been murdered since its transmission. Lapping now says they would like to dedicate the first series to Ivan Stambolic, the ex-President who Milosevic removed. In the programme Stambolic says, 'Milosevic was always walking behind me. Can you be surprised that he thought of stabbing me in the back?' He had said it to the team off the record but was reluctant to say it on camera. They persuaded him.

Stambolic became a public figure again after the programmes were shown. He was the opponent Milosevic feared the most because people respected him. One day, when he was out jogging, a white van stopped and he was bundled in. His body was later found in the mountains. There is little doubt that Milosevic's secret police chief was responsible. The same man is also suspected of murdering Djindjic, the Prime Minister.

Israel and the Arabs was transmitted in 1998. It tells the story of the 50 years' war in the Middle East. It provided the first real refusal for Norma Percy. Try as she might, she could not get Yasser Arafat to appear. Instead, they used archive to put his point of view. Unusually for this much respected group of producers, this series created a controversy which attacked their integrity. At a Conference at the Imperial War Museum in London, a historian suggested that a sequence in programme one included archive film which was not accurate. Norma Percy, who was on stage at the conference when the issue was raised, defended her programme robustly but still the newspapers, on an anti-factual television 'Find the fakes' campaign, picked up the story. Given the scrupulous attention to detail and the huge amounts of time that the Percy programmes devote to research, it did seem to some of us that there were other more deserving targets for the nit-pickers to attack. But the argument went on and on.

Norma Percy with executive producer Brian Lapping at the BAFTA Awards, 2003

The problem with this kind of debate is that the archive world contains many serious scholars who are always worth listening to, but there is also a small minority of others who are the archive scholar equivalent of what British people refer to as 'anoraks', those strange people who stand at the end of train station plat-forms, writing down the numbers of passing engines. The Scots refer to them, more kindly, as 'trainspotters'. Many walks of life have anoraks and the historical documentary world has more than most. It is always going to be difficult, if not impossible, to con-vince such people that the archive film they dispute is accurate within the bounds of reasonable research, given the poor records kept by most libraries, especially in a war zone.

The debate over Percy's programme was started by an academic who claimed that footage she had used in programme one was not accurate. The sequence concerned an attack on a Palestinian village when the Israelis were still trying to ensure supply lines to Jerusalem and were attacking Palestinian villages along the road. The academic argued that the film shown could not possibly have been shot at the time of the famous battle it supposedly depicted. The battle of Deir Yassin, he said, had happened at dawn and the footage shown was clearly shot in daylight. Others argued that the battle had gone on for some time and the light had come up while it was in progress. Nobody challenged the fact that the footage accurately showed the invading Israeli-supporting Stern Gang. The uniforms were right. The place was right. The soldiers were Stern Gang. So why all the fuss? Nobody I know tries harder than Norma Percy to get facts right. In all the years that she and Lapping have been working together this is the only challenge – if it can seriously be called a challenge – that I can remember. Pretty impressive, as track records go.

Endgame in Ireland, four programmes transmitted in 2001, tells the story of the British government's attempts to reconcile the Catholic and Protestant communities and bring peace to Northern Ireland. Once again, the production team were walking into the lion's den. The series ends with the Good Friday Agreement, a time of great hope, which has not as yet borne fruit.

In one very disturbing part they tell in detail what happened in one of the bloodiest and most tragic weeks in Ireland's history. It started on a Saturday when a bomb exploded in a fish shop in a Protestant area of Belfast, killing innocent people who were simply shopping. The IRA (Irish Republican Army) planted the bomb in the hope of killing Johnny Adair, leader of the loyalist paramilitary group, the UFF (Ulster Freedom Fighters), who had his headquarters above the shop. It had been a botched operation, the bomb went off early and an IRA man was also killed. Archive film shows the shock and sorrow of the Protestant bystanders as the bodies are carried out.

The film now cuts to an interview with Adair himself. He is a fearsome-looking individual and a caption explains that he is out of prison on licence. His expression of disgust at the wickedness of bombing innocent Protestants is hard to take, given his own violent history. But somehow this short interview encapsulates the tragedy of Northern Ireland. Both sets of paramilitaries believe themselves to be justified in their actions and both condemn the other side as murderers.

The UFF reaction was swift and vicious. Interviewed in silhouette and identified only as loyalist paramilitaries who were in jail from 1993 to 2000, Protestant gunmen tell us what happened next. They received a phone call telling them to keep Saturday night free. They were ordered to go to a little pub in the country where Catholics would be having a quiet drink, burst in and kill as many of them as possible. They took an AK and a nine-mil gun and were told to take two magazines for each. So there would be a lot of shooting. The film cuts between the terrorists' account of what happened and the memories of some who escaped. It was Hallowe'en and as the gunmen ran into the pub they shouted 'trick or treat'. Then they started shooting. Seven people died.

The Irish and British Prime Ministers at that time were Albert Reynolds and John Major. They had been talking to each other for some time, trying to come up with a peace plan which would be acceptable to both Catholics and Protestants in the North and also to the people of the Republic of Ireland – which historically claimed that the North belonged to them – and to the people of the United Kingdom. As is the pattern with all these programmes, the Prime Ministers had been asked to describe what happened in certain key meetings. They both answered the same questions and were surprisingly frank in their revelations. In one particular episode, they talk about a serious row they had. The background to this exchange had been explained earlier in the film. A senior British civil servant had been given the unpleasant task of breaking the news to Albert Reynolds that the *Observer* newspaper was about to break a story revealing that the British had been having secret talks with the IRA for years and never told the Irish government.

Commentary:	The two Prime Ministers met alone.
Reynolds:	I said John, this is bad faith in any sense of the word. I can't buy it, I won't buy it. There will be no summit and we will leave it at that.
Major:	He sat there looking at me in a bit of a sulk, I think over the problems we'd had.
Reynolds:	Am I being fooled all the time? Am I being fooled by my friend, John Major? Was this an act we were going through over previous months?
Major:	I had a big pile of papers under my arm which I slammed down on the table and I said, 'Where do you think this came from, Albert?'

(Cutaway to newspaper headline – North and South: The Blueprint for Peace.)

Major:	You know the problem this caused with the Unionists. Where did that come from? It must have come from Dublin. It can't have come from London.
Reynolds:	What's he take me for? Thinks I'm a stupid blinking so-and-so?
Major:	When this sort of nonsense breaks out how can I stop the Unionists believing all sorts of deals that they will never find acceptable? If this goes on we just won't reach a deal.
Reynolds:	That's the way it was, it was high tempered stuff.

An Irish political adviser then tells how, after the meeting, he asked Reynolds how it had gone. 'Grand, grand. Well he chewed the bollocks off me but I took a few lumps out of him too,' said the Prime Minister of the Republic of Ireland.

When Norma Percy first asked John Major for a research interview, she arrived to find him surrounded by papers. He said that he had started revising his own archive so he could be sure to be accurate in everything he said. He felt he needed a lot more time. She would have to come back again for another talk. In the end he did five research interviews, before giving a bravura performance on film. Percy thinks that it is important to give the subject of your interview all the questions in advance and all other information possible, like what other people in the same situation remember. That way you get truth and accuracy. Like me, she does not accept the argument that you lose spontaneity if you warn people of what you want to ask. This series, like the rest of her work, proves her point. It is also important to ask people to check back through their papers, because otherwise they have the perfect excuse to avoid awkward questions by simply claiming that they cannot remember. Norma also says that one of the ways she gets people to relax and act naturally is to say to them, 'What did you tell your wife when you got home that day?' I had always wondered how she managed to get normally pompous politicians to be so relaxed and animated. Now I know.

FILMOGRAPHY

Norma Percy has been responsible (with Brian Lapping) for developing a particular style of political documentary in which Presidents, Prime Ministers and their advisors tell the story of how key political decisions are taken. These series, usually made for the BBC, and Public Broadcasting Corp. or The Discovery Channel in America, are shown all over the world.

The BBC's statement of future programming policy (1995) described this work as:

> . . . *virtually a new genre of documentary which retells momentous events from the recent past with meticulous objectivity and with most or all of the principal actors recording their version of what happened. The narratives that emerged from* The Second Russian Revolution *and* Watergate *were revelations.*
> (*Alan Yentob and Liz Forgan, BBC's* People and Programmes)

Last month Norma Percy was awarded an honorary Doctorate of Arts by London City University. She was made a fellow of The Royal Television Society in 2000. In November 2003 she was awarded City University's James Cameron Prize for the year's outstanding work in journalism (both print and broadcast), and became the first person to be awarded a second Cameron award.

Lapping and Percy have won several lifetime achievement awards from the industry's top professional bodies. In 2003, they won BAFTA's Alan Clarke award for outstanding creative contribution to television. In 1995, they won the Royal Television Society Judges' Award recognizing 'an outstanding contribution to TV journalism over many years'.

In 2002, a conference of the TV news executives awarded them the first News World Documentary Award for their *Avenging Terror*, in which members of President Bush's administration, Presidents Putin and Musharaf and Prime Minister Blair and their foreign ministers and advisors described the secret diplomacy after 9/11 (shown by Britain's Channel 4 plus 22 other broadcasters worldwide, on the first anniversary). The citation said: 'These programmes turned heads of state into talking heads to tell a story that was, in its way, as vivid and startling as the most graphic news bulletin images.'

Born in New York City, she came to the London School of Economics to do an M.Phil. in Politics. She began her career in the House of Commons as a researcher to the Labour MP, J. P. Mackintosh.

In 1973, Lapping offered her a job at Granada Television for one year working on a series about what was wrong with Parliament; they have been working together ever since. In 1988, she left to join with him in a new independent TV production company, Brian Lapping Associates. She was a director of this company and remained a director when it merged to become Brook Lapping (1997), and in 2002 became part of the Ten Alps group.

At Granada, she produced all four programmes made by a novel format Lapping devised for getting inside political decisions which were so secret politicians would not talk about them on camera: 'journalists' reconstructions' in which top political correspondents research and re-enact secret discussions in Cabinet and at European summits: *Chrysler and the Cabinet* (1976), *The Loan from the IMF* (1977), *Inside Europe – The Summit* (1978), *Mrs Thatcher's Billions* (1980) and *The Lady Is Not For Turning* (1981).

She was producer of two dramas based closely on Cabinet records, official papers and the accounts of the main participants.

In *Countdown to War*, Ian McKellen portrayed Hitler in a recon-struction of the diplomacy leading up to World War II. *Breakthrough at Reykjavik*, a recreation of the 1986 summit between Reagan and Gorbachev, was a finalist in the 1988 Prix Italia and won a gold medal at the New York Film and Television Festival.

She was a producer of two programmes on Brian Lapping's Granada TV historical series *End of Empire* (Cyprus and Rhodesia) and on programme four of *Apartheid*, which won the Broadcasting Press Guild Award for 1986.

She worked with Roger Graef and Brian Lapping on two ground-breaking fly-on-the-wall films: first, the only time permission was granted to film Ministers and civil servants working together on a bill going through all its stages in the House of Commons, *State of the Nation: Parliament* (1973), and to follow one law in the making through the European Community's Council of Ministers, *Inside the Brussels HQ* (1975). She also produced nine *Hypotheticals* (1981 and 1988) based on the Harvard Law School teaching method, which looked at ethical questions facing decision-makers.

She lives in London and is married to Dr Steve Jones, Professor of Genetics and Biology at University College, London, Reith Lecturer on the BBC in 1991, *Daily Telegraph* columnist, broadcaster and author.

As series producer

The Second Russian Revolution
1991

Watergate
1994

The Death of Yugoslavia
1995

Won 15 major awards and was named on the recent British Film Institue list as one of the top ten documentaries ever made.

Endgame in Ireland
2001

As executive producer (with Brian Lapping)

Woolly Al Walks the Kitty Back
1992, BBC, TDC
On the diplomacy of the Falklands War.

Playing the China Card
1999, PBS, Channel 4

Avenging Terror
2002, Channel 4, PBS

The Fall of Milosevic
2003, BBC, TDC

Currently

Joint series producer of *Elusive Peace*, for the BBC, PBS and Arte, a sequel to her *The 50 Years War, Israel and the Arabs* (1998). She has interviewed many world leaders, including King Hussein (for over three hours for that series), Bill Clinton, Tony Blair, Shimon Peres and Jacques Chirac.

7   Brian Hill
The musical documentary

Brian Hill

If you had known Brian Hill as a student, nothing in his background would have led you to believe that, one day, he would develop into an influential figure in the world of television documentary. He says himself that he was 'not meant for television'. Born in Rochdale in Lancashire, he grew up wanting to be a community activist. After reading Sociology at Leicester University he became a social worker, very much involved in grass-roots local activity. As a result of this experience, he gained a reputation for himself and, eventually, a BBC producer asked him to act as a consultant/expert on a people's rights programme. This experience ignited an interest which eventually took him into television production, at first still pursuing his interest in community affairs.

Then, in 1992, he was approached by Paul Watson, who was setting up a new project to be made in Australia, a documentary serial about the daily life of a 'typical' Australian family. Watson wanted two directors to film over several months while he executive produced. Brian Hill accepted the challenge and was teamed with director Kate Woods. This was the first of a series of successful collaborations with different working partners which has become a feature of Hill's work. The series was called *Sylvania Waters* and created a huge debate when it was broadcast by the BBC in prime time.

Paul Watson is used to controversy. Ever since he created a major stir with his series *The Family* (BBC TV, 1974), Watson has been challenging television's conventions and upsetting the establishment. For Brian Hill and Kate Woods, the publicity surrounding their films was something new. *Sylvania Waters* was divided into 12 episodes, transmitted weekly in a popular slot on BBC1 and played to an audience of six million, a respectably high rating for a documentary series. But *Sylvania Waters* was no ordinary documentary series.

From the beginning of programme one, the viewer was invited to enter a different world. A montage of sunny scenes, a relaxed, rather romantic theme tune with colourful graphics over pictures of a watery location, the title sequence of *Sylvania Waters* conveys the mood of a comfortable, bourgeois American soap opera. Then comes the surprise. The first scene, an interior of the kitchen in a fashionable Sydney suburban house, shows two characters, arguing fiercely. The woman is pacing around the kitchen, the man sitting behind the work surface which divides the room. She says, 'For God's sake, of course he can have a bloody birthday party.' The man replies, 'Of course he can, but he's just saying they'll all bring friends and there'll be about a million people here. We haven't got the room.' She says, "Strewth, Lawrie, I swear that one of these days I'll pack my bags and I'm going out of here.' A teenager suddenly appears. He is the focus of the argument. The scene is now repeated, with the boy's animated intervention. It is exactly the same scene, repeated shot for shot, but now we understand what the couple are fighting about. The boy storms out of the room and the mood changes again.

Now we see a street scene in a comfortable middle-class suburb. Music over the opening shots continues, on and off, over the next few minutes. The young man we met briefly in the previous scene is now in close-up, talking directly to camera. He is Michael Baker and this is his family. 'This is our life,' he says. In between street scenes of the affluent suburbs of Sydney, Michael, in voice-over, introduces us to the characters whose lives will be examined over the next 12 weeks. They all speak directly to camera. First there is Mom, Noleen. Blowzy, blow-dried, heavily made up, she tells the camera, 'I'm me. I can't be nice. I can't be [shrug] Joan Collins. I'm just me.' Then comes 'stepfather' Lawrie. The couple are not actually married but he plays the patriarch in spite of that. He likes racing cars: 'It's like going with a good woman. Very exciting.'

The rest of the family are now introduced. First, Paul, who left home at 16 because he could not bear his stepfather. 'We kids were not allowed to watch television. When he and Mom went out, he took the knobs out of the television. He even hit me sometimes. He's not my father.' Paul and his girlfriend Dianne are expecting a baby. Meanwhile his stepbrother, Lawrie's son Nick, is still riding motorbikes and racing cars, just like he did at 16. He says his girlfriend, Yvette, 'understands'.

So, in episode one of the 12-parter, the cast is introduced, in typical soap opera style. Brian Hill explains:

> In Sylvania Waters *we set out to follow some soap opera conventions. We chose three families – all related to one another, but three separate households. There were different age groups and certain events that we knew were going to happen in the course of filming – a birth, for example, and a marriage.*

Therefore, according to plan, each week the programmes follow the trials and tribulations of this colourful and highly argumentative extended family. Finally, at the beginning of episode 12, Noleen and Lawrie are about to set off for Europe, where they plan to get married. As we have come to expect from this quarrelsome couple, they are arguing again. This time because Lawrie does not want Noleen's family staying in their house while they are away. Once again they are in the kitchen: she is pacing, he is sitting at the room-divider. The scene recalls the beginning of the first episode, when Lawrie did not want too many of Michael's friends coming to the house for his birthday party. At the end of the episode, Noleen has pressured all of her family to come to the airport to see the couple off on their romantic journey. They are still arguing. The last shot shows a plane taking off. In voice-over, Noleen gets the last word. 'I hope when we come back they will all start treating me like their mother, not like a doormat.' So the series begins and ends in the neatest possible way, the characters have been introduced, entertained the audience for 12 weeks and now we must say goodbye to them. For the moment.

Brian Hill describes the filming process of *Sylvania Waters*: 'You could never do it now. We were filming for six months and editing at the same time. We had three cutting rooms. Sometimes we would spend 16 hours with one of the families and only shoot half a roll. The important thing was to be there. At the end of filming our ratio was 15 to 1. Nowadays, shooting on digital, it would be more like 100 to 1.' Kate Woods and Brian Hill divided the work between them – there was only one crew, so they took turns to go out filming, one week on, one week off. The director who was back at base worked in the cutting rooms.

Paul Watson, the executive producer, was based at the BBC in England, but came out to Australia three times during the making of the series. Before filming started, together with the co-producers, the Australian Broadcasting Corporation, he chose the family which would be the focus of the series. He flew out again when the directors had assembled a rough cut of the first programme. Brian Hill says, 'Kate and I had put together maybe 15 cuts of the first episode and we just could not get it right. We wanted to start with all of the characters introducing themselves, talking to camera. But it all seemed so deadly dull. Then Paul came out and worked with us and came up with the idea of starting with the argument.' Watson then had another original idea – to repeat the footage of the argument, therefore giving an impression of unreality within a genuine reality, before going into the conventional soap-style opening that Hill and Woods had devised. After the last important decision was made – to use the teenager, Michael, as narrator – the directors felt that they now had a clear idea of how the series should be cut. Watson came out on two other occasions, working in the cutting rooms and discussing ideas. In between, rough cuts were sent to him and he would respond by phone or fax, sometimes giving notes, sometimes agreeing picture lock. It was a very harmonious relationship and one from which the directors felt they learned a lot.

I recently showed episode one of *Sylvania Waters* to the new first year postgraduate class at the National Film and Television School in the UK. The students were from many countries and studying different disciplines in film production. Many of them were frankly puzzled and found it hard to believe that this was documentary. Some genuinely suspected that the film was a fake and the characters were all actors. They felt uncomfortable with the editing techniques, like the use of incidental music to enhance mood and the parallel editing which cuts back and forward to different characters in different locations. The students also questioned the choice of the 15-year-old boy to act as narrator, which seemed to ask the audience to believe that the point of view of the series was his, not that of the film-makers. Since the programmes were shot on film they have a glossy, even glamorous, look which enhances the ambiguous mood which I understand the film-makers were trying to convey. They would not be dismayed in any way to know that the series still causes controversy, 12 years after it was first transmitted.

In a footnote to the *Sylvania Waters* debate, a session at the Edinburgh Television Festival in 1994 discussed the ethical issues surrounding 'real people serials'. Lawyer Helena Kennedy invited the producers of *Sylvania Waters*, Brian Hill and Kate Woods, together with Noleen, who was by then becoming something of a media celebrity in her own right, to debate the issues. Baroness Kennedy also invited producer Derek Guthrie and one of the four families who had appeared in the weekly documentary serial *Real Life* that he had produced for Scottish Television. The Brown family had six children and they lined up in order of height on the stage, waving to friends they spotted in the audience ('Oh look, it's our film crew!'). They explained how they had loved being on television for six weeks and were delighted to come to the Edinburgh Festival to say so. They enchanted the hard-bitten audience of television producers who had evidently come along looking for a fight. It was a big relief for me personally, as I had commissioned the series for STV and co-executive produced it with Bernard Clark. (See Chapter 12 for more on *Real Life*.)

While Scottish Television was vindicated by the Brown family, Hill, Woods and the BBC were not quite so lucky with their star performer, the Aussie matriarch.

Noleen was particularly incensed about the editing in episode four of *Sylvania Waters*. Dianne, Paul's partner, is having her baby and the camera concentrates on the emotion and anxiety the two of them feel as they wait for the baby to be born. It is a scene we have seen often enough before in documentaries. What makes this one different is the use of parallel editing. Instead of staying inside the labour ward, the film cuts away to Noleen, who is at the hairdressers having her hair blow-dried. She claimed at Edinburgh that this made her look like an uncaring mother who is not concerned about the welfare of her grandchild. She also claimed that the hairdressing episode happened on a different day, so it was even more unfair to her to intercut it with the birth scene. This is one of those debates that are always going to be hard to settle, particularly if the producers are shooting on film and there is no easy, digital access to records of filming dates. In the end it comes down to who people believe. Make your own mind up. However, the discussion raised some important issues about fairness in the production of documentary in general, but most particularly for those films which enter the private lives of people who have no editorial control over the final transmitted product. It was a particularly salient lesson for Brian Hill who, in future films, would be delving into the private lives of people who were often facing crises in their lives. How much do you tell people about what your intentions are in making the film? Do you show it to them before transmission? How much consideration should you give to the effect the transmission of the film will have on them and their families? Hill now opts for openness at all times. In a sense, even the people who appear in his films are now his collaborators, along with the rest of the production team.

In 1994, Hill made his first film for the prestigious and long-running Channel 4 series, *Cutting Edge*, again in collaboration with Kate Woods. The film, called simply *The Club*, was a portrait of Northwood Golf Club in the south of England. It is a gently ironic film, beautifully shot and sensitively edited, which reveals more about the British class system than any sociological tract could possibly manage. The tone of detached amusement is set from the start, when the character chosen to guide us through the film speaks directly to camera. His statement is a reminder of *Sylvania Waters*, echoing as it does the attitude of the very different but equally alienated character of Michael, the 15-year-old narrator of the Australian 'docusoap'. Our guide through *The Club* is Preston Lockwood, a mature and distinguished-looking gentleman who is a retired actor. He makes his attitude clear with his ironic first comment, 'Golf clubs are great places for disappointed men.'

At the beginning of the film a retired member of the club committee explains that most members are the kind of people who work in the City of London, at the Stock Exchange or as managing directors of national companies. There are, however, he says, now also some quite 'humble people' who have recently joined the club. General views of the members at play are accompanied by jolly, chirpy-sounding music, very English in its tone and reminiscent of the background music which often accompanies cinema depictions of that other, once aristocratic traditional pursuit – foxhunting packs in action.

We are 13 minutes into the film before we meet the 'Lady Captain' of the club. She explains what 'Lady Members' are not allowed to do. They cannot speak at the Annual General Meeting and they cannot play on Saturday or Sunday mornings. Twenty years after the birth of the Women's Liberation Movement, the 'ladies' of Northwood still knew their place.

The film cuts back and forwards from actuality sequences of members on the golf course to interviews with key characters. Because it never leaves the chosen location, the characters never go home, the film has a claustrophobic atmosphere – in spite of the sunshine and the manicured lawns. The climax of the film comes at the Annual General Meeting, when an expelled member of the club committee rises to put his objections to the membership. Naturally, he is repulsed. But it is a dramatic moment, the feeling being that maybe, at last, the twentieth century is creeping through the window. But no, one more time, the establishment has prevailed. *The Club* ends with the club committee displaying the same note of self-satisfied conviction as it did at the beginning.

In the next two years, Hill made four films, all reflecting his interest in how society works. *Tough Love* was a film about a group of 30 disturbed British kids who took part in experimental group therapy with visiting American psychologists. The film was shot on Hi8 – the only lightweight video available at the time – over a period of one week. There were four cameras; Hill shot on one of them himself.

The film simply recorded the experiment, leaving the audience to decide for themselves.

Next came *Jumpers*, a film about showjumping. Then *Pommies*, about British people living in Australia. Then, again for *Cutting Edge*, *Men at Fifty*, about men born on the same day as Prince Charles. All of these films, for me, revealed a point of view characteristic of Brian Hill, which is essentially non-judgemental, standing back from the action, often poking gentle fun but never condemning. In my view, these films, entertaining and enlightening though they often are, were merely a training ground for Hill for the next group of projects on which he was about to embark. The new partnership he entered into, with the poet Simon Armitage, has produced a body of work which is not only groundbreaking but also popular and entertaining, with an original vision which often comes close to outright anarchy.

Hill had been commissioned to make a film for the first series of the BBC's late and much lamented *Modern Times*. Programme editor Stephen Lambert was committed not only to finding new talent, but also to allowing experienced film-makers to experiment with form and content. These were heady days for documentarists and everybody wanted to make films for *Modern Times*. Hill had pitched an idea, which Lambert had accepted, to make a film about what ordinary people do on Saturday night. He had chosen the city of Leeds as his location and he and his assistant producer Dominique Walker had been working for months, getting together storylines and characters. They interviewed about 150 people until finally they met a junkie called Ian, who talked in such a way that Hill felt there was something poetic in his speech patterns. At the same time he felt that the city itself, Leeds, should be a character in the story. He was reminded of *Under Milk Wood* by Dylan Thomas and thought that this should be the inspiration for the film. So he would need to work with a poet. He had recently read a poem about the housing estate in Lancashire where he had grown up. The name of the poem was 'Xanadu' and the poet was Simon Armitage. He phoned Armitage and asked if he would be interested in collaborating on a film.

Simon Armitage is no ordinary poet. When he left university, he worked for some years as a probation officer. In his spare time he wrote poetry. After some years he was in a position to write full time. When Brian Hill asked if he would like to write a poem for a film about Leeds on a Saturday night he was naturally intrigued. He had worked in the probation service in Manchester and still lives in Yorkshire, and the similar backgrounds of the two men meant that they quickly became friends as well as collaborators. At first Armitage was cautious about the Leeds project because he says that films with poetry are often, from his point of view, unsatisfactory. 'Sometimes the poetry is used like subtitles for the film. Sometimes the film just illustrates the poems. I like it best when there is a friction between the two.' He thinks that poetry and documentary can work well together because they are in many ways similar. 'Both are subjective and authored,' he says, 'nobody believes in "objective" any more.' He says he is not precious about his work; he understands that in the cutting room it will be treated 'like so much fabric, to be slashed and tacked and stitched into the film. Too many writers have the attitude: "You can't touch that. That's *poetry.*"'

For Armitage, the film, *Saturday Night*, was a true collaboration. This is the way he likes to work, not like an employee or being made to feel 'like a guest in somebody else's house'. The idea for the film was, on the surface, quite conventional – to explore what people in a northern British city like to do on Saturdays. But the approach of the film-makers is refreshingly original and they have created something which rises above the normal run-of-the-mill television documentary to create a genuinely artistic work. *Saturday Night* is shot on film, in sombre black and white, which somehow

Simon Armitage

enhances the brooding beauty of the Leeds cityscapes that dominate the film. It has a narration in verse, spoken by the poet.

The film opens with a montage of drugged-up young people, partying. A male voice-over explains how he loves taking drugs. The
man then appears, in close-up, telling us the drugs he takes. Up
comes the title, over an exterior shot of a pub at night. So far, so
conventional. The next shot is the first of the cityscapes and it is
daylight. A male voice with a strong northern accent then cuts
through the background electronic music. The delivery is short,
staccato, with the greatest emphasis always on the name of the
town. This is the poet Simon Armitage with his very personal
view of the Yorkshire capital:

> *Leeds. Where the M1 does its emergency stop*
> *And the lines of houses fall into line and number off – acting*
> *   their age.*
> *And the roads go round in rings*
> *Or spider off like varicose veins.*

The poem continues over a variety of images of the city and
develops into an imaginary world which the poet develops from
the unrelated images that are presented in montage form. Brian
Hill picks out this section as being the unique combination of
montage and poetry, a reality which Armitage interprets, purely
from his own imagination. Shots of ordinary-looking houses are
followed by a woman walking with a child up a hill. A cat wanders
into the undergrowth. A boy plays with his dogs. More traffic.
A kid rides a bike by a playing field. The poet says:

> *Leeds on a Saturday afternoon, beginning to cool*
> *Leeds in a different light*
> *A Leeds of the mind.*
> *Where a woman drags a kid up the north face of the great*
> *   pyramid*
> *And a Bengal tiger disappears into the foliage*
> *And a boy trains dogs for the Chinese state circus*
> *A motorcade speeds down the Avenue of the Americas*
> *And a boy rides a bike through the goalposts and out of the*
> *   known universe.*

The film shows us an evening in the life of four characters. They are all introduced with poetic voice-over. We first saw the druggie, Ian, in the pre-title sequence. Now we meet Jackie, a middle-class southerner who 'came up from the smoke and can't get the hang of it'. She is preparing for a dinner party and 'making a meal of it'. The third character is Mike, who owns a carpet-selling business. He is 'a household name in the parish of Leeds'. He is a millionaire with a mansion and indoor swimming pool. Finally we see a transvestite, preparing for a night out. In a parody of the Kinks' classic song, Armitage says, 'She's not the world's most passionate guy, but there's more to Lola than meets the eye.'

The film follows the lives of the four characters through a typical weekend evening. At the end a complex, skilfully edited sequence brings together the ideas and emotions which have previously been expressed, including the highly atmospheric, non-human presence, the city of Leeds itself. This is a visually complex montage, owing something in its editing style to the pop video. Super8 film footage is mixed with 16 mm and an air of unreality prevails. The dominant images are of Ian and his friends partying in a nightclub. Intercut with these scenes are short visual reminders of the other characters in the film. There is no dialogue and the soundtrack is mixed between the specially composed mood music, which is one of the most successful stylistic features of the whole film, and the strong northern voice of the poet, Simon Armitage.

> *What drugs is, is your own tattoos*
> *Coming alive on your skin*
> *Opening the door*
> *And letting the light in*
> *Is what drugs is.*
> *Is what drugs is.*

The words of this final poem are taken from the interviewees themselves, primarily from Ian, the drug user. While Simon Armitage has skilfully woven them into a poetic form, the thoughts are those of the characters in the film. This is the first example of a style of writing which Hill and Armitage continued to develop in their next four films. The experiment gets more complicated as the ideas become more ambitious, reaching its zenith with the award-winning musical about a young offenders prison, *Feltham Sings*. As is so often the case, the decision to experiment in this way came about by chance. The film had always had a co-operative, group imperative, with regular gatherings in the cutting room of the director, poet, cameraman, composer and editor. This last sequence caused them problems, because while they were filming in the confusion and chaos of the noisy night-club, the sound recordist had not understood that he should be turning over. When the film came back from the labs, it emerged that the footage was impressive but unfortunately there was no sound.

Simon Armitage saw the rough cut of the silent scene and asked if it could be made visually more complex, 'more layered' as he put it. He had an idea for composing a poem that would reflect the ideas of the people in the film, in contrast to the earlier verse, which had represented his own, poetic vision. But his idea required even more than that. He says, 'I wanted to set up a tension between two polarities. The images were rather disturbing so I wanted to write verses which were often funny; putting the two together should create a kind of friction.' The editor recut the sequence, the poem was written and recorded, and a whole new sub-genre of documentary was about to be born. *Saturday Night* was described by a member of the audience at the Sheffield Documentary Festival, where I ran a masterclass about the work of Hill and Armitage, as 'The best *Modern Times* ever'. There will be few who disagree with that verdict.

Simon Armitage describes most television schedules as 'full of garbage'. He says anything that jolts the audience, wakes them up, is worth trying. With the next Hill–Armitage collaboration, the film-makers really took a risk. Once again the subject was one which appealed to Hill, the ex-social worker, and to Armitage, one-time probation officer. The pervasive British culture of excessive drinking is well-trodden ground and there have been many films dealing with the subject. But *Drinking for England* is quite unique. Like *Saturday Night*, the film looks at its subject from a non-judgemental point of view. The films have a detached air, showing us actuality without what Armitage calls 'the usual wagging finger – telling people how to live their lives'. I feel sure that this detached attitude, which reappears in all of the joint works, is largely as a result of their experiences working in the social services. Hill says that he is not convinced that the attitude can really be described as 'detached', but he is prepared to agree on 'non-judgemental'. When pressed on the subject and asked why the work they do together inevitably shows us the lives of people who are to some extent alienated from society, and often outside the law as well, 'behaving badly', Hill shrugs and with typical self-deprecating humour says, 'Look, Simon and I just enjoy making films about drugs and alcohol and violence.'

Drinking for England pushes the experimental form a little further. Once again, the film combines poetry, actuality interviews and sound. The difference this time is that the characters speak the verse, not the poet. In the initial stages of production, Katie Bailiff, the producer, went out to find people who were prepared to talk on film about their dependence on alcohol. She found a variety of characters – among others, a middle-aged man whose wife drove him home from the pub every night, two pretty young women friends, a middle-class fellow who was convinced he drove his car more safely after a drink, a woman clearly inebriated as she per-forms her poem, revealing the fact that her mother was also an alcoholic, and a likeable young man who tells us he will never give it up, even if it kills him.

Perhaps the most touching character is a woman who is about to go into rehab to dry out and hopefully kick the habit. She has a young son who is supportive and mature beyond his years. And a long-suffering mother.

The methodology for putting together the poems and songs in *Drinking for England* was painstaking and complicated. Simon Armitage never actually met the people for whom he wrote. After the producer had found suitable characters who were willing to co-operate on the film, she made sound recordings of her research interviews. These interviews would then be sent to Simon Armitage, who would study the tapes. He says he was, primarily, 'listening for speech rhythms, phrasing and cadenzas'. He chose not to meet the people because he thought it better to work 'at arm's length'. He was trying to capture the mood and the personality of the characters simply by listening to them. For example, he points out that the woman called Donna – the one whose mother was also an alcoholic – spoke slowly and chopped up her sentences. Armitage copied this and gave her a poem which he hoped reflected her speech patterns. She was delighted with the poem he had written for her and performed it with a stunning honesty and self-awareness which is really moving. Armitage points out that if the interviewees felt he had got them wrong, they would not have been able to deliver the poems or the songs. They needed to feel comfortable. None of the characters in *Drinking for England* objected to the poems written for them.

It is always difficult to persuade people to appear in a self-revealing documentary like *Drinking for England*, and I asked Brian Hill how he had managed the double feat of also persuading the characters to perform songs and poems for the camera. He says, 'I just asked them.' But pushed further he reflects that all of the people in the film were, on the surface, unremarkable and then, suddenly, they were being given a chance to show some hidden talent, like singing or reciting poetry. Millions would see them on television delivering a script which had been written especially for them, based on their own words and speech patterns, by one of Britain's leading poets, a man who has often been tipped as a future Poet Laureate. This must surely have been a validating experience for them.

The poetry in this film has a very different character to that in *Saturday Night* because Simon Armitage is now experimenting with using other people's imagery and speech patterns. The wild flights of fancy we encounter in *Saturday Night* are now replaced by a more mundane descriptive style. In an odd way, this makes the performances even more startling, because it is clear that we are seeing a totally accurate reflection of the lives and thoughts of these 'ordinary' people, but somehow they have transformed themselves, purely as a result of appearing in this film. Now they are no longer ordinary. Now they are artists and they are being given their spot in the limelight, their moment of fame.

Among a series of surprising scenes, two for me stand out. The first features the character called Duncan. We have seen him at the beginning of the film in a conventional interview situation, talking about his love of alcohol and how it has affected his life. He is a youngish man, attractive in a raffish sort of way, and the results of his overindulgence are already showing on his face. Later in the film he appears again, leaning against a wall, and suddenly he begins to sing. The accompanying music has a strong country and western flavour and he is a very good singer. He moves into the pub and continues singing, while the drinkers around him ignore the camera and appear to accept this bizarre situation with equanimity. He sings:

> *I'm a drinking man, I like a good drink*
> *I'm a thinking man, I like a good think.*

The scene is shot with the slick professionalism of a rock video, straight out of a popular chart-toppers programme on television. Brian Hill explains how the scene came about. In the course of talking with Duncan about his love of drink, it emerged that he has two brothers who were members of the very successful rock group UB40. His father was a folk singer. Hill says, 'So I asked him, "Can you sing too?" He said, "Yeah, I can sing." So I said, "Why don't you sing for us?"' Simon Armitage was suddenly presented with a change of plan. Now there were going to be songs in this film. He responded with 'Drinking Man', which is good enough by any professional standard but, suddenly appearing in the middle of a serious documentary, it provides the audience with the kind of jolt that Armitage always relishes.

The other extraordinary moment, for me, in the film features a character called Jane. She is interviewed in her house the night before she is due to go into a rehabilitation unit. She seems like a sad woman, fighting an addiction so that she can look after her young son, who bravely talks about how he feels and how much he wants his mother to get better. Later we see Jane inside the rehab unit and she, too, bursts into song. The subject is familiar – how sherry is the love of her life. It is another shocking moment, not least because the people working in this professional medical centre appear to think there is nothing abnormal about this strange performance.

Making films like *Drinking for England* obviously raises all kinds of ethical questions. While it is probably reasonable to assume that adults can make up their own minds about how they present themselves to the world, even if they are not particularly sober when they agree to be on camera, the question of the little boy is more troubling. I wondered what effect the screening of the film on television would have on the child, particularly in his relationships with other children at school. Brian Hill dealt with this potential problem in advance by talking to the teachers at the child's school and offering to come in and show the film and discuss it with them before transmission. In fact, the school did not take him up on this offer but reassured him that they were planning to talk to the students themselves and did not want to make too much of a fuss about it in case that should be counter-productive. It emerged later that not only was the boy not ashamed or embarrassed by his mother's appearance in the film, but he was very proud of her and thought that she had been brave and honest and, more important, she seemed to be winning her battle against addiction.

The next collaboration, *Killing Time*, took the methods developed in *Saturday Night* and *Drinking for England* even further. The genesis of the film was also different. Simon had been commissioned to write a 1000-word poem to celebrate the year 2001, the dawning of the Second Millennium. He sent what he had written to Brian, suggesting that they might make it into a film. This was a totally different departure for the team. While earlier films had started as documentaries, in the purist sense of the word, then developed into something more complex, this time they were beginning with a work which was completely imaginary. *Killing Time* developed into a 90-minute film which aspired to reflect the cold reality of life on Planet Earth, now about to enter a new era with all the hopes and fears that will always arise from such an auspicious date. The resulting film is a mix of actuality, drama documentary and pure drama.

Actors Christopher Eccleston and Hermione Norris play characters reflecting contemporary depictions of the medieval mystery play characters – Everyman, this time with a female partner. These characters wander around the UK, meeting all kinds of people, talking with them, trying to understand the world we live in today. Dramatic sequences are intercut with interviews and actuality in a mix that is not always comfortable. One sequence in the film caused a lot of controversy, mirroring the fuss over the printed version of the poem that Armitage has published. This refers to the massacre at Columbine High School in Colorado in 1998. In order to tell the story in an allegorical way, Armitage had decided on a conceit which substituted flowers for weapons. So, throughout the poem – and this idea was also echoed in the dramatic film realization which Brian Hill created – flowers represented guns and bombs. In one scene, the image of a flower, stuffed into the barrel of a gun, recalled the Spring Offensive of Czechoslovakia in 1968, when students in Prague attempted to bring down the Soviet Empire with slogans of love and peace and by offering flowers to the occupying army. The sense of a nightmare scenario is increased by the use of slow motion photography and a muted soundtrack. School students cower under desks in the library while sinister young men, carrying flowers, cause havoc and death. It is a deeply moving sequence that has disturbed many people. These scenes were shot at the school in Blackheath where Brian Hill's son is a pupil. His fellow students act out the roles of the killers and their victims. I would have thought that this was a dangerous experiment to play with young people who are not professional actors. However, Hill says that the school found that it actually helped the students who took part and made it easier for them to make some sense of the nightmare events that occurred to people of their own age in Columbine.

When Simon Armitage was asked about the Columbine sequence, he acknowledged that many people found it shocking, while others were moved. He said that he quite likes it when there is what he calls 'a split decision'. This reassures him that, like it or not, he has at least helped the audience to 'exercise their minds'.

Feltham Sings was a different kind of collaboration for Brian Hill, this time not only with Simon Armitage but also with Roger Graef, the veteran British-based American documentary film-maker. Graef had been negotiating for some time to get access to film at Feltham Young Offenders Institute. Not only is he an influential and multi-award-winning film-maker, he is also an expert on penal reform and well connected in government circles. Very few people would have had a chance of getting permission to film at Feltham at a very difficult time for the authorities when there had been a lot of damning press publicity. Against the odds, Graef got access. Feltham was notorious in penal circles for its tough regime and the worrying statistics of young men harming and even killing themselves while in custody there. Commissioning editor Peter Dale at Channel 4 had been considering the idea of approaching this difficult subject in an unconventional way. He suggested to Graef and Hill that they should get together and make a film about the prison – but no ordinary film. He thought they should incorporate the ideas which Hill and Armitage had been refining and, while treating the subject with the seriousness that it deserved, they should make a musical.

The finished film is a remarkable achievement and deservedly won the BAFTA Best Documentary award in 2003. It was the first completely digital film to be made by Brian Hill, and the ingenuity shown by him and his team was impressive. They followed their usual pattern of research. Katie Bailiff and her researcher spent months coming and going to the prison, getting to know the young offenders and staff and deciding which of them to feature in the film. They used a second unit director for the first time. Morgan Matthews also spent a lot of time getting acclimatized to the place and the people. Negotiations with the authorities were not easy. Hill says 'everything was fought over'. In the end, filming was confined to Teal Wing – all the wings in the prison were named after birds. Teal was one of the better wings and its name is the reason for the image of the exotically plumed duck which opens the film. The selected characters came from different parts of the prison, but they were all moved into Teal for the filming.

As usual, the researchers conducted long interviews with their chosen subjects and the tapes were sent to Simon Armitage for him to write lyrics, then to the composer, who wrote different kinds of music to match the character of the individuals who would be singing them. In some cases the young men could not read, so they had to listen to demo tapes to learn their lines. Surprisingly, only two of the subjects rejected what Simon had written for them. They were dreadlocked Jamaican boys who were sharing a cell and said that they would rather write their own rap song because they thought Simon's version was 'naff'. Their performance is arguably the best in the whole film.

All of the songs talk about the crimes the singers have committed and also talk about their lives before they went to jail. One remarkable young man whose song comes near the opening of the film was given a chorus which describes the fact that he was born in Holloway Prison, where his mother was a prisoner. He delivers his lines in a matter-of-fact way, showing no self-pity, and that only makes the whole episode more shocking and sad. Prison guards also sing their own song as they carry out their duties, guarding prisoners, patrolling corridors and locking people up for the night. Another dreadlocked man, this time a member of staff, sings about the drug habit he has kicked. He is a counsellor in the prison.

Filming in prison is always difficult, but this project was much more complicated than the average observational film. Normally people who record music will go to a studio, where sound technicians will ensure the best quality possible. None of the characters in this film could leave the prison, so the producers had to build a makeshift studio in the jail. They were also restricted by working on a documentary budget – admittedly a top-of-the-range figure, but still considerably less than a normal drama production. They took over an empty cell and soundproofed it with eggboxes and mattresses. The composer and sound man recorded the prisoners with an ordinary microphone onto a Mac laptop. They then filmed the performances to play back and the boys mimed the words. This would have been tricky for professional actors, so it is extraordinary to see the complex routines the prisoners and staff mastered to achieve what the director wanted. All the songs are shot in a number of different locations and rapidly cut, pop video style. The surprising thing is that it all looks beautifully professional.

The picture quality is also impressive. They shot on DV, on the DSR 500 camera, and deliberately underexposed it to give the look of a movie set in a prison. To ensure maximum quality, they recorded separate sound on DAT. Like all the Hill films, it is skilfully edited, with a terrific sense of pace. Alan Mackay, the editor, also worked in the prison, so he could not bring his Avid with him. He cut it on Final Cut Pro. This film is an impressive testimonial to the benefit of working with lightweight digital technology, particularly since the production team had been previously wedded to the idea that you can only get real quality on film.

To date, the last collaboration of the Hill–Armitage team is a film, provocatively entitled *Pornography – The Musical*. After *Feltham*, it had been hard to guess what on earth they would do next to shock the audience. This was it. At first they say they found it difficult to see a way through this difficult subject. Hill says that films about sex are 'usually comical or anatomical'. They wanted to give women who work in the sex industry a voice. Hill thinks there is a lot of hypocrisy about 'porn', but there has been a huge shift in the last 20 years. He thinks that pornography is quite fashionable, no longer stigmatized and lots of people use it. They found a way through the obvious problems, both legal and logistical, of filming people creating pornography by building a studio and recreating explicit sex scenes specifically for their own film. They intercut between the studio performances and conventionally shot interviews with the sex workers. The musical sections are also filmed in the studio.

It is possible that Hill has overestimated the ideological shift in public opinion on this subject. Reviewers were brutal about the film and some even found it as pornographic as the subjects it set out to examine. It seems to me inevitable that this will be the last in this particular genre of documentary that these innovative collaborators will tackle, not because the film was so controversial but because I suspect that the team have exhausted their ingenuity in this particular sub-genre of factual film. Having moved all the way from a black and white documentary with a poetic narration to a highly stylized studio-based musical drama, it seems obvious that the next production will be drama, pure and simple. They have explored so many options for telling the stories of the alienated and neglected in a way – with the possible exception of *Pornography* – that audiences found entertaining as well as enlightening, while still sticking, more or less, to documentary form. What will they do next? Hill says they are having discussions about making a feature film based on Armitage's first novel. Hill has already directed one fiction story for television and also written and directed another. Both explored the same sort of ground as the documentaries – one was about domestic violence, the other featured stories of children in care. However, he says he will never stop making documentaries.

I asked Brian Hill why he and Simon Armitage were so interested in the kind of people they always seem to film – outsiders usually living on the fringes of society. I pointed out that their subjects are never what most of us would describe as 'ordinary people'. He replied with a question:

Well who is ordinary? People are always ordinary till you get beneath the surface. That family in Australia. I bet their friends and neighbours think they are ordinary. But they are in fact dysfunctional. But that makes them normal for me, normal in the sense that all families, one way or the other, are dysfunctional.

Armitage is less concerned than the others about moving away from documentary. He says it is simply a category, a way in which television departments can be organized or budgets allocated. But it has no more status as 'reality' than any other form. 'I don't accept the idea of "reality",' he says. 'Authors have their own reality which they bring to everything they do.' Whatever form they choose for their next production it will surely be innovative and use the technology in some original way. Hill and Armitage will never stop experimenting, pushing back the boundaries, surprising the audience.

FILMOGRAPHY – BRIAN HILL

Brian Hill is managing director of Century Films, a UK-based independent production company. Century specializes in documentary production but is increasing its drama output.

Brian started his career in BBC Education as a researcher on social action programmes. He then moved into the independent sector and worked as a producer and director for a number of independent production companies in London before forming Century Films.

Director credits

Class Rule
December 1991, 4 × 50 min, BBC2
Films about the class factor in British politics.

Sylvania Waters
1993, 12 × 25 min, BBC1
Series about life in an Australian suburb.

The Club
1994, Channel 4
Film about a golf club for *Cutting Edge*.

Nominated for Flaherty Award BAFTA
Winner BAFTA, Best Editing
Nominated RTS, Best Documentary

Tough Love
1995, Channel 4
Cutting Edge film about disturbed teenagers.

State of Marriage
1996, Channel 4

Feature-length film about people who got married in the same year as Charles and Diana (for *True Stories*).

Jumpers
1996, Channel 4
Cutting Edge film about showjumping.

Saturday Night
September 1996, BBC2
Film about a night out in Leeds (for *Modern Times*).

Trouble with Money
1997, 50 min, Channel 4
Film about Lottery winners (for *Cutting Edge*).

Pommies
September 1997, 3 × 50 min, Channel 4
Films about British people living in Australia.

Political Ambitions
1998, 3 × 50 min, Channel 4
Films about wannabe MPs.

Drinking for England
November 1998, 50 min film, BBC2
Drinking set to verse (for *Modern Times*).

Winner of Best Documentary – Royal Television Society, 1998

Men at Fifty
November 1998, 50 min, Channel 4

Film for *Cutting Edge* about men born on the same day as Prince Charles.

Burglars
November 1999, 50 min, ITV
Film for ITV's *Real Life* series.

Killing Time
1 January 2000, 75 min, Channel 4

Film based on Simon Armitage's millennium poem of the same name. A mixture of drama, documentary and animation.

The Tyre
2000, 10 min, theatrical release
Drama starring Christopher Eccleston.

Winner of the Yorkshire Film Award
Leeds International Film Festival, 2000

Nobody Someday
January 2001, theatrical release, transmitted March 2002, Channel 4

Feature-length documentary about Robbie Williams's European tour in 2000.

It's a Cow's Life
March 2002, 50 min, Channel 4
Film about the life of a cow from birth to plate.

Falling Apart
October 2002, 63 min, Channel 4

Drama about domestic violence starring Hermione Norris and Mark Strong.

BAFTA Best New Director – Fiction, 2002
BAFTA Best New Writer, 2002

Feltham Sings
December 2002, 50 min, Channel 4

Musical documentary featuring the inmates and officers at Feltham Young Offenders Institute.

BAFTA – Flaherty Award for Best Documentary, 2003
Ivor Novello Award – Best Original Television Music, 2003
Shortlisted for Grierson Award and RTS Best Original Score

More Precious Than Gold
Theatrical release at various cinemas, appears on DVD *Robbie Live at Knebworth*, VHS Lilya Forever

Awareness-raising short for UNICEF about child trafficking.

Pornography – The Musical
October 2003, 50 min, Channel 4

Musical documentary featuring porn stars singing and talking about their work.

Bella and the Boys
15 February 2004, 75 min, BBC2

Drama about the lives of three young people who grew up in a care home.

Series producer and executive producer credits

Deadline
1995, 6 × 25 min, Channel 4
Films about life in a TV newsroom.

Shot
1999, Channel 4
Cutting Edge film about the experience of being shot.

The Facemakers
1999, 50 min, BBC1
Film for *QED* about facial surgery in the Philippines.

Bondi
June 2000, 6 × 25 min, Channel 4 and ABC Australia
Films about life on Bondi beach.

Teenage Kicks
TBA, 6 × 30 min, Channel 4

Series about the lives of a group of teenagers at a London school as they tackle their 'A' levels.

Care House
May 2003, 90 min, BBC4
Film examining the lives of the residents and carers at a care home.

Rude Girls
TBA, 90 min, BBC2

A film that looks deeply into the personal stories and lives of girls behaving badly.

FILMOGRAPHY – SIMON ARMITAGE

Xanadu
1992, BBC2
Writer and presenter

A 30-minute film in verse, commissioned by BBC2 for their *Words on Film* series, *Xanadu* is a 'poem film for television' set on the Ashfield Valley Housing Estate in Rochdale, Lancashire, where Armitage used to work as a probation officer.

Looking for Robinson
1993, BBC2
Writer and presenter

A 50-minute film on the life and work of American poet Weldon Keyes, in prose and verse. Armitage goes in search of Keyes, who, it is thought, leapt to his death from Golden Gate Bridge in

San Francisco. Armitage visits his grave and his San Francisco beat haunts.

One Foot In The Past
1993, BBC2
Writer and presenter

A 10-minute film in verse for BBC2's heritage and landscape programme, focusing on Emley Moor Mast.

Building Sights
1995, BBC2
Writer and presenter

A 10-minute film about the Humber Bridge for BBC2's contemporary architecture programme, *Building Sights*.

Words From Jerusalem
1995, BBC1
Writer and presenter
A commissioned poem for Easter.

Saturday Night
1996, BBC2
Writer and narrator

Based in the city of Leeds, *Saturday Night* is a 50-minute poetic commentary to a documentary about nightlife in Leeds. Part of BBC2's *Modern Times* series, it was made by Century Films and was directed by Brian Hill, who directed *Sylvania Waters*.

Drinking for England
1998, BBC2
Writer
Poetry and song for a 50-minute documentary on alcoholism.

Killing Time
2000, Channel 4
Writer

A 90-minute television film based on the millennium poem of the same name, filmed for television and broadcast on New Year's Day, 2000. It was performed by Christopher Eccleston.

The Tyre
2000, Century Films
Writer

Ten-minute feature film based on the poem of the same name from CloudCuckooLand.

8 Victor Kossakovsky The Dogme from St Petersburg

Victor Kossakovsky

Victor Kossakovsky opened his masterclass at the UK National Film and Television School in 2003 by telling the students, 'Nobody knows everything about film. So forget what I tell you. This is only my experience.' This was a typically modest introduction because Kossakovsky has developed into an influential figure in the world of documentary. He is a true auteur in that he directs, shoots and edits his own films. He says he would not like to work with a cameraman because he has to feel something is just right before he films it. Then he says, by the time he could explain exactly where he wants to look and how it should be shot, the moment has passed and it is gone forever. He has very strong views about form and has invented his own original approach to the genre.

Kossakovsky was born in St Petersburg – then Leningrad – in 1961. He is a big favourite on the international film festival circuit.

Since his wildly individualistic film *The Belovs* was released in 1993, his new films have been awaited with great anticipation all over the world. But he takes his time in making them. He says, 'I am very lazy. I have only made seven films.' Actually, this is typical Kossakovsky irony. He only makes films when he really cares about the idea. And he refuses to be lured by commercial imperatives.

He says, 'You must really need to film something. It's like an illness. A feeling that you have to film it or you will die.' He makes an analogy with the behaviour of a typical cat. He says he believes that documentary makers should emulate the attitude of cats. 'A cat can jump from the ninth floor to the fifth floor. Nothing happens.' No harm comes to them because they are always ready. Like a cat, the documentary maker has to be constantly at the ready for any kind of situation. But they must never be predictable. 'If you know what you want to say, don't do it. It must always be something new for you.' He says he can find a film to make every day but he has to lose sleep over an idea before he will definitely decide to make it.

I first met Victor when he came to England for a screening of his film *Tische*. One day I was walking down a road with him in West London and he asked me, 'What does this mean?' He pointed to a sign, painted on the tarmac in the street which said 'Look Left'. On the other side of the road, a similar sign said 'Look Right'. With his usual deadpan humour he asked me, 'Is this a political message?' Of course he knew perfectly well that the road signs were not a condemnation of the rightward shift of the Blairite Labour government, surreal and disconcerting as that might have been, but simply a warning sign to careless pedestrians to watch out for one-way traffic. Later he described the scene to my students. 'This made me think, I could make a film about democracy here. That could be the title, "Look Left, Look Right". But the problem is, do I want to live with this idea? Do I want to spend so much time in London?' He finished the point with a warning for the young film-makers, 'Never compromise your work just for money.'

Kossakovsky has a number of rules which he follows and urges other documentarists to consider. Some of them are, on the surface, eccentric, in that they work for him but might seem overly restrictive to film-makers with a more pluralistic approach. But given the influence he has had internationally, it is worth listing the Kossakovsky guidelines, which in many ways remind me of the original statement from Lars von Trier and his colleagues in the Danish feature-film industry, who published their manifesto, *Take the Vow of Chastity*, in 1995. Now universally known as the Dogme Rules, a fading photocopy still hangs on my office wall. I think of it as an important artefact of historical significance for the cinema. I have found that many young film-makers, in Europe and the Americas, feel a natural affinity to Victor Kossakovsky and his films. Maybe, one day, the documentary form as outlined by him will prevail in our industry. Who knows? But, for the record, here they are:

THE RULES OF DOCUMENTARY (according to Kossakovsky)

1 There are no rules. Only go with your instincts.
2 Cinema was invented with one single shot. Without a story. (The Lumière brothers, *Workers Leaving the Factory*, 1894.) There is too much emphasis on story. In documentary structure can be absolutely abstract.
3 Never make interviews.
4 You need a brain when you are making art. But don't use it when you are filming.
5 Never put cutaways in a documentary. Never even film it.
6 You can't repeat life. You can't repeat the moment. Never ask anybody to repeat an action.
7 People have to trust you, or they will not behave naturally.
8 Sometimes we have to make harsh decisions about what to include in a film. *Nice people should not make documentaries.*

Kossakovsky tells a story to illustrate Rule 3. He says that when he was 18 he worked on a film about a famous Communist Party worker-hero. They filmed an interview with him talking about his childhood. He told the story well, he even cried. The picture was later damaged in the laboratory, although the sound was fine. The director decided to film the interview again. The editor thought there had been a mistake because he had been given, he thought, the old sound. In fact, it was the later interview. The two sound-tracks were identical. The old man had told the story so many times that he had it by heart, even the emotional outburst of crying. In fairness to the interviewee, most people have favourite stories to tell and often repeat themselves. However, Kossakovsky is simply stressing his need for spontaneity when he is filming.

The Belovs, made in 1993, follows the Rules to the letter. The film is about a brother and sister, sharing a farmhouse in the Russian countryside, ekeing out a precarious living and growing old together. It has no story as such, although there is a strong emotional narrative. The mood of the film swings back and forth from anarchic humour to moments of something close to despair. In my view, the family will be instantly recognizable to any reader of nineteenth century Russian literature. There is nothing of the smart, hip and sophisticated new Russia about them. One scene in the film encapsulates this. The two main characters are usually alone but, one day, two brothers visit them. They sit around a table arguing loudly about politics. They talk about Lenin. They want to know what is the point of living. A lot of drink is taken. Kossakovsky calls them 'a typical Russian family'. The scene could be taken, as he says, directly from Dostoevsky.

It is obvious right from the first second that this is no ordinary film. In pre-title, we see an old man sitting at a table. A dog is licking his nose. The shot is held without camera movement throughout the scene. It looks like a silent black and white movie, tinted with sepia. The old man talks to the cameraman, Kossakovsky himself. The man explains that the dog always knows when there is something wrong with him and will always lick him to help him get better. He sighs and takes out a cigarette. He sounds slightly drunk. He says, in a ponderous, even preachy way, 'This is my message to everyone. Let human beings develop in a natural way.' The screen cuts to black in the middle of his pronouncement, which continues simply in voice-over. Then comes the title, in Cyrillic script, one word, 'BELOVS'.

After the title comes an extraordinary scene. It is a journey in a boat down an unidentified river. The camera is constantly moving from close shots of the water itself – often the screen is filled with rippling water – to changing scenes on the river bank. At one moment it moves slowly past rocks protruding from the river. There is something primitive about these rocks; they look like fossilized animals. Immediately after the rocks, the boat arrives at a port and then moves out into the sea. The boat is moving quickly, bouncing over rough waters and once again the screen shows only water. What makes the scene truly bizarre, however, is the choice of music. It is a strange Bollywood number with a woman's voice apparently singing a lament, interrupted from time to time by a foot-tapping male chorus. The scene is exhilarating, hilarious, if only because it is so weird. It is a full four minutes long.

At no point in the film do we get an explanation of the river scene and its accompanying music. I understand that the river is near the location of the filming, the family's farm, but since no obvious connection is made in the film, this is information only assumed later. The river in the film has an ending but no apparent beginning – the sequence starts with the river already in full flow. Kossakovsky explains the reason for this. According to him, there is no obscure, David Lynch-type mystery here. He was shooting on 35 mm with a ratio of 3:1 and the early shots of the river were damaged. So he could not use them. As always with Victor, you are never quite sure if he is being serious or pulling your leg. As for the Bollywood music, he says that it would not seem unusual to a Russian audience because Indian pictures are very popular there and they would not find it a strange choice. Obviously, the film is read differently by different cultures. In my case, when I saw the film for the first time, my reaction was one of complete incomprehension. There is always a moment at the beginning of any film when you have to decide whether to trust the film-maker. I had no background information about Kossakovsky or his movie, but decided to relax and enjoy it for one simple reason. This director, whoever he was, must be good because in the first few minutes of the movie he had already made me laugh.

After the river, the next scene begins with a mysterious picture, a blurred, dirty window with a shadowy figure behind it. The window slides open. An old woman stands there, scarf around her neck. She says, 'I am coming my darlings. Granny is coming, my little darlings.' She is speaking Russian, so at least we know what country we are in. Soon the old lady is milking a cow, whispering encouragingly to the animal. A normal enough country situation. But, because of the two scenes which went before, this is still bizarre enough to make us imagine we are in some kind of spooky alternative universe; everything that happens from this moment seems strange.

The music in the film is massively important but also, unusually, not exactly clear in its direction for an international audience. The viewers have to bring their own sensibilities and experience to a reading of the film. This is in complete contrast to normal use of music in documentaries (or, for that matter, most fiction films), where music will be used to underline a point, increase tension, step up the emotion, tell the audience what to think. Here, you are on your own, your imagination is challenged. You have to read these music scenes for yourself.

After the puzzling Bollywood opening, the next big music break is tightly edited, more that any other in the film, cutting from shots of Anna, hitting the cows in the field with a little branch, to hens running around aimlessly, another Anna and a cow shot, then to 'wildlife programme' close-ups of ants racing around to a shot of a tractor, driven by Mikhail, racing towards the camera. Next we see a pensive hedgehog gazing into a stagnant pool of water, then suddenly galloping out of the way as the glorious progress of Mikhail's somewhat erratic tractor drive, now accompanied by his dog, continues. Meanwhile, a Cuban band is singing its cheerful message. 'Arriba, Arriba.' The mood of the scene, for me, suggests that Mikhail as he appears to be, lazy, irresponsible, even debauched, is the one with the spirit of joy and adventure in this picture. Anna, who is presented as the always complaining, downtrodden, hard-working woman, is a bit of a bore. That impression is to be seriously challenged later in the film.

At the end of the deliriously crazy tractor ride, we see an open road, dust rising. Along comes a car, baggage on top. This is the Dostoevskian moment in the film, the visit of the brothers.

Anna and her brothers sit at the table arguing. They have a habit of declaiming rather than conversing, so the language has a rather theatrical quality. This idea is enhanced by the fact that the camera holds the same shot for several minutes, like a simple recording of a stage performance. One brother says, 'Anna, you have absorbed the worst aspects of the soviet system.' She is the only one who talks normally. She says, 'Yeltsin is doing his best.'

The conversation continues. Anna has left the table, the camera has changed its position but still frames the whole table, holding the same shot. Anna is outside, whistling to the animals. The men continue to pontificate.

> 'The Russian Empire conquered vast territories and trampled on people's national feelings.'
> 'Other countries evolved naturally. I don't know where Russia is.'
> 'Shut up Karamazov.'

The picture now cuts to a family photograph from years earlier. They are all staring solemnly at the camera; one of the boys is in uniform. This shot is held, again without camera movement, for a full two minutes while the bizarre conversation continues. One talks about the siege of Leningrad. Another says, 'I'll meet you at the Elbe.'

Victor says that he used the family photograph because he had run out of film while the sound was still running. It is difficult to know if this is another example of his ironic sense of humour. He enjoys teasing over-earnest interviewers. On the other hand, he says, 'Sometimes a difficult situation demands another way of thinking.' The challenge is to do something which is not obvious and possibly more creative. This is interesting because it is exactly the argument used by the Danish director, Thomas Vinterberg, who made the brilliant *Festen* under Dogme Rules. Thomas says that having lots of technology, props, lights, specially composed music, etc. readily available can encourage lazy thinking. The Dogme Rules forced him to think of new ways of approaching his subject, therefore it stimulated creativity.

While Victor's explanation makes sense, it still does not explain why there is no camera movement at all for two minutes while we look at a still picture. It is obviously a deliberate choice and it works. Because the shot is held for so long, we do the work ourselves. The eye moves around the picture, picking out details, leading us to wonder how these clean-cut young people with their strict-looking mother have turned out as they are today. The very stillness of the picture leads cleverly into the next scene, which is full of movement and stunningly beautiful to look at. The three old men are in a traditional Russian sauna. Light streams through a window into the otherwise dark room where they are sitting, beating themselves with twigs. Their naked bodies seem to glow in the dark. There is a strong visual reference to silent films from the early days of the revolution showing hero mineworkers, toiling in the dark. We see that their lips are moving but we cannot hear them because there is no natural sound on this scene. Instead, we have another incongruous but nevertheless inspired choice of music. At first we hear only the instrumental introduction. It is a big band playing a tango. Then the male vocalist begins. He is English.

> *The moon was yellow*
> *And the night was young*
> *A smile brought us together*
> *And I was wondering whether*
> *We'd meet again some day.*

It is pure 1930s schmaltz and it works brilliantly.

Because Kossakovsky does not care about context, we only find out the names of the family members in the end credits. We are never told where the farm is situated or what is the name of the river. The weirdest example of this lack of journalistic precision occurs when Anna walks into a bedroom and shouts at somebody who is sleeping, telling him to get up. He sits up, very sleepy; he is just a boy. Who is he? Why have we not seen him before? This is towards the end of the film. We guess that he is a grandson because Anna refers to herself as granny, but that might be a nickname. This should be a disjunctive moment for the audience but somehow it is not. By this point in the film, Kossakovsky has coaxed us into his peculiar universe and we simply follow along behind. Given the early visual training of most audiences in the world, watching television where everything is spelled out in detail, this is a remarkable achievement.

The Belovs has no story, in the conventional sense of the word. Victor says that the whole film is constructed to build up to the last scene, which is the most important scene in the film. Anna has professional earphones and is listening to something being played on a nagra. She is giggling and sighing. She is clearly listening to recordings of herself and her brother made by the film crew. She takes off the phones, gets up and walks out of the door. Still in shot, she begins to sing and dance. She sings:

I shall dance and wiggle my bottom
Hey you should all look at me
What nice buttocks you shall see.

She dances and stamps her feet, clicks her fingers, apparently oblivious to the camera. Now for the first time in the film, the camera starts to move. The camera is following her around; now Victor, the cameraman/director, is also dancing.

Harken, split I was
And remade I was
Seven times gave birth
And still a virgin was.

This extraordinary, powerful scene ends the film. Victor says that he could not have put the scene in earlier because people would feel that he was being unfair to Anna, making her look foolish. Instead, by the end of the film, we have recognized her courage and forebearance. The balalaika that accompanies Anna's song was added in the edit, a rare concession to artifice from Kossakovsky. It was a good decision because it enhances the sheer, exuberant Russian spirit of the scene. Of all the music sequences in the film, this is the only one with genuinely, historically accurate, Russian music. Right at the end of the film we finally hear the authentic sound of the country. In spite of that, this film could not be set anywhere else; the spirit of Russia permeates every frame.

When the crew first arrived at the farm to begin filming, they did nothing for three weeks, just little jobs around the place, no filming. Then they started to shoot. Victor says, 'They thought we were mad. Then they stopped taking notice of us.' The brothers arrived on the second day of filming and the next day Anna asked if she could listen to the recorded sound. He gave her the machine but did not film it. The experience had, he says, a 'big effect on her'.

They knew they had to leave because they had made her self-conscious. They stayed away for two months and then went back to start again. But he says he knew that, when the right moment came, she would ask again to hear the sound and this time he would film it.

When Victor was 25, he had to get himself a passport. This was the law in Russia at the time. So he went to a photographer to have a passport portrait taken and a few days later went back to pick it up. So far, so just like everybody else. When he got to the shop, the photographer told him to find his picture, which was somewhere lying in a pile that had just been developed. As he sorted through the photographs, Victor started to wonder about all these young people, all born at around the same time as him, there in St Petersburg. He says he thought about how, every day in the world, maybe 50,000 people die and another 50,000 people are born. Like theatre, somebody changes the cast. He says he was always wondering, 'Why am I Victor? Why am I Russian?' He could not get it out of his head. He decided that if he could find all of the people born on the same day as himself, in the same place, maybe he would begin to understand more about himself and how the world works. He spent four years finding the people and two years making the film.

My copy of the film is the one transmitted by the BBC in the *Storyville* strand. It starts with a full screen caption:

> On Wednesday 19th July 1961, 101 babies were born in what was then called Leningrad.
> One of them, Victor Kossakovsky, grew up to be a film-maker.
> In 1995, he scoured the city of St Petersburg to find those who share his birthday.

An admirably clear, concise example of how to write text for television. But if Victor had anything to do with it, I will be very surprised indeed. It is very BBC but not at all Kossakovsky. The real film begins with a man shaving. We don't know who he is and he is not identified. In the next shot he is outside in a courtyard talking to a young lad, being interrupted by a woman, hunkered down by a wall and smoking. The boy says he is on strike. She shouts at him, reminding him that people on strike do not eat. This is the new age for Russia, post-Soviet Union. The man says it is his birthday then walks up to the camera and stares into the lens, first saying nothing, then muttering conspiratorially. He says, 'Life's not bad. OK so far. The future is uncertain. The weather bad. I don't like talking in front of all these people. Let's go somewhere else.' In spite of the huge cast of characters in the film, we never see that man again.

This film is, in many ways, different to *The Belovs* and, it could be said, comes close to breaking some of the Rules. Throughout the film there are exchanges between Kossakovsky and the people who share his birthday. Depending on how you define the word 'interview', it could be argued that there are a number in the film. However, if you accept the American, 'direct cinema' definition, you will say that these are not 'interviews' but 'conversations'.

While many of the scenes in *The Belovs* feature a static, locked-off camera, recording events as they happen in front of the lens, this film is shot in the observational style, often handheld, with very fluid action sequences. There is also a great deal of intervention from the film-maker. We hear his voice, the characters sometimes call him by his name and in two of the episodes we actually see him, although he is not identified for the benefit of the audience. This is at least a consistent decision, since none of the many characters in the film are identified, unless another person mentions their name in a natural way.

In the course of researching and filming, Kossakovsky met and talked to 70 of the 101 people who had been born on the same day as him. A number of them are seen fleetingly and never appear again. One character, a heavily pregnant woman, features throughout the film. She is seen in the fast-cut montage early in the film, in the delivery room at the hospital, her baby being born, on camera. The film then moves back to the waiting time before she goes into hospital and cuts back and forward to her story as she and her partner wait with increasing anxiety to know if a hospital bed will be available for her. Close to the end of the film, when the birth scene is shown in full, a wonderful moment comes when she is afraid that there might be something wrong with the baby who has just been born. She does not cry out to the doctors, as anyone would expect, she says to the film-maker who is shooting the scene from the bottom of her bed, 'Is she alright, Victor?' And he says, 'Yes.'

Wednesday was Kossakovsky's way of investigating his own world, trying to make sense of it. From the point of view of a non-Russian audience, it has an additional interest. It gives a sharp, detailed and very honest picture of St Petersburg, a few years after the collapse of the Soviet Union. Most of the people in the film are suffering badly, financially; there are signs of the rise of a corrupt new capitalist class; the police come out of the film with no credit whatsoever. (One scene shows a respectable, educated man who has been taken into hospital after a beating by the police. The doctor says, 'This is the second one in two days.') At the end of the film, Victor meets the last of the birthday group still living in his home city. The man has been avoiding the filming because he has spent time in prison. He asks if any of the other birthday people went to jail. Victor explains that some got into trouble in the army, some went to live in Novgorod or Chad, some left the country and went to live abroad. But most are still there, ready to share their lives with a stranger with a camera.

I found the whole film fascinating, as an insight into the new Russia. But I was also often profoundly moved by the honesty and, at times, the vulnerability that the characters revealed. And I was impressed by the loyalty and pride that they still showed for their beautiful city, in spite of everything. The last caption of the film recalls, but I think betters, the opening announcement. It says, 'We would like to thank the people of St Petersburg, who were born in Leningrad on 19th July 1961, for their participation in this film.' Born in Leningrad says it all.

Kossakovsky's latest film on release is different again from anything we have seen before. It is called *Tische*, which means, literally, 'hush' or 'keep quiet'. It is a clever, satirical film, but also amusing and beautiful to look at. Kossakovsky's smart idea was to make a film from one camera position only. The camera would be placed in the window of his office in St Petersburg. It would never leave the room and the entire film would be shot from there, looking down on the street below. It is possible to spot many cultural references in the film. Most of the time, it is a silent movie with a musical score, specially composed and performed for the film.

Filming *Wednesday*

Victor says that he was influenced by realist and abstract paintings when considering the look of the film. It also seems inevitable that Hitchcock's *Rear Window* must have been sometimes in his thoughts.

When a friend first told me about this film he said, 'Kossakovsky's new film is about a hole in the road. He has filmed this hole from his window for a year.' Not, at first, the most compelling idea for a film but, given the track record of the film-maker, I was prepared to suspend my disbelief. *Tische* has one central conceit, which is the progress of road works which continue for a year but never seem to rectify the original damage caused by a hole in the road. Victor says that the film is not about the story of the road or any other story for that matter, although it does have an emotional development. If pushed, I think he would probably accept a description of the film as being about laziness and corruption in public building organizations, as observed over the period of one year in one particular place. The location happens to be St Petersburg, but it could be anywhere in Russia. Indeed, not only Russia. There are many countries in the world where this particular metaphor would be recognized and appreciated by long-suffering taxpayers.

The film begins with a scene of public workers sweeping the pavement below. The action is speeded up and, viewed from above, the little figures sweeping and the pedestrians walking by look like little toys. The soundtrack has a fast, jolly piano accompaniment, reminiscent of the silent cinema. This opening sets the mood for the rest of the film. It is clear that there is something slightly unworldly, vaguely theatrical and above all funny about this world we are about to enter.

The film covers all four seasons and the hole in the road is the main feature. The works become more and more farcical as, however many men or machines are engaged in sorting out the problem – whatever that might be, we are never really clear about why the works got started – it gets worse and worse. Huge holes are now being dug; the whole road has to be closed from time to time, causing major inconvenience to motorists and pedestrians. It has an Orwellian feeling, like the brave new world once again engaged in a battle which will never be won and no-one remembers why the war started in the first place.

At times, the camera lingers on a detail which is enhanced to the point that it looks like a painting. Sometimes it is a close-up of the road surface, sometimes a fierce blizzard of snow, or the moon reflected on the window. These beautiful visual intervals, accompanied by the original, specially composed music, give breathing space for the audience to relax a little before the next excess of bureaucratic lunacy.

Meanwhile, little cameos of everyday life are recorded. A couple appear to be arguing in the street, then they make up and embrace in the middle of the road, nearly getting themselves killed by passing traffic. A police van stops and two criminals escape out of the back of the vehicle, but are apprehended by a violent civilian who has to be restrained by the police when they finally notice what is happening. An old lady is looking for her dog. She is calling out his name: 'Tische, tische.' ('Hush, hush.') The film finishes with the roadworks no nearer to completion, but the old lady finds her dog and gets him into the house.

Victor says that he was not sure that he really had a film until he saw the old lady. He was halfway through his shoot when she appeared. She appears to symbolize so much. At her age, she will have lived through much of the old Communist Party government and now be adjusting to the new western-style regime. But she still remembers how to keep her own council, however long it takes to mend a hole in the road.

The shooting days for the film were, as usual with Kossakovsky, very economical. He filmed for seven days over a period of a year. The editing took considerably longer. Altogether the film took a year to make. It has been shown in 60 countries, understandably, because it is not only a beautiful, skilfully constructed and funny film, it also has the universal appeal of an instantly recognizable message – and no dialogue.

Kossakovsky is a fiercely independent spirit and only makes the films he really wants to make. I was with him in London when a friend of mine, an executive in a big independent production company, asked him if he would be interested in making a film about the new owner of Chelsea Football Club. Victor looked genuinely surprised. He said, 'Why would I want to do that?' My friend misunderstood his reason for saying no and asked him if he was worried about getting enough access to the man. Victor, usually very good-natured, looked positively offended. 'Of course I would get access. Putin has asked me three times to make a film about him. I don't want to make a film about him. Or Mr Abramovich.' Later my friend asked me to try to persuade him. I e-mailed the request and got a polite but short reply. 'Tell them thank you. But no.'

Victor usually finances his own films from the sales of the one before and from prizes which he regularly wins at film festivals. He spelled out for me the money he had been paid by European broadcasters, including the BBC, for his last film and I was surprised and impressed, and had to admit that this is a perfectly viable way to work and a good way of preserving independence and control. Of course, you have to be totally confident in your own ability to pull it off. It works for Kossakovsky but he, of course, is very, very clever.

FILMOGRAPHY

The Belovs
1993

A sister and brother live together on a farm in the middle of the Russian countryside. The film documents their daily lives and features a visit they receive from some lively relatives.

Wednesday
1997

Kossakovsky sets out to find all of the people who were born on the same day as him, 19 July 1961, in St Petersburg. The film gives a vivid insight into the lives of the citizens of St Petersburg at the end of the twentieth century.

I Loved You
2000, BBC TV (subtitled 'Three Films About Love')
The series tells three stories, each featuring a different generation.

One is located in a children's nursery. A little girl tells the filmmaker that she loves one of the boys in the group. A rival for his affections emerges. They are heartbroken when the boy has to leave because he is now old enough to go to school.

The second film is about a young couple getting married.

The third is a moving film about an old Russian couple who have gone to live in Israel. He is incapacitated and very unhappy, missing Russia. She is selfless in her devotion and loyalty.

Tische
2002

Kossakovsky documented the life of St Petersburg in the course of a year by filming life in the street below his window. The film follows the progress, or lack of progress, of a hole in the road which is regularly being worked on by municipal employees, with no apparent improvement being seen. An old lady living opposite searches for her dog, shouting out his name, Tische. The word is translated into English as 'hush' or 'quiet'.

9   Sean Langan
Journalist with a camera

Sean Langan in Afghanistan

Sean Langan's career as a documentary film-maker started almost by chance. At the time, he was a print journalist, a features writer who had previously been Economics Editor of *The Guardian*. He says that, for years after he started working in television, he thought of himself not so much as a documentarian, more as 'a journalist with a camera'. Nowadays he accepts the label 'film-maker' but still tells stories, at his own expense, which illustrate his lack of interest in the finer points of the technology. He specializes in films made in highly volatile, often dangerous, situations. The BBC reflected this by calling his first specially commissioned series *Langan Behind The Lines*.

As a child, Sean lived in the Algarve – he is half Portuguese, half Irish. He says the conditions of the house in which the family lived was, by contemporary standards, very primitive. This might be one of the reasons why he is so comfortable in himself when working in foreign countries that sometimes offer only a modicum of creature comforts. He made his first film in Kashmir, for the BBC Video Diaries Unit. It was commissioned in December 1997 by Bob Long and was, in theory at least, supposed to be a modest affair.

The video diaries people had pioneered a new kind of documentary. The producer who invented the original format was Jeremy Gibson and the series had launched in 1990. People who had never made a film before were invited to make one for the BBC. They would shoot it themselves on a lightweight video camera. The story would be told in diary form and would be narrated by the film-maker. This narrative technique had been used in many films in the past, so in one sense it was not a particularly new idea. The stroke of brilliance in the BBC's diary concept was to get the producers to film themselves, reflecting on the day's events, and intercut these ruminations with the action. The pieces to camera, filmed every morning and evening, were often the most entertaining aspects of the programmes and the new form, rough and unprofessional though it often was, injected a freshness into the schedules. It became hugely popular and has also been immensely influential in the documentary world.

The diarists were given three weeks training in technical matters and storytelling techniques. Sean Langan, who is never completely predictable, was unable to do the scheduled three weeks training because he was finishing another project and needed to get off on his diary story as soon as possible afterwards. So instead of three weeks training, he had three days. In those early days, the video diaries were shot on Hi8 cameras. Given the lack of time and Langan's clear disinterest in the minutiae of the new technology, the BBC engineers advised him to keep the camera on automatic all the time. One even advised him to 'gaffer tape' up all the other switches, leaving only On/Off free, in case he made a mistake and went into manual mode by accident. This advice was not entirely satirical in intent. After some discussion, Langan also decided to opt for a wide-angle lens and a clip microphone.

The wide-angle lens meant that he could be sure he was getting everything he needed in shot without necessarily having to check the viewfinder all the time. On the Hi8, this was a bonus, particularly for a diarist who was keen to get up close as much as possible and also film himself in action. This is where Langan broke the mould in the video diary field. Normally the diarists would only film themselves in static situations, where they could place the camera on a steady surface and keep their image in focus. Langan decided to film himself as he walked around and talked to the camera. This method required a degree of ingenuity. He had to hold the camera at arm's length and talk to it, as one would to a good friend. Of course, it is only possible to shoot this way if, like Langan, you have long arms. It became an important feature of his work.

Although this first film was initially commissioned as a video diary, *Murder in Paradise* was eventually shown as a three-part special on BBC2. It is an extraordinary story and took five months to film. For Langan, it was a personal journey as well as a professional commitment. He was paid the normal rate for a video diary, so the long period of time he chose to give to the project was to a large extent financed by him. At the same time he has immense respect for Bob Long, who was prepared to wait for the story and not put him under pressure to finish on schedule as most executive producers would have done. Langan says that, for him, time is a key factor:

> *Time. Lots of it. It makes the difference between what I do and, say, CNN. Two days in a country tends to reinforce the ideas you already had before leaving London on an assignment. Two months in a place and you see things differently. It hopefully means you get closer at least to the views of the people in that country, which is something I definitely try to achieve. It might not be any more accurate but it definitely means a different view is aired of a particular event or situation.*

In Kashmir, the story began when a group of European tourists were captured by insurgents and held as hostages. Some members of the group were eventually released, but four continued to be held and were eventually killed. Close relations of the dead hostages went out to Kashmir to try to find out what had happened, why the hostages had been murdered and who killed them. Langan decided to go with them. The relatives found that no-one wanted to talk about the killings. In heartbreaking scenes in the first part of the film, they are seen showing photographs of their family members and asking local people, 'Have you seen these people?' Nobody had seen anything or, to be precise, nobody was admitting it. Eventually the families left, but Langan decided to stay on. The film follows his journey as he goes to look for the people who murdered the tourists.

The search is a long and painful one, both for the film-maker and his audience. Kashmir is a stunningly beautiful country, once part of the old hippie trail, when young people came to 'find themselves' in the awesome beauty of the mountains. Now it is a country torn by strife and violence, where warring factions in the fight of the Muslim people for independence from India commit, on both sides, army and rebels, some of the most savage acts of brutality known to modern man. Langan is taken by the people who are helping him look for the rebels to see some shocking scenes. He meets people who have been tortured and visits a place where a mass murder has taken place and the surviving people are traumatized. In this village, 23 people have been brutally killed, including a little boy. Langan points out the pathetic sight of washing, still on the line, with the child's trousers hanging there, drying in the breeze. He films the evidence of the murders inside the now deserted houses with forensic accuracy, using a style reminiscent of a police video.

He talks to the witnesses and survivors. A man asks him, 'What do you want here? What are you looking for?' and he replies, 'The truth, I suppose.' The man looks at the camera, 'You will not get it.' Reluctantly, Langan says to him, 'I agree.' In a piece to camera, Langan asks himself why is he filming these things, what is his role in all of this. In a sense he feels that he is part of the process. Maybe these horrors are created solely for the press to turn up and film, giving publicity to the cause of the perpetrators. And there he is, with his camera. This kind of introspective self-questioning is one of the features of Langan's work and is rare in television journalism. But this is not journalism. It is documentary.

In the course of his research, he gets a lead to one of the surviving killers, the man who was probably the head of the group of kidnappers, a rebel leader whose code name is Ibrahim. A go-between promises to arrange a meeting, and much of the tension in the third part of the film surrounds the proposed meeting with the hostages' murderer. Meetings are arranged and cancelled and Langan spends a lot of time in his hotel room, waiting for news and filming his thoughts in a searingly honest way, confessing his doubts and depression.

In between all the horror and the suspense, he has made friends with a local man, a tailor who learned his English from the British Army, for whom he once worked. The visits to the tailor provide some light relief. He has a picture of the royal family, the Queen and Duke looking very young, possibly at the time of independence for India. Every sentence ends with 'sir'. He is given to saying things like: 'God has made you a man, but only the tailor can make you a gentleman, sir.' Langan has a suit made for him and enjoys the fittings and showing off to the camera his elegant new clothes. He says now that he had lots of calls and letters about the tailor at the time of transmission and people still remember this handsome, dignified man, who adds some welcome warmth to a chilling story.

Eventually, the real call comes and Langan is on his way to meet Ibrahim. It is a tough journey, ending in a physically draining long mountain walk, particularly difficult for a man who smokes a lot, even on camera. The rebels are impressed that he is prepared to undertake such gruelling conditions. But he has waited five months for this meeting and although he is nervous, on his own with these people, he is optimistic that at last he will find out what happened to the hostages and why.

The disappointment is almost overwhelming when, just outside the rebels' village, the group meet some Indian soldiers who proudly tell them they killed the local insurgents' leader the night before. Langan asks, 'What was his name?' 'Ibrahim,' they tell him. As he continues to trek towards the village, Langan expresses his frustration and suspicion. Is this a coincidence or a conspiracy? He meets a group of villagers who are mourning the death of their leader. They say that 11,000 people came to the funeral. Langan had arrived at the outskirts of the village at 20 minutes to one. Ibrahim was buried at 12.30. The man had lived in those mountains for 10 years and Indian troops killed him the night before a British-based journalist came to interview him. Langan wonders if he should stay on and continue to pursue the story. He is convinced that the hostages' bodies lie somewhere in these mountains and somewhere there is one other survivor of the kidnap gang, the other 18 having all been killed. But now he is told by some of his contacts that his own life is in danger. He decides to go home. It is a powerful ending to a tragic story.

This film bears very little resemblance to the video diary form that was originally commissioned. It is stylishly edited by Mark Summers and the combination of highly crafted editing and the use of evocative eastern music to underline emotion or heighten tension moves it onto a whole different plane. This is yet another variation on the documentary form. It is not a video diary but it is also not a presenter-led television feature programme. It has all the suspense of a television movie thriller, but it is real. It also looks beautiful. Langan has a good eye for an arresting picture and there are many shots of the stunning Kashmiri landscape. These are intercut with handheld action shots and pieces to camera, usually filmed at night in a hotel room. The title sequence describes it as 'A Personal Story' and perhaps that is as good a definition as any of the successful hybrid form that is *Murder in Paradise*.

After the first project, technology had moved on and the BBC issued him with a new digital camera, then state of the art, the Sony PD100. He was also given a beech box and more sophisticated microphone in place of his earlier preferred sound recording gear on the Hi8 – camera mike and clip mike. The camera has a flip-out viewfinder so it is possible to hold it, film yourself and at the same time check that you are getting what you need in the frame. This kind of filming means that the camera is very close to the subject so there can be a certain distortion in the picture, but this does not seem to bother Langan. He still sometimes uses the more traditionalist diarist's method of placing the camera on a flat surface and filming himself in mid or wide shot, talking directly into the lens. But he has resisted advice to do what he considers to be the normal current affairs set-ups, always useful in the cutting room, of walking in and out of shot. It seems to me that he is right to do so, because the whole mood and style of his work is friendly and informal and any resort to the accepted conventions of television documentary would lose the feeling of intimacy that he manages to create.

As an experienced journalist, Langan's working methods are different from many established documentary makers. He does a lot of paper and Internet research before he makes any kind of contact. His stories are always overseas and usually in unstable countries, so the first thing he does after the initial research period is to hire, before entering the country, a fixer who is also driver and translator. When he arrives, he spends several weeks simply hanging out, absorbing atmosphere, getting the feel of the place. He is not looking for a story at this stage. He then starts filming and the film is always a journey of discovery. The story develops and the process itself is filmed. He never does recces and he never talks to people before filming them. Everything is immediate, filmed as it happens. His easygoing charm and sense of humour often gets him to places or talking to people who would never have granted an interview if approached officially.

While this all sounds a little chaotic, his journalistic training makes him keep meticulous notebooks. He has an appointments diary, notes on research background that he may need for voice-over or interviews and, every evening, he looks at his rushes and logs what he has filmed that day. He keeps lists of scenes that he needs to film and the general views (GVs) that will be needed for illustrative purposes or simply to help the film 'breathe'. So behind the easygoing façade, there is a lot of careful planning.

Langan describes his motivation, 'The starting point for me is to find a story I can really connect with. As a journalist I used to write hundreds of articles a year, bashing them out at the last minute. But the experience of making *Murder in Paradise* made me realize that, if you can find a story you can personally get involved in, the audience will also connect.' He also thinks that personal involvement makes the films more honest. 'It affects how I respond to situations and I hope my reactions and comments are therefore more honest, closer to the truth. I know it is a contentious word and maybe a bit pretentious, but seeking some kind of truth is lingering there at the back of my mind and one of the guiding principles in all my documentaries.'

The next series of *Langan Behind The Lines* covered Afghanistan, Iran, Iraq and Gaza. The programmes were made and transmitted in 2000, shortly before the attack on the World Trade Center in September 2001, so the scheduling was fortuitous. At a time when the western world was reeling from the shock of the destruction of the twin towers by Islamist suicide bombers, the BBC could at least claim that it had recognized the growing international threat and tried to understand.

Again, Bob Long was the producer. Langan spent three months looking for a story, at first thinking he should concentrate on Israel and the Middle East crisis. Then he realized the real focus he wanted was Islam, of which, at that time, most western hemisphere/Christian people knew little. He realized that the starting point had to be Afghanistan, where the Taliban were firmly in control. He applauds Bob Long for his patience in allowing this dramatic change of plan. The series took 15 months to film.

Langan Behind The Lines opens with him arriving in Afghanistan for the second time, having tried to get in and been thrown out a month and a half before. This time he has been instructed to travel straight to Kabul, so the journey starts with point-of-view shots from the car on the way. He stops for a while and soon a vehicle on the road stops and he is surrounded by men who want to know what he doing. What at first seems a threatening situation soon dissolves into laughter, with everybody wanting to see themselves on camera. The tension dissolves and the men leave, taking no action.

Later, in part two, he is stopped again and we next see him sitting on a hilltop, surrounded by Taliban, deep in conversation.

The discussion is surprisingly relaxed. After all, the Taliban had offered protection to Osama Bin Laden, soon to be the White House's Enemy Number One. The last thing one would expect is that they could be such pleasant hosts to a law-breaking westerner. One of the men tells Langan he spent the previous night with his family. When Langan says he is about to be married himself he is told he should have been married long ago. The men offer him tea and teach him how to play the Afghan egg game. The conversation is interrupted by another Taliban patrol on the road below. Eventually we get the translation. The passing troops want to know what the men with Langan are doing with a foreigner. His new friends cover up for him by claiming that they have arrested him for filming – in a country where filming and the taking of photographs is forbidden. The troops move on. He is saved, again.

Langan then has to get to Kabul as soon as possible because he has to get official permission to film – a rather optimistic ambition. Inevitably, his application is rejected once more, but then it emerges that his fixer/driver has a useful contact, a relation with influence, and he is able to get a meeting with a very important member of the Taliban to discuss his status as a journalist in Afghanistan. This meeting is crucial but also dangerous and Langan now resorts to the standby for all investigative film-makers – the hidden camera. A specially constructed bag, containing the camera, has been made for him by the BBC engineers and he places it beside him and expresses his worries about the situation while he squats on a balcony outside a door, waiting for the VIP to talk to him. But, typical of Langan, instead of conforming to journalistic norms and admitting his concern while keeping a stiff upper lip, he sees the humour in the situation. 'What am I doing?' he says, looking directly into the hidden lens, 'A grown man, talking to a bag.' Against all the odds, he is given leave to stay, although he is not – officially at least – allowed to film.

He is taken to a prison, run by the quaintly named Vice and Virtue department of government and a spirited discussion takes place. The main topic of conversaton had been the execution, by stoning, of people caught in fornication. Sometimes women adulterers are stoned to death in the local football stadium. Will there be an execution this week? Until the last moment, nobody knows. Langan makes his way to the football stadium, sets up his hidden camera and waits. Eventually it becames clear that, this week, no woman will be executed. A football match will take place instead. Langan gets out of the stadium as quickly as possible and in an old airfield, beside the wreckage of Russian planes, he discusses with the camera his feelings about this experience. As a journalist, he has to think about the story and a public execution is a good story. As a human being, his attitudes are very different.

He continues his intrepid tour of Afghanistan and encounters, memorably, a school run by women for girls, the women taking great personal risks, not only in their work but also in allowing themselves to be filmed and interviewed. This is a country which has reintroduced the rule that women must wear the burka at all times and have no need of a sophisticated education. The interviewees' faces are pixellated to protect their identities and somehow this editing decision makes the whole scene more powerful and moving.

In the last sequence of the two-parter we see Langan talking to a group of traditionally dressed men, who look just like the Taliban fighters we have seen earlier. But these men are not militia, they are farmers. To be precise, poppy growers. They are the people who supply the raw material for 80 per cent of the world's heroin. With breathtaking logic, they explain to Langan that they would be more than happy to give up the poppy growing in exchange for outside investment in schools, hospitals and jobs. If the western world wants to stop the supply to the heroin growers, all they have to do is give economic subsidies to the farmers of Afghanistan. At the moment there is no other way for farmers to make a living, so right now they have no choice but to supply the world drug market. They say that the Americans were happy to help them defeat the Russians, but they do not want to help them now. The implication is clear – responsibility lies with the west. The discussion is terminated when the senior man announces that it is time to pray. No more questions. The opium growers are off to say their prayers.

The final programme in the series is called 'Life's a Beach', a typically ironic reference to the famous American satirist's quote, 'Life's a bitch, then you die.' The film is about life in Gaza. Langan visits Palestinian homes, cavorts on the beach with young militants, watches children being given military training and attends a press conference given by Sheik Yasid, the spiritual leader of the insurgent group Hamas. He asks for a private interview and the Sheik invites him to come to his house. The Hamas leader is a paraplegic, yet is considered to be one of the most dangerous men in the world. During his discussion, Langan asks him, 'Is this a holy war or a war of liberation?' The Sheik says, 'Call it what you like.' This is not an easy interview. In response to Langan's suggestion that bombing women and children in coffee malls is contrary to Jihad and not true to Islam, the Sheik says that what he is saying is incorrect. Islam allows you to treat the enemy as they treat you. They have driven our people from their land. We are not the aggressors, he says. Afterwards Langan castigates himself for not being tougher in his questioning. Most journalists would think that accusing the leader of Hamas of being unIslamic was quite tough enough as questions go, but Langan is a perfectionist.

In 2004, the Sheik was targeted and killed by an Israeli missile. Other people died with him, including a child. In a widely discussed, extremely controversial statement, the Israeli government argued that they had evidence that he was responsible for the Palestinian militants' suicide bombing campaign and for that reason they were justified in executing him.

Later, two more programmes for this BBC series were made in Zimbabwe, just before the election which brought President Robert Mugabe back to power. Once again, Langan was banned by the Ministry of Information because he was working for the BBC, which had been blacklisted by the Zanu-PF government. In programme one he enters the country and tries to get the decision reversed. Not surprisingly he fails and on his way to the airport decides to drop by the headquarters of the *Daily News*, the one newspaper which stands up to the government. He talks to one of the journalists, a very brave man with the integrity to tell it like it is. Langan decides not to give up.

He leaves, officially, then comes back in as a tourist over the Zambian border at Victoria Falls, one of the wonders of the world. He has to tear himself away from this idyllically beautiful place and makes his way to Bulawayo, the capital of Matebeleland, an area historically unfriendly to the governing party. While he is there he reads the local paper and is shocked to find that he is a wanted man, the government knows where he is.

He decides to find out what is happening anyway and travels to Harare, seeing squatters occupying white farms on the way. He explains that land distribution is a fair idea, too few whites own too much land, but the intimidation and violence is growing. He goes to a memorial service for an enemy of the government who has disappeared and says that one in four people in Bulawayo are said to have gone missing. He meets farmers and politicians, goes to a football match, is stopped by a member of Zanu-PF and asked what he is doing. In a Harare nightclub, a black comedian entertains a largely white audience with sombre humour about the increasingly deteriorating political situation. In a suburb, a by-election is taking place but the voters are afraid of the violence that might occur. Everywhere, Langan hears the same story and everyone tells him that it will be worse when the presidential election takes place. The programmes add up to a sad indictment of a troubled land.

When I asked Sean Langan about his own political philosophy he said, 'My generation rejected the militancy of the 1970s. I was at university in the Thatcher era and I suppose I was a bit of a yuppie. But I was very concerned about the environment and was anti-globalization. I call myself a Radical Moralist. Apart from that, I am not interested in making political tracts. I go into a story with an open mind, no political agenda.' It was in this spirit that he approached his next series, this time made for Channel 4, *Travels With A Gringo*.

Once again, he started with a concept. He wanted to make a series about globalization. South America seemed the right place

Sean Langan filming in South America

to examine this phenomenon. He had been reading Che Guevara's Motorbike Diaries and saw an interesting way of linking his own contemporary journey with Che's travels in the past. He would follow the itinerary taken by Che, like him recording his analysis of the state of the continent. But, being a 1980s sceptic, he was not starting out with a clear political agenda. This becomes obvious in the series, especially at the moment when a striker in Bolivia asks him if Che is his hero. Langan replies that Che did his journey twice, once as a medical student on a voyage of discovery, the second time as a politically committed revolutionary. He explains that he empathizes with the ambition of Che's first journey and that is his aim also. He is on a voyage of discovery. The man is deeply disappointed.

Discussions with Channel 4 in the setting up of the series were not always easy and Langan had to work with an independent production company, very different from the BBC. This time he would not be allowed the freedom and unlimited time that he had valued when working with Bob Long. He also had to deal with editorial input from Channel 4 executives. After buying the project, a senior executive (now no longer at the channel) told him he should not emphasize the Che Guevara story because, he said, 'Nobody is interested in a 1960s South American revolutionary.' Given the fact that Che is, without doubt, one of the great fashion icons of the western world and in many places still a major political influence, one has to wonder just how out of touch some of these executives are. Langan was told – and as the comedians say, you couldn't make it up – that he must not mention Che until he was 15 minutes into his first programme.

Bizarrely enough, at the same time as one executive was declaring Che to be of no interest, another, in the Film Division of the channel, was commissioning the brilliant Walter Salles film, *The Motor Cycle Diaries*, soon to be a worldwide, award-winning success. This is a story I often tell to students and it always gets a laugh. Especially in Cuba.

Langan's series starts in 2002 in Argentina, Che's birthplace. The country has just defaulted on its debt to the World Bank. Local banks are refusing to release money to account holders. The middle class are in revolt and the police are clearly sympathetic to the regular protests in the streets. Lots of young, well-dressed women are out there. 'Best looking demo I've ever seen,' says Langan. World Bank representatives are in Buenos Aires, holding secret meetings, and Langan tries to 'doorstep' them in the hope of getting an informal interview. He asks a local journalist how many times she has spoken to the delegates. She looks puzzled. 'Never,' she says. 'They never talk to us local people.' He gets to film a group of the delegates and asks a World Bank spokesperson which countries really make the decisions, who has the power. After a certain amount of obfuscation, he gets his answer. She says, as if it is obvious, 'The rich countries.' The Bank's verdict on the future of Argentina's economy will be announced shortly. From Washington DC, as usual.

The World Bank leaves town and Langan goes up north to Cordoba, where Che started his journey by motorbike. Langan experiments with a motorbike but decides that filming and riding at the same time would not necessarily be a good idea. He settles for conventional transport, with the support and companionship of an Argentinian journalist. They visit Bolivia, where the miners are on strike and eventually win their demands, primarily that the pits should be renationalized. This has been made easier because the Anglo-US company that owned the mine has been declared bankrupt. Nevertheless, it is a historic victory and Che's image is everywhere. 'In Latin America, Che is a living icon, not just a cultural icon like he is in Europe' says Langan. In Bolivia people tell him they blame Yanqui imperialism for their economic problems. Langan says, 'Yanqui imperialism and globalization are the same thing. Either way you are stuffed.'

He meets the leader of the coca farmers, Eno Morales, who is running for President. He is a native Bolivian who is fighting for the right of his fellow farmers to earn their living as they have for many years, growing coca leaves, without interference from the USA and their local allies. Coca is the base for cocaine. The scene is reminiscent of the encounter with the poppy farmers in Afghanistan. Morales introduces Langan to President Chavez of Venezuela, who is himself about to be almost ousted in an orchestrated coup attempt. Chavez invites him to come to see him in Venezuela, which he does. There, he attends another big rally, with the President. Langan concludes, after his experiences so far, that anti-globalization is the mainstream view in Latin America. After eight years of teaching documentary students from all over the region, I absolutely concur with his conclusion.

The last programme in the series takes him to Honduras and Guatemala, and pressures of time were being emphasized by the production company back home. He spent two weeks in each country and produced a perfectly respectable film, again concentrating on the exploitation of the local workforce, including children, by First World companies. Langan's regret was that this programme feels like conventional documentary because he did not have time to find the characters and the stories that would give it the personal vision which he values so much. The programme ends in Mexico, with young people risking their lives to cross the border illegally, by sea, so that they can earn a decent living in the United States. One is a 16-year-old girl, who is reaching the end of her pregnancy and wants her baby to be born in the USA.

His latest film, *Langan in Iraq*, is interesting not only for its content, but also because it was a hard film to get commissioned. His experience in getting this film on air – and now, finally, in the cinema in the USA – is something of an object lesson for all documentarists who want to make their films without interference from the strait-jacket of television bureaucracies but still want them to be widely screened. As Langan relates, George Bush declared 'mission accomplished' in May 2003, after the invasion of Iraq by coalition forces. Around August of that year, Langan started to get calls from friends in the Middle East and from Arab exiles in the UK telling him that there was a real and growing insurgency spreading across Iraq.

He took the story to the usual group of commissioning editors. Everyone turned it down. He says, 'One quote I can remember – "Baghdad, been there, done that." Another, "The war is over."' Langan reflects:

> *After 15 years in journalism, looking back now, I really have lost faith in the media. The story – whether it was weapons of mass destruction or the level of insurgency in late 2003 – the media got it wrong. Again and again. The* New York Times *later issued an apology, which the British media have never done.*

He finally got to make the film in 2004, having pitched the idea to a frankly unlikely commissioner, the style magazine *GQ*. They liked it. And so, 'With £4000, some expenses and minimal insurance,' he says, 'I went to Baghdad. I was without a television commission and that was a great feeling. Rather than being worried, it was completely liberating, it took off all the pressure. Although I did have to push myself. I knew it would have to be something strong, I would have to get what nobody else was getting.' There were very few journalists there at the time and Langan says he wondered, at times, if he had got it wrong. Maybe all those executives who had turned down the story were right after all. But still, deep down, he knew he was onto a major story.

He was filming in an American military hospital one day and helicopters were landing every 20 minutes. 'It was so noisy, like the roof was coming off. I was brought up in the seventies and this scene was, literally, like a Vietnam War movie.' Then, he says, he would read the papers or watch television and the stories were all about reconstruction in Iraq. 'There was a big gap between what you were watching on the news and what was happening on the ground. It felt like full-scale guerrilla war to me.'

Langan filmed with the Americans, who gave him excellent access, but he also filmed the Iraqi opposition, including members of the resistance. He was the first journalist to get access to the insurgents and took huge risks to do so. He says he spent a lot of time sitting in the back of cars waiting for contacts to arrive. Often he was let down, but he also got some amazing material. He points out that, because he was on to the story much earlier than most, the resistance had not yet introduced their policy of kidnapping and beheading foreign journalists. He says the rebels were often more scared than he was because there was always a chance that behind him would come a Bradley tank full of Americans.

He spent three months filming and this gave him a certain amount of security. In one memorable scene in the film, he goes to a small town and is filming when he is set upon by a very angry mob. He says, 'Being attacked by a mob is, by definition, one of the most dangerous things that can happen.' He believes that he would not have got out alive if it had not been for the people he had met on previous occasions, who spoke up for him and calmed down their companions. At the time he was only aware of the danger and the need to keep his head. He kept on filming. Looking at the rushes later, he could spot faces in the crowd that he knew. These people saved his life. In the film we see him being led to safety by some very brave local people, who are 'talking down' their angry neighbours. They take him into a building and close the security gates. An hour later, he was taken to a restaurant in the same town and when he tried to pay for the meal, he was told, 'No, you are our guest.' He said to himself, 'Hang on a minute, just an hour ago, some of these people were trying to kill me.'

One thing that added to the stress during his filming trip was the fact that he felt a conflict inside himself, making him question his own identity. He has filmed in many dangerous situations, but never felt bad about 'sneaking behind the backs of the Taliban to get an interview'. But sneaking behind the backs of the Americans made him feel uncomfortable. 'I would be at an American base, chatting easily to people I got on well with, speaking the same language, knowing that the next day I would be meeting with people who wanted to kill them.' He says he made it clear to the insurgents that he did not want to know any details about their operations in advance. That way he could maintain an objectivity about the conflict and not take sides.

In another extraordinary scene he is out on patrol with American tanks. He is walking alongside the Americans, chatting to them. One of the tank commanders says, in laconic, even ironic, style, 'We would never bomb a country that has a McDonald's.' Langan asks, 'What about Burger King?' Just as everyone is relaxing, the bombardment starts. The convoy is being attacked and Langan is racing, hiding behind the tanks, to protect himself. He is still talking to the camera. He keeps up a constant dialogue as he runs. Later, when I interviewed him, he explained that he had left his flak jacket in the car. But he remembered the camera. There speaks a true, if slightly gung-ho, documentarist.

This film also revealed the first evidence about the abuse of prisoners in Abu Ghraib. Langan says you just had to drive by to be told what was happening. Heartbreaking scenes of friends and relatives outside the jail told stories of what was happening inside. Yet it took the world's media some time to catch up. When he returned

209

to the UK, Langan finally got the attention of the TV mandarins. Although, with almost comical misunderstanding of the reality, on the ground, one of them told him they had 'enough people doing dangerous things in dangerous places'. Personally, I would have been tempted to reply, 'As Evelyn Waugh nearly put it – "Well, up to a point, Lord Executive Producer."' Fortunately, reality kicked in and the film was recognized as being a serious piece of journalism, and an important contribution to the evidence which would later be examined in the aftermath of the war, one of the first serious reports from a massively important international conflict that will surely have huge implications for the future of the entire world.

At the time of writing, Langan is on his way to Afghanistan to make a film for the BBC. He was a little reluctant at first because he wasn't sure that there is enough of a story there at the moment. Afghanistan would not be my idea of a safe and rather dull location. I am sure there are great stories there and that Langan is the man to find them.

FILMOGRAPHY

Nightmare in Paradise
1998, 3 × 40 min series, BBC2

A video diary special following Langan's attempts to find four western tourists kidnapped in Kashmir.

Langan Behind The Lines
2001, 5 × 40 min series, BBC2

Travelled from Kabul to Gaza for series about the Middle East. Included the first ever in-depth documentaries on the Taliban regime in Afghanistan in episodes one and two, 'Tea with the Taliban' and 'Kabul Vice'.

BAFTA nominated

Langan in Zimbabwe
2002, 60 min, BBC4

Undercover film on Mugabe's policy of violence and intimidation against black opposition in Zimbabwe.

Travels With A Gringo: Langan in Latin America
2003, 3 × 60 min series, Channel 4

Followed Che Guevara's travels through Latin America. Langan travelled from Argentina to Mexico, to witness the impact of globalization on the region.

Mission Accomplished: Langan in Iraq
2004, 90 min film, BBC4/BBC2

Showed how US policy in Iraq helped turn an underground insurgency into a popular uprising (*Sunday Times*: 'A brilliant, brave and humane piece of journalism.' *Evening Standard*: 'The film that changed my mind about the war.') Theatrical release in America, March 2005.

10 Clive Gordon
The Berlin aesthetic

Clive Gordon

Clive Gordon has an unusual background for a documentarist. He started his working life as an academic. In his thirties he went to work as a researcher for Yorkshire Television on *First Tuesday*, its monthly documentary slot for the ITV network. Clive made his first film as a director in 1992. He moved to Berlin in that same period and has been there ever since. In my view the cultural, historical and creative drive of that city informs every film he has made since.

The style and form of his films have evolved over the years but they have had certain features in common, even from the beginning. He hardly ever uses interviews, simply observes people and events. What makes his films different from other film-makers who follow the same rule is that they are not 'observational' in the sense of American style 'direct cinema'. Clive describes his style as being, he hopes, 'cinematic'. The films are beautifully shot and the pace of the editing varies according to the mood he is trying to create. Sometimes leisurely, even slow, sometimes very fast, lots of ideas, challenging the audience. There is no doubt in my mind that if Clive Gordon had been commissioned in the USA, France or Germany, he would have been making his documentaries for the cinema. As it is, he really is making cinema films, except they are mostly shown on television. They are often dense, not easy to read and at times, for some, 'too difficult'. But multi-award-winning prizewinners all the same.

Why 'difficult'? Because the viewer has to do some work, think, 'make up your own mind'. Television documentary is often led by explicatory commentary and in a Clive Gordon film there is usually none. Absolutely vital information is carried in text on the screen. Always short sentences, couched in simple language. Carefully paced, easy to read. But the audience is always being challenged. Music is very important in all the films and often indicates the mood that the film-maker wants to convey. Sometimes it works as counterpoint, like the best written commentaries can also do. A distinctive feature of all the films is the sense of humour, usually ironic, often angry, which is a characteristic of the work of Clive Gordon. The films are always political, always controversial and often set in dangerous situations.

Any young film-maker who wants to study the art of opening a documentary, getting the first few vital minutes right, should look at the films of Clive Gordon. In this chapter I have concentrated to some extent on the first moments of some of Clive's most feted films.

Probably my favourite Clive Gordon film – certainly the most amusing – is *Moscow Central*, a film which follows a strange group of candidates running in Moscow's first truly democratic general election in 1993. It is that rare treasure – a genuinely funny documentary. The humour comes mainly out of the situations in which the people find themselves, but it is helped along by the film-maker's approach, both ironic and, at times, anarchic.

The first shot in the film shows a man sitting on a swing with a spinning globe suspended from the ceiling and hanging immediately above his head. He speaks to camera. 'If I were president, the first thing I would do is say, "People, at last you can do anything you want. The only thing you mustn't do is harm nature or animals or your neighbours. Don't harm anyone . . .".' It seems highly unlikely that this man would ever be president. After the title sequence, which quickly summarizes with archive footage the bloody fall of the old Russian regime and the new liberalization, we see him again. It emerges that he is indeed a candidate in the election, running as the prospective representative in the Duma for Moscow Central. He is seen canvassing in the street, handing out his manifesto. A DV camera on a tripod stands beside him, unmanned. He is filming himself for his evening programme on Liberty TV, a cable station with one staff member, where Vostrikov (for it is he) is the managing director, engineer, DJ and interviewer.

One after the other, all the candidates are introduced, in an increasingly bizarre scenario. There is Krashnov, named by some as having serious mafia links. He shows us round his underground currency headquarters with its high security, bodyguards and heavyweights, now his temporary election HQ. Then there is Tarasov, the first Russian to make a million in the Gorbachev era. He had been forced into exile in 1991 and was only able to return now because he had registered as a candidate in the election and under the rules could not be arrested as long as he is running for office. And the candidate who was the favourite, Alexander Mishkin. Brave, handsome, a popular journalist with obvious integrity, he is the only character in the film who is not funny, so he will probably win.

In a sequence which obviously amused the production team as much as it still does the audience, we meet a young man in a fur hat and tinted glasses. He is on a metro train when familiar rock and roll chords start up on the film's soundtrack. Soon the Rolling Stones are belting out 'Sympathy for the Devil', which has resonance for anyone with a knowledge of documentary history or, for that matter, rock music. It is the song which Mick Jagger claimed, in the Maysles' famous 1970s documentary *Gimme Shelter*, always seemed to lead to some kind of terrible luck. (In the Maysles' film, a man is murdered, on camera, by Hell's Angels during Jagger's performance of the song.) This man in the Moscow subway looks tense, nervous. He is followed by the handheld camera as he leaves the train, rides up the escalator, into the street, lighting a cigarette, walking quickly. The Stones words keep coming. 'I was in St Petersburg . . . killed the Czar and his family . . . Then the Blitzkreig came . . . Pleased to meet you, hope you guessed my name.' The man walks past a crowd into an auditorium, goes up onto the stage and finally the commentary introduces the sinister-looking guy. He is Alexander Frolov, rising star of the Party, the Communist candidate. The camera lingers on a vicious-looking old man in the audience and pans down to his lapel badge, a picture of Josef Stalin.

The film follows the candidates as they conduct their varied campaigns. One hilarious scene shows Vostrikov of Radio Liberty conducting a phone-in programme with Tarasov. (Vostrikov has previously been to a clinic to get a paper certifying his sanity. He told them he was applying to be a private detective.) They start to argue about the need for strong leadership, as in China. Vostrikov is against this idea and gets very angry. Tarasov storms out. '*La commedia est finita* – as they say in France,' says Vostrikov.

As election day approaches, the situation becomes more bizarre. Although the Communists are tipped to do well, they are suspicious. The film shows a group of heavy guys walking towards the camera, talking about the likely result. Konstantinovich says, 'I expect the results to be falsified. And so my comrades will be monitoring the election because we have great experience at falsifying elections.' 'How?' asks a voice off camera. 'There are lots of ways, we don't need to go into that now,' says a man walking beside the candidate, obviously anxious to shut him up. 'We know how to do it and we will be watching.'

The next sequence in the film is even more bizarre. The police have found a way round the immunity of political candidates and have come with a warrant to arrest Tarasov.

'Are you refusing to be arrested?'
'No, I'm not refusing.'
'OK, shall we say 11 a.m. tomorrow.'
'That's not convenient, I have many meetings. I could do the 12th
    [election day]. I have nothing on then.'
'Very good, then, the 12th at 11 a.m.'

Polite handshakes all round. Tarasov goes into his press conference, where a big crowd of journalists wait for him. He tells them
how pleased he is to be back in Russia.

On polling day the police wait for Tarasov but he does not come.
They say they cannot find him, which is strange because the film
crew do find him and film him buying toys for his two-year-old son
before sneaking off, into hiding again. When the results are
announced, Frolov, the Communist, has managed to get a seat,
but only as a party list candidate. Over shots of the city at night, a
caption tells us the election result.

'The winner, by a few hundred votes, was the millionaire from
    London, Artiom Tarasov.'
'In hiding at his Mayfair headquarters, he became the new MP for
    Moscow Central.'

Another of Clive's films, *Men in Pink* made in Rwanda in 1999,
could, in theory, not be more different from *Moscow Central*. It
deals with investigations into the genocide in Rwanda, after the
war was over. Of course, there was a lot of current affairs television coverage of this tragic situation at the time. But, as usual, the
Clive Gordon film had a very different approach – more intelligent,
more complex and altogether more stylish.

It has a brilliantly crafted opening sequence, which is worth looking at in detail. Like many of his films, it opens with a head and
shoulders shot of a man looking directly at the camera. He says,
'My name is Basesayose. I am 41 years old. I am accused of
genocide.' Three other men follow, uniformly dressed in pink.
One by one they introduce themselves. All are accused of genocide. Now we see a group of men behind bars, staring out at the
camera. Music begins to play, guitar music from Mali. Men in

prison uniform walk past the camera. The title comes up: MEN IN PINK.

A caption follows, white text on black screen, another regular feature in a Clive Gordon film. It says:

> 'In 1994 nearly one million people were killed in Rwanda because of their ethnic background.'

Prisoners now walk past the camera, over a wet road. The picture fades to black for another caption:

> 'For generations Tutsis formed a privileged minority in Rwanda. The colonialists turned them into a governing elite.'

That word, 'colonialists', gives a clear signal to the audience of how they should read the attitude of the film.

It is followed by a quick montage which consolidates the feeling that this will be an angry film, peppered by irony – a mood that had already been signalled by the title. The movie *Men in Black* had recently been on the circuits in Europe and the posters were everywhere.

The montage begins with people in a theatre, preparing for a production. It cuts to the four prisoners, in a car, being driven somewhere. Then we see a queue of people going into a building, presumably the audience for the production; travelling road shots follow, on the side of the road are men with machetes; the men in pink get out of the car and walk into an unidentified building; close-up of people handing in theatre tickets; another man with a machete on the road; fade to black, the music ends.

Extracts from the theatrical performance will be used for punctuation and emphasis throughout the film. It is a savage comedy, played in a slapstick way, and the audience laugh uproariously at the antics of the actors. The subject – the history of the genocide. The film follows two trials. The case of the men in pink is heard in a Rwandan court. The other case is that of Clement Kayishema. He is being tried by the United Nations International Tribunal in Arusha, Tanzania.

Clive Gordon makes clear his attitude to the UN before the film reaches the second trial. In a particularly gruesome sequence, we see men murdering prisoners on the road, striking at them wildly with machetes. He cuts to two troops from the UN force. A caption follows:

'The United Nations response to the genocide.'
'They left.'

Clement Kayishema is first seen surrounded by officers of the court and guards, being brought into a courtroom. A caption reveals that this is the UN International Criminal Tribunal for Rwanda. The film cuts back and forth between the Arusha court and its National Park. A white man is taking pictures of the giraffes. Eventually his identity is revealed. He is James Stewart, the UN's chief prosecutor for the Criminal Tribunal. The giraffes become a symbol for the black comedy that often bursts forth in this angry film.

At the end of the film, all the people on trial are convicted. A quick montage sequence includes the white lawyers from the UN talking to their clients who have just been found guilty. 'We are just going to eat now,' one says. 'Keep your spirits up.' As he walks away, the prisoners shake their heads in disbelief. Clive says that he wanted to put a caption just before the end credits. It would have read:

'Kayishema and Ruzindana were convicted of genocide.
On a technicality they were found not guilty of crimes against humanity.
But never mind, there's lobster thermidor for dinner.'

Peter Dale, the Channel 4 commissioning editor, vetoed the last line, rightly in my view. He was not very keen on the giraffes either. But Clive won that battle.

The music used at the beginning of the film is not indigenous to Rwanda. It is Malian and it belongs to the genre now called 'world music'; in other words, it is original African music that has been adapted for western consumption. I discussed this choice of music with some students at a workshop in Ghana. Students had come from all over sub-Saharan Africa and I was interested in their views. I was surprised that they were not offended by the use of music from another country. They pointed out that the director was British and the film was strongly authored, very much a personal point of view. So he could use any kind of music that helped him express his personal feelings. The important thing for them was the artistic integrity of the film, not the literal accuracy or otherwise of the choice of music.

Filmed in northern Uganda in 1997, *The Mission* tells the story of the children who were kidnapped by rebel leader Joseph Kony and forced to fight in his army or, in the case of the girls, work as prostitutes for the soldiers. When the members of his group, the Lord's Resistance Army, kidnap Catholic children from a school run by Sister Raquele, she decides to go and rescue them.

It is always interesting to look at the context in which films are shown. Channel 4, which has funded all of Clive's major work to date, is a commercial channel and it is surely not possible to ignore the effect on the audience for a disturbing political film that is preceded and interrupted at least three times by advertising. I have looked again at *The Mission*, a film I saw on its first transmission in the UK, to question what effect – subliminal or otherwise – the advertising which punctuates this extraordinary film might have on an audience.

'Before the advertised programme' – as the television continuity announcers often say – what was shown on Channel 4 before the first ever transmission of *The Mission*?

First, an advert for L'Oréal cosmetics (still running today). Lovely actresses tell you they that they need pampering with these rejuvenating products – the catchphrase: 'L'Oréal – because I'm worth it.'

Then comes a pitch for Time computers. Why pay more? Don't pay a penny until . . . .

Now, the product called Organics, which apparently can be good for your hair because it has advanced protection agents, even with curling tongs and hairdryers. 'Where there is heat, there is beautiful hair.'

Then, 'We are always looking for ways of improving your wrinkles.' French, male accent. 'Reducing fine lines in four weeks. Roc, we keep our promises.'

219

And finally, a trailer for a C4 programme. White print on black. 'Little did she know when she made this speech.'

Then the face of Princess Diana, picture reduced, filling half the frame. Surrounded by black. She says: 'My interest is humanitarian, that is why I felt drawn to this human tragedy, that is why I wanted to play my part in working towards a worldwide ban on these weapons.'

But over the picture of the dead princess the titles, still white on black, say: 'What little difference it would make.'

More compressed frames in black pictures, the famous footage of the princess walking through a landmine site in Angola. The captions and voice-over say: 'Diana, The Wrong Crusade? Wednesday at 9. On Four.'

This is the mood created by the advertising department at Channel 4 for the first public showing of the sad and moving film *The Mission*. Channel 4 have not always been so lacking in sensitivity. Jeremy Isaacs, the founding controller at 4, defended the fact that it was part funded by advertising. He had been head of programmes at Thames Television, where I had worked for him and admired his integrity and vision. He said about ads at C4. 'They cheer up the screen and give us a break.' Many times this is true. (Indeed, I could not complain about ads between my own programmes transmitted by 4.) Jeremy Isaacs had left the channel when this programme was transmitted, so was not himself responsible for what seems to me to be crass insensitivity. What was it saying about *The Mission*? To me it said, 'Here comes another woman, not quite so beautiful as the goddesses we have just been watching, but every bit as idealistic and doomed to failure as the last one, Diana.'

Immediately after the trailer came a continuity announcement – a woman's voice over the opening of the generic title of the series *True Stories*. She says, 'Now on 4 the true story of one woman's mission to rescue children from a life of fear and brutality.' Television schedulers have a tendency to treat the audience as slightly dumb, but this was a completely redundant announcement. The pre-title sequence of the film explains the background to the story very clearly. A uniformed officer from the Ugandan army talks to camera and tells how a rebel army makes raids into northern Uganda, attacks small villages and kidnaps the children. The lieutenant's vivid account is punctuated with simple text, white on black, giving more details.

> 'For ten years a rebel army of kidnapped children has been on the rampage in Northern Uganda.'
> 'They are led by a mystic, Joseph Kony.'
> 'The children believe that Kony has supernatural powers. He orders them to kill or be killed.'

The soldier describes how the children are made to pray and sing. Then Kony goes into a trance, wide open eyes, sweating, shaking. Then he gives them their orders. 'The Holy Spirit has said the following.' The children believe him.

The soldier's account is followed by a music sequence. It is stunningly well shot, on film, like all the work Clive did with the brilliant cameraman, Jacek Patricki. The scene is dark, and men and boys are dancing and singing. There is something ritualistic in the mood and the rhythms and movements of the dancers. Just for a moment we see that one of them has a machine-gun slung over his shoulder. In the next shot another man with a gun is standing with his back to the camera, watching the others. The scene lasts for about a minute, a long time right at the beginning of a film, but it creates the mood that permeates the film and takes us into the title: THE MISSION.

After the title we see soldiers again; this time they are clearly identified as the Ugandan army. They have captured some rebels and are about to take them to a therapy centre, World Vision, where they will be de-programmed before being sent back to their villages. Part one of the film cuts back and forth between scenes of the army pounding down the road, singing in the distinctive harmonies of sub-Saharan Africa; therapists at the centre, welcoming and working with the captured rebels; and an editorial meeting at a newspaper, where the decision is made to try and find the rebel leader, Kony. (It seems that nobody knows much about him – except that, like many wicked people before him, he was an altar boy as a child.) Just before the adverts, photographs of the rebel leader, first seen in the newspaper office sequence, are reprised, this time with crash zooms, cut to music. Indeed, music runs through the whole segment, working as counterpoint or underlying emphasis. The photography is breathtakingly beautiful at times and the editing intelligently and sensitively judged. But no major characters have emerged. Part one is context, background, even mood. But where is this woman who was featured in the continuity announcement? A brave decision, some might say, to make no reference to your main character for the first 20 minutes of a film made for television. But very Clive Gordon.

Part 2 begins with travelling shots underlined by more local music, intercut with a meeting at which a district commissioner describes to a visitor the mayhem that has been caused by the rebels. Over a thousand killed, many injuries, robberies, destruction of property. This device acts as a way of providing vital information without the usual devices of commentary or too much text on screen. The contrast between the matter-of-fact statistics, the vibrant, life-enhancing music and the shots from the road showing damaged houses gives an air of unreality, even surreality, to the whole sequence which is particularly effective. The music fades as an abrupt cut takes us into a scene which is quite unexpected. A nun, a white woman, is closely questioning a local man who appears to be an employee. Neither are identified. They are standing beside a security gate and he is explaining that he heard it slam. 'Why did you not call me?' she asks him. He had been expecting the local defence force and thought it must be them. 'Did you ask them?' Yes. 'What did you ask them?' I said are you the men from the LDU. No answer. 'Were there many of them?' Very many. Throughout this exchange we do not know where we are or who the people talking are. The look of concern on the woman's face and the intensity of her questioning simply implies that something terrible has happened. The film cuts to a wide shot of a long room full of young people, then to a close-up of two young people looking very distressed. A caption on the wide says 'St Mary's Convent School, Adobe'. Both shots have natural sound, a low hum, nobody talking. A man then asks for a list of the names of the people who have gone out this morning. He will call a general assembly to check. Now, at last, we find out what is going on.

Unusual in a Clive Gordon film, the important information is given in a conventional interview. The nun begins the story.

'These rebels divided into two groups. One group went straight to the dormitory. Another group passed in front of our house and we were still in bed.' She points to a worker. 'One of them came to my window, knocked and said, Sister, the rebels are here.' Two children describe how the rebels came and took them away. They were not allowed to wear their white clothes and were marched off, naked. They walked all night and were beaten if they delayed. 'Then in the morning we heard that Sister is coming. She is following us.'

The film intercuts scenes of the therapy centre with the continuing story of the abduction of the children. Others contribute to the story but the central character, Sister Raquele, is the main witness and she is a brilliant storyteller. She tells how she and her helpers finally arrive at the rebel camp, how 40 soldiers in a row point their guns at them and shout 'Hands up', how she calls the leader of the group by his first name and begs him to give back the girls. He agrees to give her 109 but will keep 30 more. She describes, word for word, the pleas of the girls who have to remain with the rebels. 'I can still see their faces,' she says, tears in her eyes.

The film continues to follow this extraordinarily courageous woman as she tries everything she can to get back the girls, who, we learn, have been 'given' to rebel leaders and are being used for sex. We see her meeting with military intelligence, who tell her that the girls are in Sudan, a foreign country. When she says she will go there to try to negotiate, the exasperated soldier tells her that the only option is a military one.

Finally, in part four, we arrive at the camp of the Lord's Resistance Army. Sister Raquele is not there but a negotiator from the Ugandan government has been meeting with Joseph Kony. He and his lieutenants, including Mariano, who kidnapped the girls from the convent, are shot on a long lens – understandably – and this, together with the shimmering heat, gives the pictures of these heavily armed assassins a nightmarish quality. Kony makes a speech, surrounded by bodyguards. He says he is the son of God. He says he is not afraid to die.

The film cuts between scenes in the LRA camp and Sister Raquele in a travelling shot. It seems likely that she is on her way to see Kony, despite the advice of a number of concerned army officers. At the rebel camp, Kony is still speaking and the film cuts, surprisingly, to a computer screen. A man's voice is explaining how the Internet works. The screen now shows the manifesto of the Lord's Resistance Army. Sister Raquele is there, staring in wonder at the screen. 'You mean this can be read all over the world?' She begins to dictate a letter, 'To Mr Joseph Kony.' She is asking him to return the girls. As she reads out the names, the film cuts back and forth between Kony speaking and the nun dictating, tears running down her face. The words continue over the shot of an African sunset, which also features in the title sequence, and the end credits begin to roll.

Probably Clive's most admired and 'awarded' film is *The Betrayed*. The film follows the attempts of desperate Russian mothers who have come to Chechnya to try to find out what has happened to their sons, conscripts in the Russian Army, who have disappeared.

The film opens in the now familiar Gordon style:

> 'On New Years Day, 1994, 3500 conscripts of the Mayakovsky brigade were sent in to attack Grozny.
> They were wiped out.
> For four months the Russians have tried to conceal what happened.'

A surreal shot of night-time fighting fills the screen until the title is superimposed: THE BETRAYED.

Then, in a large, semi-darkened room, we find a group of Russian mothers, tired, worried and hoping against hope. They explain how they feel.

'Don't look for him, that's what they said. You won't find him anyway. And that one today, he said, he's alive, he'll come back,' says the first, and others carry on in the same despairing tones.

A caption appears:

> December 1994
> The Russians move into Chechnya

There follows a montage sequence accompanied by a heavy metal Russian rock group. We see planes, troops, trucks, helicopters, all looking particularly menacing because of the aggressive music track.

Then a car draws up and a friendly Russian officer gets out and walks towards us. He is identified as Colonel Kosov, Liaison Officer. This is the man who will, we will finally discover, betray the mothers. But now he is greeted with warmth and delight. He has, they believe, come to help them. The film shows scenes of the city of Grozny, bombed, destroyed, like images of the Second World War. The Russian rock band's music accompanies the scenes of hopelessness and destruction.

A mass grave is discovered. A Chechen man tells the camera, 'They shot them, then they buried them alive. After dying you don't bleed.' That is how he knows the Chechen people were still alive when they buried them. A teenager finds a purse. It is his sister's. Then they find her body. He is totally devastated. The inarticulate grief of this young man is almost impossible to bear. As the people look for their relations, Russian armoured personnel drive by. This is one of the most harrowing scenes I have ever seen in any film – fiction or non-fiction.

The next scene shows Russian military might again. The heavy metal is accompanying the scene. As usual in a Clive Gordon film, the point of view is clear. Nothing, so far, prepares the audience for the awful truth. Kosov arrives at an unknown location. We quickly understand that it is a Chechen meeting place. Kosov wants to talk about the mothers. The Chechen leader, Isa, gets straight to the point:

> **Isa:** Why are you torturing these women, why do you drag them back and forth? Why can't the Russian command say 'Your sons are dead.' We asked you to take the corpses because the dogs are eating them . . . Why bring them to Chechnya, to make us out to be monsters? . . . You want me to meet the mothers?'
>
> **Kosov:** I'm asking you to tell them.
>
> **Isa:** To upset them? I will never do that.

And so it becomes clear that Kosov knew all along that most of the sons were dead.

Clive admits that he has come a long way as a film-maker. There is a clear development from the Chernobyl film for ITV's *First Tuesday – Children of Chernobyl* (1992) – to the latest, *The Lost Boys* (2003). 'Chernobyl was much more journalistically orientated, The latest, *The Lost Boys*, is different. On the edge of normal grammar. Lots of silence. I used classical music for the first time.' *The Lost Boys* tells the story of a group of young refugees from the war in Sudan who, having walked for years – literally – find themselves in a transit camp where some of them will be selected to start a new life in America. The film follows them as they adjust to this strange new life in the United States.

The opening is, as usual, key to an understanding of the film. This one – and the previous film, *Pimp Snooky* – was made with different collaborators. Both were shot by Paul Otter, a brilliant cameraman, and edited by Gregor Lyon. He was responsible for the lyrical first sequence. A travelling shot follows the white line on a road. A young black man, close-up of his face, right of frame, is looking at a postcard of the Statue of Liberty; he is in a bus and through the window we see indistinguishable scenery – we do not know where we are. Now out of the window we see a hilly desert landscape, Africa. A caption says that thousands of boys fled from the Sudan and began an epic journey through the wilderness. They arrive four years later in Kenya. Then we are back on the bus, American landscape out of the window. Now the window is on an aeroplane, Africa. Then the US again. Intercut are shots of young black men sleeping. In voice-over, the boy tells us that he dreams about his mother and father, but when he wakes they are not there. 'Me, Moses and Simon, we are the lost boys.' We are in the cockpit of an aeroplane. It is landing. The white line again. A glorious African sky. The title.

The opening sequence has dreamy classical music, very melancholy. The constant cutting from African landscape back to the United States is confusing, deliberately so. But the sequence works because it takes us into the world of this sad young man, whoever he is, wherever he is. We are on his side from the beginning. The film follows the boys for their month in America. Some scenes, like their arrival in the States, where they are falling about on the moving pavement at the airport, or when

Filming *The Lost Boys*

somebody shows them how to flush a toilet, some of their job interviews and conversations with the charity workers who are supposed to be helping them, are funny – but in a way that makes you laugh at the Americans, so well meaning, so unable to understand or communicate with the young Africans they are trying to help. The film could be read as a series of humiliations for the boys.

At the end, one of them goes on a trip to New York. Scenes of him on the ferry going round the Statue of Liberty are intercut with his new job as a doorman at the Radisson Hotel. All his hopes and ambition have come to this. The last shot in the film shows the twin towers. It was filmed just days before the terrorist attack. The message is clear. Clive admits that this is not an easy film for some members of the audience. 'It is difficult,' he says. 'Difficult and arty. But it's there for the audience to understand.' I told him about a conversation I had with Nick Fraser, editor of BBC's flag-ship documentary series *Storyville*. Nick had said to me that he thinks Clive is a brilliant film-maker – but, he said, he has been in

Berlin too long. He should come back home now. 'He is getting too Brechtian.' I thought that was a very perceptive comment – although I would also argue that it is no bad thing to be Brechtian. Nick said that what he meant, in this case, is that the films are getting more cynical. I put this point to Clive, who said that he sees the point being made but he thinks it is more a question of detachment in attitude and the films are ironic, not cynical. Perhaps a better word, he says, is 'clinical'.

Clive Gordon, who has German ancestry, likes living in Berlin, partly because he feels like an outsider when he is there but also feels like an outsider when he returns to England, where he was born. 'Right,' he says. 'I am looking at everything through a window. Not getting emotionally involved with the people in the films, or very rarely, anyway. Is that a weakness? I used to worry about that. But not any more.'

FILMOGRAPHY

Children of Chernobyl
1991, 52 min, 16 mm
The Chernobyl disaster and how the Soviets tried to cover it up.

Ten international awards, including:

Gold Medal, New York International Film and TV Festival
British Film Institute Grierson Award
British Academy Award for Best Film Editing

The Unforgiving
1993, 78 min, 16 mm

As their forces close in on Srebrenica, a Serbian mother seeks the body of her 11-year-old son, who was tortured and killed by Muslims in Bosnia.

Awards include:

British Academy Award for Best Documentary, and Nominations for Photography and Film Editing
Special Jury Prize, Golden Gate Awards, San Francisco
Best Documentary Award, World Television Festival, Japan

Reviews:

'A story . . . with the force and mythic simplicity of a tale from the Old Testament' (*Sunday Times*)

'This is a masterpiece which may well come to be seen as the definitive film from the killing fields of Bosnia' (*Sunday Telegraph*)

'. . . the mother of all atrocity documentaries . . . will have a profound effect wherever it is shown' (*The Guardian*)

Moscow Central
1994, 72 min, 16 mm

A black comedy about the outrageous campaign to elect the Member of Parliament for Moscow Central in Russia's first free elections since 1917.

Reviews:

'. . . great comedy . . . a fascinating portrait of a country in terminal chaos . . . don't miss it' (*Daily Mail*)

'. . . hilarious, an eye-opener' (*Time Out*)

'A marvellous, bleakly comic documentary' (*Mail on Sunday*)

The Betrayed
1995, 79 min, Super 16 mm

As the Russian forces advance over the plains of Chechnya, a group of Russian mothers search for the conscript sons they believe have been captured by the Chechens.

Awards include:

British Academy Awards for Best Documentary, Best Photography and Best Film Editing
Prix Italia
Prix Europa
RTS Best Documentary

Reviews:

'. . . a brilliantly filmed and extraordinarily painful documentary' (*The Guardian*)

'Clive Gordon's film has a sledgehammer impact' (*Evening Standard*)

'Finest war documentary ever' (John Willis, *The Guardian*)

'This is a brilliant piece of film-making, achieved under almost impossible conditions and telling its story with devastating force' (*Daily Mail*)

'. . . a disturbing and truly memorable film' (*Daily Express*)

The Mission
1997, 74 min, Super 16 mm

Deep in the Ugandan bush, an Italian nun tries to get back 30 of her convent school girls who have been abducted for sex by an army of children led by a mystic claiming to be the son of God.

Reviews:

'. . . haunting imagery . . . the visual sumptuousness underlining the obscenities described . . . *The Mission* is unbearably moving' (*Time Out*)

'. . . a shocking documentary [turned into] . . . a terrifying drama' (*Sunday Times*)

'. . . an authentic horror story from the other side of the globe . . . pure *Heart of Darkness*' (*The Observer*)

'. . . this is what documentary making is all about' (*The Guardian*)

Men in Pink
1999, 79 min, Super 16 mm

As a student theatre troupe tours Rwanda with a comic re-enactment of the genocide, a group of killers and two of the leaders of the genocide are on trial – and a priest is investigated for the murder of five children. A dark comedy about the aftermath of the genocide in Rwanda.

Reviews:

'Quite the most stunning, if numbing, documentary of recent times' (*Daily Express*)

'Gordon's brilliant use of form forces us to examine our own consciences and voyeurism . . . when you think your eyes can't cope any longer, Gordon lets your ears take the pain of these unspeakable horrors . . . Stunning' (*Time Out*)

Pimp Snooky
2000, 92 min, Super 16 mm, Channel 4 version, re-edited in 2001 for theatrical release

The adventures of Snooky the pimp on the mean streets of Milwaukee.

Reviews (C4 version):

'Think Tarantino, only this is real' (*Heat*)

'One of the most exhilarating pieces of television to come this way for a long time . . . Clive Gordon deserves to be showered with awards' (*The Guardian*)

'. . . a fearsome documentary . . . captures magnificently the paranoia and rejection behind the lingo and bravado' (*The Observer*)

'. . . as Clive Gordon's film prowls the impeccably-shot suburban streets . . . we almost succumb – like his teenage prey – to Snooky's razor-edged charm. But not quite. A quite enthralling study in ghetto economics, sexual exploitation and ruthless power games' (*The Guardian Guide*)

The Lost Boys
2002, 77 min, DigiBeta

Orphaned by the war in Sudan, and raised in a desert refugee camp, Moses and his young friends are suddenly invited by the US government to start a new life in the 'land of the free'. Never having turned on a light switch, they arrive in Boston . . . (to be screened autumn 2003).

Gull
In production

A psycho-thriller written by Paul Laverty, in production at Slate Films/Morena Films for release in 2006.

11 Sean McAllister
Director/cameraman
with attitude

Sean McAllister

I first met Sean McAllister when he was a student at the National Film and Television School at Beaconsfield in the UK. I was head of the Documentary Department from September 1993 to January 1995 and he was studying Documentary Direction. Sean was already developing a very individual voice. He was always keen to get his hands on any of the new technology gear available at the time and, while other students were still commited to working on film, Sean was experimenting with Hi8 and entering into correspondence with industry boffins abroad about improving the sound quality for single-camera operators.

Ricky Leacock, the legendary American cameraman/director, was, by then, living in France. Leacock was one of the founders of the American movement called 'direct cinema', sometimes known as 'fly on the wall'. For years, he always shot on film. Now he was experimenting with lightweight video equipment. Sean was regularly in touch with Ricky, picking his brains for the latest advances in the new technology which would improve camera and sound quality for one-man-operated shoots. Through Ricky, he got in touch with an engineer in Switzerland who was making hand-built stereo microphones for lightweight video cameras. The school bought one. I was immensely impressed by this student who was kicking against the grain and the aesthetic sensibility prevelant in the school at that time, convinced that his was the way of the future. Of course, he was right.

McAllister was born in Hull, went to university there and then did a course at the Bournemouth Film School. After that, he came to the NFTS. His application film was about the workers on the night shift at a frozen food factory in Humberside. Crudely shot and edited, the film still revealed the empathy and commitment that McAllister always feels for the underprivileged members of our society. He has continued to follow those interests while honing his skills and becoming more sophisticated in his analysis.

One day I was working in my office at the school and I received a call from one of the ex-students. Danny Cannon was at Shepperton Studios, preparing to direct a big-budget film starring Sylvester Stallone, *Judge Dredd*. Danny suggested that the NFTS Documentary Department should provide a team to film the progression of the film from empty sets through to completion for a 'making of' feature that would be used to publicize the finished movie. Our students would send their footage to Hollywood, where it would be edited and distributed. The film was to have complicated special effects, all kinds of electronic wizardry and big stars. The producer, Beau Marks, wanted us to shoot two days a week, recording the building of sets, construction of the electronic robotic characters, rehearsals of the actors and final takes.

When I held a departmental meeting at the school to explain what I thought was a very exciting project, I was astonished by the lack of enthusiasm, even contempt, expressed by many of the students. I was very new to film school life. I had worked in television since graduating from university and been trained on the job in the film departments of CBC Toronto and the BBC in London, so I was mystified as to why film students would not seize the opportunity to rub shoulders with big stars, the world's best special effects people, and work with a young director who was highly regarded and also one of our own graduates.

Danny Cannon helped me to understand the situation. I left him a message at the studio saying that I was surprised to find it difficult to recruit a team but was optimistic that we would get there in the end. Danny sent me a heartfelt letter, handwritten, commiserating and bemoaning the arrogance and snobbery that so often pervades the corridors of major film schools. He told me about some of his own depressing experiences as a student, how his understandable desire to go to Hollywood and earn a decent living was often derided by self-defined 'artists' with serious intellectual pretensions and – not always – a lot of discernible talent. Thank goodness, economic realities and more realistic recruiting have made those attitudes less common. Although, in pockets, they still remain.

The upside, for me, of this experience is that a number of students emerged from the pack, volunteering to work on the *Judge Dredd* project. The students were a bright and talented group. (One of them was camera student Lynne Ramsay, who has since achieved international fame with fiction films that she directed and scripted – notably *Ratcatcher* and *Morvern Callar*.) The self-appointed leader of the group was Sean McAllister. He came with me to Shepperton to meet the film's producer Beau Marks and discuss financial arrangements. In the end I left most of the talking to Sean. Beau seemed to like him – I think he admired his cheek.

Sean negotiated generous expenses for the students and also persuaded this tough Hollywood producer to let them shoot on Hi8. As a result of that decision, Beau agreed to buy a camera and tripod for the production. This was donated to the school at the end of the shoot. The camera was kept in the *Judge Dredd* office because Beau would not let the students take it away, in case it mysteriously 'disappeared'. When I went to pick up the equipment at the end of shooting I discovered that, as a further precaution, Beau had insisted that the camera batteries were kept locked up in another office. He obviously knew his film students well.

Sean worked on a number of films while at the Beaconsfield school, including two in his graduate year. One was a group project called *Just People*, where some of the students hired a bus and driver and travelled around the UK, looking for 'celebrities'. It took the form of a classic picaresque adventure but it was also anarchic, disrespectful and not entirely sober. The high spot for me was the episode where they find the house of television chat show hosts, Richard and Judy, who had a networked daily programme of the same name. In the time-honoured tradition of the paparazzi, the students decide to riffle through the TV stars' dustbins, looking for 'evidence'. Then they get caught. For the record, Richard Madeley handled himself well in his confrontation with the 'burglars' and let them go after a firm telling-off. *Just People* was actually broadcast by Channel 4 in 1998 – a brave decision.

Sean's other graduate film was very much a personal story. *Hitting Thirty* is about a friend of Sean's from Hull, his partner and his gang of mates. Sean is not happy with the film nowadays, feeling that he should have written a commentary to clarify the storyline. But, like the rest of the documentary students in those days, he felt that commentary is 'television' and therefore beyond the pale, artistically speaking. I know all about that attitude. I was his supervising tutor at the time. However much he now feels reluctant to show the film, it remains a warm portrait with some intimate moments that reveal the promise which he was to develop in his later, professional work.

Sean admires Molly Dineen, also a graduate of the NFTS, who makes very personal, character-based films. She is something of a role model for many of the students and comes in to teach from time to time. While she is always a character in her own films, she is the unseen presence, the voice off. She and Sean once discussed the differences in their approaches. While both film their own material and are attracted to unusual characters, Molly thinks that Sean is much more of a presence in his films than she is. He is very much 'in your face'. At the same time Sean says that Molly and another extremely successful graduate, Nick Broomfield, were inspirations for him at the beginning of his career. Sean started to develop the style of filming which is now his trademark with his first television commission, *Working for the Enemy*.

A UK independent, Mosaic Films, were putting together a series called *United Kingdom* and were looking for new young film-makers to shoot for them in different parts of the British Isles. The rushes would then be edited by the series producers, who hoped to make programmes that would give some revealing insights into the state of Great Britain at the end of the twentieth century. One of the producers came to see me at the Scottish Film Council, where I was then chief executive, having left the NFTS in 1995, to ask for suggestions for potential contributors. He told me that they were having problems recruiting Scottish film-makers. I was not surprised, given the title of the series. The words 'United Kingdom' did not play well in many parts of Scotland at a time when calls for devolution from UK government and the restoration of the long-defunct Scottish Parliament were the popular causes of the day. I suggested that Mosaic might be better off if they included a question mark in their title. I was also sure that most strong-minded young Scots, if asked to film an aspect of life which reflected the state of their nation in that period of time, would not be prepared to give up editorial control to an English production company. However, I recommended Sean McAllister because, in spite of his Scottish name, he was born and brought up in England, in Hull. I was sure that he was also strong enough to cope with the conditions imposed on the film-makers.

Working for the Enemy, transmitted by the BBC in 1997 and shown at many festivals, is a revealing, even intimate, portrait of a controversial character, the sort of man who is central to the ever-raging debate in the UK about welfare payment. By the standards of the Tory Party and the right-wing press, the subject of the film is 'a scrounger'. The film opens with a travelling shot of a man and his girlfriend walking down a street in Hull. Voice-over commentary from McAllister says, 'When I first met Kevin he told me he had been on the dole for 18 years. Kev is 35, Robbie is 19. A couple of mates in Hull suggested I made a film about them. He's never worked. She's been working since leaving school. Kev sees his life on the dole as his right.' Pause. 'But the system doesn't.'

The tone of the commentary is conversational. The phrase 'a couple of mates in Hull' makes it clear that this is no conventional approach. The film-maker is one of the lads. The use of the term 'the system' suggests that this is also not a film that will be putting the government's line. Now we see exterior shots of an official-looking building. The title comes up and is held for seconds, accompanied by a sinister sounding cord of music: WORKING FOR THE ENEMY. It is clear that this is going to be an authored documentary, without the usual constraints of having to strive for objectivity or – that much abused word – balance. The film-maker is clearly on the side of the rebels.

The film cuts to an interior. It is an introductory meeting for a group called in by a government-sponsored organization called Jobsearch. Kev is in a classroom with other people having a spirited exchange with a course leader. We learn that this is a seminar for the unemployed, an annual event for people on the dole. The men are being asked for their qualifications for working. Part of their discussion is as follows:

> Kev says, 'I left school in 1978. I did four weeks temporary work in 1990. It's now . . . what . . . 1996.'
> 'Wow,' says the instructor, looking sympathetic. 'Have you been forgotten, Kev, do you think?'
> 'I wish I would be. I don't want to be here.'
> 'Well nobody wants to be here.'
> 'No I don't want to work.'
> There is a look of surprise and puzzlement on the face of the instructor. Kev adds an explanation, 'Its like skydiving. I just don't want to do it.'

So the tone of the film which follows is established. The unshockable McAllister followed the anarchic Kev and his friends for weeks and became, in a sense, part of the gang. Meanwhile, back in London, the producers of *United Kingdom* were waiting for the rushes, which they expected to edit. Sean says that when he explained the conditions to Kev, 'We bonded over it. In a sense, we were both "Working for the Enemy", which became the title of the film as well.' He says that when Colin Luke, the series editor got the rushes back, he was in something of a dilemma. For one thing, Sean had made sure that he was himself very much a part of the film. He had become a character in the drama. But also there were cultural and ideological attitudes that were not those of the series producers. The film is full of references, visual and verbal, to characters taking illegal drugs. Sean remembers a discussion in which Colin asked him, 'What *is* smack?' Colin decided to let this particular film-maker into the cutting room to edit the film – just what McAllister had planned all along.

After the extended sequence with Kev and other unemployed rebels jousting with the men who are trying to help them find work, often hilarious exchanges, intercut with scenes of the young girlfriend Robbie at work as a seamstress, we finally get the information which is key to Kev's personality. He is a graphic artist. We see some of his impressively original work as he explains in voice-over, 'I have a job, I just don't get paid for it. My great fear in being forced to work is that I won't be able to draw. And if I can't draw then there is no point in me living.' Sean asks, 'Why not frame and sell the pictures?' Kev says, 'I could not bear to. I only draw to stop myself shooting somebody.' Sean: 'You're not that mad are you?' Kev: 'No, because I draw.' Later, in a conventionally shot interview – unusual in a McAllister documentary – Kev and Robbie sit on a sofa, talking to the camera and explaining his philosophy of life. He says his dad worked from the age of 12 to the age of 55 on a building site. Now he has emphysema. 'I love me dad,' he says, 'and that's what they've done to him.'

The film intercuts between the hapless officials who try to persuade Kev to take a conventional job and the lifestyle which he and his mates enjoy. They spend a typical Saturday. The day starts in the flat where Robbie and Kev are taking a drug. The commentary says, 'Saturday is juice day. A 30-pound dose of methadone.' They go to a shopping centre, spend time by the sea. 'Love is the greatest drug,' says Kev. Back at the flat, he shows us pictures of Robbie after she has come home having taken smack. But another picture shows her as he loves her, sober and smiling.

In a later scene, perhaps the most controversial in the film, a friend, Nick, comes around to the flat. The three of them are getting out of their heads on drugs and alcohol, the language is ripe with expletives and Kev and Robbie are fighting. Robbie and Nick leave the flat, Kev demands to know what is going on, the scene is heavy with sexual tension. The camera simply observes the action, there is no interrupting voice-off, normally a feature of any dramatic scene in a McAllister film. The three seem oblivious to the camera and I have a sense that maybe we should not be watching this, it is too intimate, too private. The audience is cast in the role of voyeur, like the stereotypical busybody behind the twitching curtain, spying on the neighbours.

Eventually, the system catches up with Kev. He has a number of official interviews. He will be obliged to work or his benefits will be stopped. A hilarious scene shows him resisting the invitation to learn how to lay paving stones. The gang leader's suggestion that after his training he could even lay his own patio does not appeal to Kev. Eventually, he gets a placement in a charity shop, uncomfortable, off drugs and resigned to his fate. The law requires that he does this job but, still, it's only for 13 weeks. He will get through it, one way or the other. Sean asks him how he has found the experience of being filmed. He says he has found it helpful but somehow this has an ambiguous ring, particularly when he looks directly into the lens of the camera, smiles ironically and says 'Thank you, BBC.'

I met Kev and Nick at a young film-makers' forum in Manchester where, together with Sean, they were talking about the experience of making the film. It was an enlightening experience for me, not least because of the response of the audience. They roared with appreciative laughter when Kev expressed his hatred of the system and were highly amused by the drugs and alcohol scenes. I felt that, in many ways, Kev was seen not only as a strong-minded individual but also as a suitable spokesman for young people in the north when he refused to be bullied into a conventional lifestyle. He told the audience, almost apologetically, that he is now working for money. He had for a long time worked with a friend, doing computer graphics, because he enjoyed it. The friend could not afford to pay him at first. But the work was so successful that now his friend has put him on salary. He is doing the work he loves and making no compromises to the nanny state.

I have always been interested in the difference in perception that people who appear in a film feel between seeing it in a cutting room, before transmission and watching it go out, knowing that millions of viewers are out there, watching with the eyes of strangers. Who is the audience, you wonder, what are they thinking about me? Suddenly, you are reading the film differently yourself. Is that what I am like? Why did I say that? Is that what I look like? I asked Nick how he felt when he saw the drunken druggie scene transmitted. There he was, on television, stoned out of his head and flirting with his best friend's girlfriend. Did the film make him stop and think, contemplate a change of lifestyle? It was a serious point I was making, although possibly a little brutal. Nick told me that he had thought a lot about the film and he thinks it did have an effect on his life. Later he told me that he was a little shocked that I had asked such a direct question, especially in front of an audience. But that's my documentary training, I suppose.

It seems to me that Sean McAllister, at this stage in his career, was beginning to develop a screen persona and individual voice as a filmmaker that is quite different from any other. Documentary has many committed political film-makers, but while others on the left are often dogmatic, crusading, sometimes strident, he is quite simply on the side of the underdog. The political perspective is not clear at times. He automatically sympathizes with the outsiders, the people who normally have no public voice, and allows them to speak for themselves. He does so with empathy, humour and a gentle sense of irony, marvelling at the craziness and unfairness of the world we live in. In this sense, he is for me a true descendant of the British writer George Orwell. Like Orwell, in books like *Homage to Catalonia*, *Road to Wigan Pier* or *Down and Out in Paris and London*, McAllister is always on the side of the 'awkward squad'.

Sean's next film, *The Minders*, also for the BBC, was made in Iraq in 1997. It begins with an unusually long pre-title sequence, four minutes. Out of the black, without any text or title, the first shot in the film shows a group of men wearing protective clothing, faces masked, walking as a group down a hill in the English countryside, towards the camera. There is a spooky hissing sound, repeated three times. Then the voice-over begins. It is McAllister speaking. The delivery is flat, matter of fact, strong northern accent.

'Symptoms of nerve gas poisoning: runny nose, increased saliva, tightness of chest, difficulty breathing, headaches, dizziness, urination, defecation, vomiting. To survive, you must shut your eyes, drop to the ground, face down, place your hands under your body.' A photographer begins to snap the group, but one of the disguised figures breaks away, walks towards the camera, removes his helmet and smiles ruefully. 'I'm not too sure about this,' says Sean McAllister.

We are watching a chemical warfare training course with the British Army. Before leaving for Iraq, Sean and his producer had been sent on it by the BBC:

It was surreal, so we filmed it. We weren't going to use it at first. But these SAS bastards had convinced us that we were going to die. They told us Saddam was going to gas all the journalists in Baghdad.

The BBC executive producer, Stephen Lambert, had commissioned Sean at a time when war seemed inevitable. But the situation changed dramatically, between the commissioning process and the arrival in Baghdad. Sean explains, 'When I got there, nothing was happening. Kofi Annan had sorted it all out. Stephen was on the Satphone saying, "We want you back. The controller doesn't want another film about sanctions . . . parents saying how difficult life is because they haven't got any food or whatever."' But Sean was determined to make a film in Iraq so, after some discussion, he and Stephen agreed that instead of the war film he had planned, he would make a film about 'minders' instead. These people are assigned by many governments to 'help' foreign journalists and film-makers. In theory they obtain filming permits, advise about dangerous situations, book hotels and transport, and the rest. Most of the time what they actually do is make sure that the foreign media does not get out of line or find out something the government is wanting to keep secret. They are often colourful characters and sometimes we find a minder who is genuinely interested in helping us to achieve our ambitions. In my experience, not often.

Sean started looking for suitable characters. He says, 'I was the only one among 300 journalists who was happy that there wasn't a war going on.'

After the spooky chemical warfare training camp, the film cuts to a travelling shot in Baghdad, then an official building. Inside there are journalists milling about, an air of tension. Then it cuts to a man, in the middle of this chaos, watching a football game. The commentary explains that he is Kippah and he is one of the temporary minders who has been taken on to deal with all the extra journalists who have arrived to cover the war. In sync, Kippah says, 'Liverpool is my best club, still and forever, Liverpool is my best club.' With war looming, Kippah is watching a Merseyside derby, without a trace of rancour towards the enemy. 'I can't forget Steve Heighway, or Ray Kennedy, or Ray Clements, or Hughes. If England played with Iraq, I would support England. I like them too much.' He tells us he has a photograph of England captain Bobby Moore, holding up the World Cup in 1966 – like a movie star, a hero, blonde and beautiful, he says.

The second character in the film is Allah, a government minder with 17 years' experience. In his first appearance he is eating an elaborate concoction of ice-cream. He is 'a bit of a ladies' man'. He is interested in Sean's taped music collection and wants to copy some of them. As he drives Sean around the city, he switches on his in-car stereo and plays one of the tapes, very softly at first. He tells Sean to keep down, keep out of sight as they move through sensitive areas. The shot of Allah driving is from a very low angle – Sean is lying on the floor of the car. He keeps asking, 'Can I get up now?' and Allah smiles indulgently but says, no, too dangerous. 'Can I film that way?' No. 'Can I film that way?' No. The series title MODERN TIMES comes up as the at-first muted sound of one of the tapes he has copied begins to be audible: women's voices, 'Danny boy, Danny boy.' Then a dramatic cut to a colourful wall poster of Saddam. The track is raised to its full sound level, male voices, like a football chant:

I get knocked down but I get up again
You're never gonna keep me down
I get knocked down but I get up again
You're never gonna keep me down.

The tape continues over a number of portraits of Saddam smiling, cut on the beat, determined and defiant. The title of the film comes up, in graffiti style, to match the posters we have just seen: THE MINDERS.

For me, this is an extraordinary pre-title sequence, brilliantly edited by Olly Huddlestone. It is four minutes long, unusual for a film originally intended for television. It incorporates so many ideas, so many mood swings, in a very short time and ends on a positively subversive note. At the beginning of the sequence, the audience has been led to believe that a nasty war is about to begin. The film-maker is interested in trying to understand the enemy people by filming his own minders. One supports Liverpool and English football generally and the other loves British rock music – not what the news reports have led us to believe. It is dangerous to be seen with a camera in certain sensitive locations in Baghdad, but the minder who drives the film-maker around is not too worried about it and maintains his sense of humour. McAllister himself displays an ambivalent attitude, although he is British and is working for the BBC, the state broadcasting corporation. The music which runs through the second part of the sequence and bursts out aggressively over smiling pictures of the 'enemy' leader, Saddam, is the music of an anarchist rock band. It is clear that this is no conventional view of a well-covered news story.

Allah, the ladies' man, has his big moment when a famous film star is coming into the airport in Baghdad and the foreign media, desperate for any story to film, are arguing about their right to be on the runway or in key positions in the departure lounge and in general displaying the arrogance of the western media on foreign detail. Allah is patient and polite throughout, but he holds firm to the instructions he has been given. They are limited in the positions they can place their cameras and that is non-negotiable. (Hardly surprising, since no major national airport allows free access to cameras in any sensitive area which might be of interest to terrorists.) However, the foreign press persist in their demands. Clearly, the rudeness of the foreign journalists upsets him. The moment that interests McAllister is the one where the actress arrives and Allah meets her. 'Did you kiss her?' he asks. 'Yes, six times,' Allah says, absolutely thrilled.

It emerges that Kippah, the new recruit, has been fired by the ministry. Sean has been trying to get hold of him. He says, 'I had been knocking on the door of the ministry every day and asking, have you sacked him? They say, he's a temporary minder, we'll give you a real minder. But I want to film him. They're very suspicious. All the other crews are filming babies dying in hospitals – and you want to film him? He is irresponsible. We sacked him.' Sean goes on, 'I was on a knife-edge. Have I got a film? A lot of this kind of film-making is thinking on your feet.' So he decided to phone Kippah and film himself in conversation with his subject. This is unusual because he would not normally set up a scene and appear on camera in a situation which had not happened naturally. The scene works because it is obvious how concerned Sean is for the fate of his new friend.

The conversation leads to the most moving sequence in the film. For me, this is one of the great moments in contemporary documentary, a classic dramatic moment when one of 'the enemy' opens himself up emotionally to somebody from 'our side' and we the audience wonder, once again, why we are being led into war with these people, with whom we have so much in common. The situation is simple. Kippah shows Sean around his house. It has very little furniture, everything has been pawned for money because the economic situation, exacerbated by UN sanctions, means that he has been unemployed for a long time. Pictures of his favourite British footballers, which once adorned the walls of his bedroom, have been used as fuel, burned to heat the house. Still he will be generous to a guest. He gives Sean a kaftan, saying he can no longer fit into it. He insists that Sean tries it on. Sean agrees, puts the camera on automatic and hands it to Kippah.

In any normal edit, this would be cut out but the jerky movement during the handover stays in. An extraordinary moment, when Kippah takes control of the filming. Roles are reversed, if only for a few minutes, as Sean does a stately descent of the stairs, dressed in traditional Iraqi clothes.

The Minders is a film that will resonate long after the present stand-off between the American and British governments and the Iraqi people finally reaches its bloody finale. Totally unpretentious, often roughly shot and loosely edited, it has honesty and integrity. The intimacy and affection that develops in the course of filming between the two protagonists and the film-maker is particularly moving. At the end of the film, Kippah pawns his watch to pay for dinner for Sean and Ben, his producer, despite their protests. Kippah explains that it is the custom of the Iraqi people to offer hospitality to strangers. This act of generosity is necessary to him, although he is well aware that the strangers come from a country which is about to invade and occupy his homeland.

The BBC received letters after the programme, some of which revealed the confusion in a few members of the audience about the type of documentary they had been watching. One said that they had enjoyed the film but 'It was a shame that the journalist (*sic*) was not better trained. Inappropriate questions. Unresearched. He either enjoys playing the fool or he is a fool.' Naturally, Sean thought this was hilarious.

The next film, *Settlers*, was commissioned by Peter Dale at Channel 4. Dale wanted a film which looked at the troubles in Palestine through the eyes of two characters, one a Palestinian, the other a Jewish settler. Sean spent weeks looking for the right characters, people with whom he would feel comfortable but nonetheless would be completely committed to opposing sides. To represent the Jewish settlers he chose an orthodox American immigrant, a radio show host called Dov. Sean says, 'I had seen his picture on the front cover of *The Economist* magazine.' (Dov was pictured carrying a machine-gun in one hand and a bible in the other.) 'He was an egotist and didn't really trust me, but I quite liked that. It made the relationship more interesting. But he liked having me around with the camera.' The Arab character, Ali, is a big man in his community. He works as a tour guide and often acts as a spokesman for his people. He had been in jail for 17 years for planting a bomb. Everybody knew him. Sean says, 'He is the dude, he is the daddy, but inside he is suffering, like so many Palestinians.'

The film intercuts between the two characters' lives, revealing through their individual experiences the painful lives of their opposed communities. The film was shot at a time when Israel was handing back some of the land it had occupied to the Palestinians. At the same time, Jewish settlers were moving into property in Muslim neighbourhoods and hanging the Israeli flag from their balconies. There is violence on both sides, sometimes guns are used but more often there is stone throwing. In an interview shot at night with Dov he is standing by a window with the town below. A McDonald's sign fills the right side of the frame as he gets into his stride with his story. He is talking about the time of the intifada. 'I got many stories of rock throwing and shooting and many kinds of things . . . We were throwing rocks, we were smashing Arab windows, sure . . . Two years later I was driving through an Arab town and there's a road block there, of stones, and I stop and go out and there's this Arab throwing stones at my car. So I grabbed my sub-machine-gun, click click, and fired in the air but he is still throwing stones. Macho man. So I shot one in his direction, still didn't get hin out of the way and then finally,' Dov adopts a pose, aping the action of a man pointing a machine-gun directly at the camera, 'I aimed right at him, knowing this guy wants me to kill him and then I start talking to God. I said, Master of the Universe, if you want this man dead, then kill him yourself. And I put the gun down.'

In the course of filming, Ali's life starts to fall apart. We learn that his wife and children have left him and he is distraught. Since the film was made for Channel 4, which is funded by advertising, there are commercial breaks. This can cause problems for editors and it needs great skill to keep the momentum of the story going, particularly when the editor cannot possibly know in advance what little advertising gems are going to interrupt the story and distract the viewer. Good editors turn these distractions to their own advantage by building in some form of suspense, before the break. The audience is left wondering what will happen next. *Settlers* does this very well. At the end of part two, Ali has invited Sean to a friend's wedding party. We see him smoking a hookah, looking sad but holding himself together while, all around him, people are celebrating.

After the break, the camera follows Ali through the dark narrow streets of his town. Sean's commentary says that Ali's parents have told him that he has been drinking for days. Ali is staggering along, moving in and out of the light, so at times the screen is practically black. Ali is moaning, 'I am old, I am old.' Sean is trying to calm him. 'Let's go home and have a cup of tea.' Ali just wants another drink. Later we see him at home lying in a stupor. His mother comes in and talks to Sean, behind the camera. He does not speak Arabic and simply murmurs sympathetically in English. He can guess what she is saying. Ali has drunk 10 bottles, she has found them.

Sean told me that part of him felt ashamed to be filming a man in such a pitiful condition. Should he not be putting the camera down and helping in some way? He said he did what he could by being there and giving the mother a sympathetic hearing. But he would always keep filming in such a situation. The decision to stop comes in the cutting room. You might decide not to use the material. But you must always shoot it.

In my early days in television, it was considered to be wrong to show films to the subjects in your films before transmission. It was a question of editorial control. The theory went: show the film to your characters and they will want changes, possibly bring in lawyers, talk to the press who will kick up a row and the film might be stopped before you can show it. This is your film, your point of view, you are the author, so no outside interference should be tolerated, even from the subjects of the film. Current affairs investigative programmes often still take this position. In this litigious age, that is not surprising. When, for example, they are exposing corruption in high places, they are right. Prior restraint, as it is called, is anti-democratic. However, the issue is more complicated with films that are about the film-maker's view of somebody else's life. Roger Graef, the veteran American obser-vational film-maker, came up with a set of rules that I always rec-ommend to young film-makers. Roger will always show a film before transmission but clearly state that he will only change fac-tual errors. Point of view cannot be challenged.

Sean got a letter from Dov after he finished editing. Apparently Dov was having second thoughts about his contribution to the film. The letter said, Sean told me, that if he showed the film in public, Dov would 'sue the arse off me'. The film had already been delivered to Channel 4. 'So the next day I was on a plane to Israel with a tape and a bottle of wine. Dov said, I thought that would get you out here. Still, his ego is big so he allowed those scenes where he is getting tough with the Arabs. But Ali was dev-astated. He felt betrayed. But he agreed to the final cut, mainly out of loyalty and friendship. He saw that he should look at his own imperfections, take it on the chin.' Ali did not agree with the portrait of himself but accepted it. Dov, in the end, liked it. But maybe because 'he could not see the irony'. After transmission, Dov used to telephone Sean for a chat. Sean thinks that he missed the attention. This is quite common, only human surely. It is important that documentary film-makers build in 'aftercare' time for the people they make temporarily famous.

Hull's Angel (2002) is, according to Sean:

> . . . about a woman in Hull who sets out to help asylum seek-ers. She gets involved with one but finds out they are not all angels. Neither is she. She had walked away from a 28-year marriage, lost both her sons who don't want to know her any more. She's an old-school socialist, her and her daughter. They live in a part of Hull where you can't sell a house for £6000. Nobody wants to live there. In a way, the film is about the state of Britain.

The government has based 1500 asylum seekers in Hull, a town with no previous foreign immigration. The film's subject, Tina, is living with a 24-year-old Iraqi refugee, Khaled. She is 48, commit-ted to helping as many of the refugees as possible. She explains her ideology to Sean in a conversation where she is, as usual, cooking for the many. She is exhausted because a whole crowd came round the night before to eat and did not leave until one. She is working in a chicken packing factory. She says:

> What got me today and yesterday is I'm covered in all this blood and its splashing in me face. [She stops to check on the cooking.] I bet the prat who owns the company, I bet his wife is driving around in a Merc. And we are packing chick-ens. Now if that doesn't turn people to socialism, God knows what will.

Khaled thinks that no more refugees should be allowed into the country, now that he is safe and able to stay. He has a wife in Iraq who he wants to bring over to live with them in a *ménage à trois*. Tina is sending money to this woman. Eventually, she breaks. Sean has phoned her that evening and she has asked him not to come round because Khaled is moving out. He comes around anyway, camera at the ready. The couple are still arguing and Khaled is packing.

Three months later, she has moved away from Hull and is living in a hostel and working as a manager. Sean arrives with her worldly goods, packed in bin-liners, which her daughter has been looking after for her. She breaks the amazing news. She is going to get married to another asylum seeker, Khaled's cousin Masood, also 24. Sean interviews him and, not one to mince words, asks if he is not really looking for a British passport. Will he not leave her for a 22-year-old eventually? Masood insists that he is genuine and sincere. The last shot in the film shows Tina and Masood walking hand in hand through a park in Bradford. In voice-over she is saying that she feels bad because she left Hull and did not stay and try to put her message across. Like the asylum seekers, she has left it all behind.

The Liberace of Baghdad (2005) tells the story of Samir, a piano player, and his family, living through the turmoil of post-war Iraq, still

Samir Peter, the Liberace of Baghdad

occupied by 'coalition' forces. He is a charismatic character and a great musician. His songs and music are heard throughout the film. McAllister had decided to go back to Iraq in 2004, in spite of the fact that he had problems getting a commission. He did not have a story, just an instinct. 'What was happening on television was really depressing me. I'd been offered loads of money to do really shitty things and I thought, "Sod it. Let's go and do something interesting."' Nick Fraser, editor of the BBC's influential documentary strand *Storyville*, was the only person willing to back him. 'It was great that Nick was brave enough to commission it.' *Storyville* could not offer enough money to fully fund the film – normally they work with co-producers – so Sean decided to put up the rest of the money himself. He remortgaged his house. 'Money was tight but Nick was great. He was the person who was there for me.'

The filming took eight months. He says that being 'only half-commissioned' was great, because he did not have the usual pressure from funders. But he knew he could not afford to fail and he gave it 100 per cent. 'Round about April 2004, it was getting difficult. They were starting to take hostages and the foreign journalists were being threatened with stoning, or being taken. You're halfway through a film. What do you do? Pull out?' He says Pawel Pawlikowski once gave him some good advice. 'First you find a situation which interests you. Then you find your characters. Then the documentarist's job is to sit and wait.' He thinks that every good film has conflict and in Iraq at that time the conflict was inherent in the situation. Still, he had to wait. He says it drives him crazy when people say, 'Oh, you were lucky there.' He says the real skill is to recognize the situation, the character, 'the luck' when you see it. He sometimes teaches at his old school, the NFTS in England. Looking at student rushes, he says, you see so often a missed opportunity, a story that got away. I know what he means and it is true that this is often down to inexperience. In the words of a great American golfer: 'People say I'm lucky. But it's funny. The harder I practise, the luckier I get.'

The film opens dramatically with night shots of the sky lit up by gunfire. A voice is shouting. 'What's going on, why are they shooting?' A man turns around and talks to the camera. 'It's a war.' The off-camera voice (McAllister) asks again, why are they shooting. Samir, the hero of the film, lights a cigarette and smiles. 'Because they are happy.' Iraq has just beaten Saudi Arabia in a football match. Who is going to stop them, he asks. 'There is no government.'

Sean had arrived in Baghdad believing that reconstruction was underway and thinking that the war had been justified. Having met and befriended the piano player, Samir, he was taken round to the family home and introduced to his son Fahdi and the eldest daughter, Saha. In a scene near the beginning of the film, she is cooking a meal for him and she says, 'Sean, we don't have much freedom here.' He says, now things are different. She shakes her head, 'No, worse.' He is amazed. It cannot be worse than Saddam Hussein he says. She replies, 'In Saddam's time, we had security. Since the occupation the Americans have done nothing for us. No change.' Sean says that they say they got rid of Saddam to free the Iraqi people. 'No, no, no,' she says. Her father adds, 'If we were a poor country and did not have this petrol, who cares what Saddam was doing to us?' Saha adds that Saddam was a good man who made some mistakes. She says he knew what was going to happen but the Arab countries did not listen to him. Her mother and sister now live in America. But they will always be Iraqis.

Saha's views were shocking for Sean and indeed to many people, particularly the Americans in the audience who watched the film at the 2005 Sundance Festival. Sean says, 'She had seen eight months of so-called reconstruction and nothing was happening. She was distraught, feeling hopeless. But by the end of filming, she was the one who made the most sense. Everything she said at the top of the film made sense at the end.' Towards the end of the film, the sister who lives in America comes to visit and supports Saha and her attitude. Only Samir has any faith now in America and he too sees the contradictions. He has applied for an American immigrant visa because he wants to join his ex-wife, who is living in Arizona. But he says, 'This could have been the Japan of the Middle East. But they would not let us.'

As usual, McAllister worked on his own, shooting and recording sound. He shoots on a PD100 DV camera:

I use a Sennheiser K6 with an Omni E66 directional microphone on top and everything is on automatic except the focus. I spend a lot of money repairing sound. I've become best friends with my dubbing editor, Bob Jackson. I've stopped using radio mics at the moment but I might look at that again. Sometimes they seem to inflate the ego and people enjoy performing. Others feel wired, trapped.

He shot 110 30-minute tapes and says it was an easy edit. His regular editor is Olly Huddlestone, who has a big say in the cutting room. 'He really co-directs the edit. Nick Fraser was great. He came in after four weeks and was very happy.' Sean, who had not worked with Nick before, wondered if he was always kind to directors. But when Nick came back four weeks later he was very tough. They had recut the opening and lost the impact. Nick told them to put it back as it was before. 'He was absolutely right.' *Hull's Angel* had taken 14 weeks to edit, *Settlers* 16 weeks. This one just felt right from the beginning and Olly was able to throw away the extra material and concentrate on the main story without too much difficulty.

The Liberace of Baghdad won a World Jury prize at the Sundance Festival. Sean says the American audience were both shocked and moved by the film and it has, since then, received a great deal of publicity. As a result, Samir is now receiving offers to perform his music around the world. Sean says he has finally realized what kind of film he wants to make. There must be a political content but the dominant story will always be human. 'I don't want to be a polemicist. I want the films to be emotional on the surface but there have to be layers of meaning also. They have to be political.'

FILMOGRAPHY

Hessle Road
1988, Frontier Films

Inhabitants of a traditional fishing community in Hull are moved out to a satellite housing estate, never to return.

Toxic Waste
1988, Frontier Films

Campaign film about the illegal dumping of toxic waste on Britain's motorways.

Fylingdales
1988, Frontier Films

Campaign film, warning of the dangers and health risks from radiated toxic waste.

A Passing Thought
1989, Frontier Films

Experimental film ruminating on life under Prime Minister Margaret Thatcher.

The Season
1990, Homemade Films
Eight weeks on the night shift in a Hull pea canning factory.

Crematorium
1993, 10 min, NFTS
Behind the scenes at a London crematorium.

Life with Brian
1994, NFTS

Brian compensates for his unhappy marriage by spending his leisure time hunting rabbits and ferrets.

Hitting Thirty
1995, NFTS

Andy is 30. His partner Karen has a child – not his – and wants commitment. His head is still with the boys down the pub.

Just People
1995, NFTS; 1998, Channel 4

An anarchic celebrity hunt around the UK in a hippie bus. Made with Ashleigh Irvine.

Shoot-out in Swansea
1997, Vagabond Films, BBC
Portrait of Kevin Allen, making his first feature film, *Twin Town*.

Working for the Enemy
1997, Mosaic Films, BBC2

Leading character Kev has only worked for four weeks in his adult life. He is now 36 years old. He thinks it is his right to choose not to work but still claim benefits. The government disagrees.

The Minders
1998, *Modern Times*, BBC2

An affectionate look at the lives of two of Iraq's media minders, revealing the reality of life under UN sanctions in the period before the US-led invasion.

Settlers
2000, *True Stories*, Channel 4

Set in Jerusalem, this is a portrait of two men: Dov, a Jewish settler, and Ali, an Arab activist. The film throws light on the problems of both communities in the period leading up to the second intifada.

Hull's Angel
2002, *True Stories*, Channel 4

Tina, a middle-aged woman who has broken with her husband and family, finds refuge with young asylum seekers in Hull.

The Liberace of Baghdad
2004, *Storyville*, BBC

The film-maker meets a piano player in war-torn Baghdad and, through him and his family, sees a whole different side to life in Iraq, after the coalition invasion and the fall of Saddam.

Won a World Jury prize at the Sundance Festival.

12 Maxine Baker
Lessons for life – some of the things I have learned about making documentaries

Maxine Baker

About 10 years ago, when I was chief executive of the Scottish Film Council, the newspaper *Scotland on Sunday* asked me to write an article about my first memories of going to the cinema. It was an interesting request and made me think back to why and how I came to be the documentary film-maker I am today. I had no clear recollection of the first films I saw at the Grand Cinema in Burnopfield, North West Durham, England. I could only recall that a lot of them seemed to be American films about Cowboys and Indians, and that the films appeared to expect the audience to recognize that the Cowboys had God on their side. We kids in that

Geordie audience always cheered for the underdogs, the Indians – and they always got slaughtered. We came from a poor mining village where we all supported our local football team, Newcastle United, who in those dark days also got regularly slaughtered, at least metaphorically, in the Football League. It seemed natural for us to cheer for the victims in any disaster.

Documentary is sometimes about seeing that there might be another side to any published story. And, even as a child, I was stirred to check out the facts and the background to anything I heard or read. Not just the background, but also the detail. After watching a western movie I would ask my mother, 'Where is Arizona?' and she would tell me, 'Look it up in the Atlas.' Or 'Check it in the encyclopaedia.' A difficult word? 'Look it up in the dictionary.' So I was encouraged at a young age to question everything. For me, that is the spirit of documentary film-making. Do not take anybody's word for anything. Find out for yourself and always tell the truth, however uncomfortable that might be for you – not to mention your lords and masters.

I wrote in my *Scotland on Sunday* article about my first clear recollection of going to the cinema. This was a real, glamorous cinema, one of the old picture palaces in Newcastle, eight miles away and half an hour on the bus. Dad took me and my brother Roy to see *The King and I*, and afterwards expressed his fury about the daft picture he had wasted his time watching. From the advertised publicity, he thought it would be a documentary about British colonialism. Anyway, Roy and I loved it and I thought, looking back, that it had taught me a lot more than the 'kiss, kiss, bang, bang' movies that we regularly watched at the Grand. Looking back again now, 10 years on, I think the lessons for life I thought about then could be further refined. Now follows my 'lessons for a documentary film-maker', learned not from an old movie but from 30 years of personal experience. With apologies to Errol Morris and Robert McNamara, my lessons are somewhat less bloodthirsty than Lyndon Johnson's Secretary of Defence in *The Fog of War* (see Chapter 1), but probably more relevant to your average young film-maker. At least I hope so, for the universe's sake.

I have selected five case studies, extracted from my working diaries and chosen from many other potential stories. I hope that the advice I draw from my experiences will be of some help to other film-makers. I have always found that I learn more from my mistakes than I do from, apparently, getting it right. So the cases I have selected all tell of difficult situations where tough decisions had to be made, often with no time for reflection. The stories start in the era of film but would not necessarily have been different today – because they are to do with procedure, not technology – and end with digital editing.

CASE STUDY 1: Don't cry for me, Argentina (Buenos Aires, 1971)

As a young film researcher at Thames Television in 1971, I had one of those adventures an ambitious young thing can usually only dream about. I had been hired on a short-term contract to do film research on a little-known, dead wife of a forgotten Argentinian dictator, Juan Peron – her name, Evita. I got the job because I speak Spanish and happened to know a lot about the subject, because my landlady was Argentinian. The Thames crew were already out there with the director, Carlos Pasini, filming a documentary about Evita's life story. Apparently they were having problems. One day I got a call from the legendary Jeremy Isaacs, then head of features at Thames. We all had massive respect for him, as a film-maker and a boss. He encouraged us to be bold and commissioned all sorts of projects which would have no chance in British television today. He also backed his people. I was in awe of him. I walked into his office and he fired a question at me, using a line which could have come straight out of a 1940s newshound movie, 'Carlos needs help. I want you to fly out to Argentina tomorrow. Can you do it?' Of course, I said yes. 'OK. Go get your jabs.'

He was right, Carlos did need help. This was the period of instability in Argentina when Peron, who had been in exile for years, was about to return with his wife Isabel, who was going to run for president. The generals had not yet seized power again but it was likely that they would. The Peronists were considered to be the biggest threat to the oligarchy and any mention of the name of Evita was politically dangerous.

My job was to work separately from the crew, gathering photographs, sound recordings and archive film of Evita. On the surface pretty simple, but in Buenos Aires, at that time, political dynamite. Carlos gave me a fixer to help but I quickly found it easier to work alone as much as possible for the simple reason, still true today, no doubt always will be, that a young woman with a cute accent and a short skirt, running around asking questions, was never going to be taken seriously by the authorities.

People took alarming risks to help me. Photographs and film of Evita had supposedly been destroyed after the coup against her husband. But there were hidden stashes which Carlos identified for me and I went down there, innocent and ignorant, asking for help. I always got it. But the curators and film people wanted to make sure that they would not be implicated when the film was shown in the UK. So I had to sneak into the photographic archive after it closed. The curator rephotographed every picture I needed on 35 mm stock with an ordinary SLR camera. I was not allowed to have them processed. Rolls of unprocessed film stock in a young woman's handbag at customs surprise no-one.

I went to a movie studio where they still had some of her films, despite her own order to destroy them. In my taxi, on the way there, the driver called in and told somebody where I was going – obviously not his controller. When I got back in the car after my meeting, I was carrying what looked like a pile of dry cleaning. The driver radioed in, 'The stupid bitch forgot her cleaning; she's just picking it up.' The studio had sensibly disguised the parcel containing clips from Evita's movie career. And it never occurred to the people who were watching my movements that I could understand every word they said.

I left Argentina with hand baggage containing 16 mm copies of her brother's home movie record of Evita's Rainbow Tour of Europe in 1943, a stash of 35 mm photographs of her, which have since become very famous, and clips from the movies that should have been destroyed. At the airport when we left, there was a special security check. All bags and people to be searched. I had in my hand-baggage Evita's home movies on 16 mm film. But no camera. The crew had refused to hide the film among their kit for me because they were all aware of what a hot potato I was carrying.

One of them had said to me, 'Leave it here, love. I'm not prepared to risk my life for Thames Television, neither should you.' But once again, the daft young thing act worked. The female customs officer searching my bag found one can, then another, then another. I said, 'I was filming your city, it is so very beautiful.' No camera. Three cans of 16 mm. A tourist? She told me to go, quickly. I have never been so happy to take off from any airport. Shortly after we left, the coup happened and Argentina was plunged into dictatorship by the military.

Was the rediscovery of the story of Eva Peron, the film we made, *Queen of Hearts*, which inspired the musical *Evita* and a lot besides, worth the risks I took? For me, then, yes. Definitely. However, I was very young and very inexperienced at the time and film researchers were not supposed to be at the sharp end, so I had not prepared properly. Years later I wandered into the office of one of my colleagues at Granada. I noticed on his shelves that he had a fine collection of Leonard Cohen cassettes. I expressed surprise that a well-known Canadian depressive would be the favoured easy listening for a hard-bitten investigative journalist.

My colleague opened one of the cassettes and showed me that it was in fact an interview with a resistance fighter in South Africa during the apartheid era. He had gone in as a tourist and had been secretly filming. But the crew hid the interviews in this way so that if they were stopped by police or customs, they would not be suspected. I wish somebody had told me that years earlier.

For any investigative, undercover or otherwise dangerous location, here are a few tips:

1 Only take big risks if you are sure it is worth it.
2 Make sure you have a good cover story. We claimed we were making a travel programme but I am told that this one doesn't wash any more, too many people have used it.
3 Remember that, in situations of danger, you are probably on your own. You may be lucky and find colleagues or even strangers to help but don't count on it.
4 Don't be afraid to look stupid; don't admit you know a language if it might cause people to decide you are not as dim as you appear to be.

CASE STUDY 2: The year of living dangerously (Accra, Ghana, 1984)

I flew into Accra with my friends and colleagues Simon Albury and Graham Murray from Granada Television, and an Englishman who lived there, James (Jimmy) Moxon, who was returning after a visit home to see his mother. Simon and I were there to do recces and preliminary interviews and Graham was the film researcher. We were making a film for the series *End of Empire*, a history of Britain's withdrawal from its colonies. In that particular period in Ghana, history was dangerous stuff. A coup had recently removed the elected government and the armed forces, under Flight Lieutenant Jerry Rawlings, were in charge. The previous government had been unpopular and corrupt, and many people welcomed the military takeover. The ruling council espoused the philosophy of Kwame Nkrumah, the subject of our film. So in theory we should have been non-controversial, but of course that was only the theory.

On the plane, the chosen movie was *The Year of Living Dangerously*, about a journalist caught up in the bloody events in Cambodia when the west was pulling out to leave the people to their fate. The film certainly got us all in the mood for what we were about to encounter on the ground. We knew that there was a strictly enforced curfew and the plane had been held up in Nigeria, so we were late. The pilot added to the tension by announcing that he would be turning the plane round very fast when we landed because he had to clear Ghanaian air space before the curfew began. He said that the crew were not allowed by their union to overnight in Ghana because it was too dangerous. (It was a British plane and in those days the British still had unions.) He said our baggage would be unloaded quickly and left for us on the runway.

This was my first visit to sub-Saharan Africa. On landing, the first impression I had was of the stifling heat – like walking into an oven. The next impression was of tanks and soldiers with machine-guns. I was then picked out of the group and taken to a small room on my own to be questioned about what we were doing in Ghana. I knew that a lot of the people we were hoping to interview were sworn enemies of the military government and was naturally nervous, especially with all those guns around the place. It turned out that all the interrogators wanted was a bribe and some duty-free cigarettes.

Simon had contacted the British Embassy before leaving England and got the name of the Head of Chancery, often a euphemism for intelligence operatives. I would normally not do that, especially when working in a sensitive political climate. The new government were socialists and so am I. So I thought it would be better to stay away from the Brits and make friends with the local government civil servants. Simon insisted, because he said if we got into trouble we would need the embassy's help. Our Man in Accra turned out to be a very pleasant young man with a pretty wife and an idealistic attitude to helping Africa. Fortunately we liked each other. However, I doubted that we would call on his help. But I was wrong.

One Sunday, Simon, Graham, Jimmy and I set off on a recce around the city of Accra, looking at the places where Nkrumah and his comrades had made history. We had applied for permission to film in these places but had not yet received it. We just wanted to see what they all looked like and how easy it would be to film them. One of the locations was a prison that had been built by the British colonialists and was where Nkrumah had been incarcerated. As it happened, it was also the place where the PNDC, as the Rawlings ruling group were known, kept their own political prisoners. James Fort is in a poor area of Accra and the jail stands on a hill above the beach.

I had brought my 35 mm stills camera to take recce pictures so that I could show them to our cameraman to help him decide what equipment he might need to bring when he flew out for the shoot. I raised the camera to focus on the prison and immediately one of the soldiers guarding it ordered me to stop. Jimmy advised that I do as I am told or the camera would be confiscated and then the soldiers would find out what other shots I had taken without permission. Simon and I were schooled in the tough-guy traditions of Granada so we decided to agree to the soldier's instruction, then go down to the beach and check out the location from there. We did not notice that the soldier was following us, so that when I took a picture from the beach, he saw the sunlight flashing on the lens. We were arrested and marched at gunpoint into James Fort Prison.

It was a very scary place, the prisoners even scarier than the heavily armed guards. We were interrogated for a long time by a political officer from the army, a polite and intelligent man who seemed a bit bemused. His whole body language was saying, 'Why me? And Why on a Sunday?' He could not keep me there because it was a prison for men and they could not protect me. But he pointed out that I was probably a spy and could he trust me to come back voluntarily for interrogation by a senior officer the next day? I pointed out that there was no way we could get out of the country; an American embargo meant there was a shortage of petrol and hardly any planes coming or going. Eventually we were released after giving our word that we would come back the next morning, so we did.

The embassy sent someone to represent us. First we had to explain ourselves to the prison governor. Then we were sent to Army headquarters. Eventually, they decided to believe that I was not a spy and confiscated the film but not the camera. They said that when they processed the film if there was anything suspicious they would pick me up again and this time I would not get out. One of the soldiers explained to me, *sotto voce*, that they didn't have the chemicals to process colour film anyway, so stop worrying. Lots of handshakes and smiles followed and they extracted a promise that we would send them the film when it was finished.

When the film was transmitted in England, it was bootlegged all over Ghana because they could not afford to pay for it. I received a message from Flight Lieutenant Rawlings, via a third party. The government liked the film, thought it was fair and right to pay tribute to the Founding Fathers, even if they were now the opposition. He also said that I was an unusual journalist because I told the truth about why I was filming and kept all my promises. He invited me to come back and make another film some time.

Later, in Zambia, I told this story to a self-confessed member of Her Majesty's secret service and I asked him, 'Really, do I look like a CIA agent?' He answered without a blink, 'Actually, yes, you do. You are exactly the sort of person that those bastards would recruit if they had a chance.' So full marks to Rawlings and his educated and intelligent comrades. I might not have been so lucky in a whole lot of other countries I worked in later. But I was certainly a lot more careful.

Here are my lessons from that adventure:

1   In a situation where the country you are visiting has a government opposed by your own, stick to your local advisers and don't involve your embassy. If you do get into trouble and call up your embassy people, the police who arrest you will assume you have something to hide.
2   Never take pictures in a place that is forbidden unless you have the proper secret filming gear. And watch out for the position of the sun when you do it.
3   The above two rules do not apply to the French or the Italians, whose governments will get them out whatever it takes.

CASE STUDY 2 and a half: James Bond land (Malawi, 1985)

In another programme in the *End of Empire* series I filmed in Malawi. Our executive producer Brian Lapping had spent three years negotiating with the late dictator, His Excellency the Life President, Hastings Banda, to get an interview. Banda was not easy to deal with – after independence he had swiftly dispatched most of his Cabinet, one way or another, and ruled the country with a rod of iron, propped up by the British and Americans, who saw him as a bulwark against Communism. I was given his first interview for 30 years, but only on condition that I spoke through an intermediary and stuck to the agreed questions. In the tradition of many sub-Saharan countries, a stranger cannot speak to the chief directly but must speak through a 'linguist', even if they are actually speaking the same language. My linguist was the British ex-Governor, still great pals with the Life President.

After filming, I and my production team were ordered by Banda to go on a tour of the country and see his many 'achievements'. Effectively, we were kidnapped for a couple of hours. We were treated to a performance of traditional singing and dancing, praising the great man at the site of his old schoolhouse where he studied as a child. I was required to sit in a chair along with local dignitaries, with the people paying their respects to me. Later, to my dismay, a man speaking for the assembled people offered me an envelope, their tribute to me – an envelope full of money taken from these dirt poor people. I had no warning that this might happen and decided to accept graciously and then get advice as to how to hand it back. I was told that it would be very rude, so I donated it to a local charity. Later, my colleague John Sheppard said that I was a great loss to the royal family.

Towards the end of the day we were taken to see a school that Banda had built in the bush for the brightest students, who were taken from their homes to be educated by white people at a boarding school modelled on the English public school system. The kids played cricket and learned Latin. I was getting very close to losing it when the assistant cameraman said to me with a smile, 'Don't worry, I've just found out where we are. We're in a Bond movie.'

My lessons from this trip were:

1   Be ready for anything. Think on your feet. But never insult local traditions, however outrageous they may seem to us.
2   People like Banda always insist on questions in advance. Don't try to slip in the odd unscheduled one when dealing with a ruthless dictator. You will only endanger the lives of your local helpers. And maybe your own.
3   Always vet your crew for a sense of humour. In a place like Banda's Malawi you are going to need people around you who are fluent in the language of the surreal.

CASE STUDY 3: Winter of discontent (Holland Park, London, 1987–8)

Tony Benn, the veteran leader of the left in Britain, has always been a hero of mine. As a Cabinet Minister in successive postwar Labour governments he had kept a diary, which he spoke into a Dictaphone every night without fail and later had transcribed. These diaries began to be published in the 1980s when Labour were again in opposition, with Margaret Thatcher in full cry, leading a very right-wing Conservative government. I had tried to make a film with Tony in the early 1980s but other projects got in the way. Then, in 1987, I was phoned by the legendary Ray Fitzwalter, head of the investigative programme, *World in Action*, and known to the London office as His Excellency, the Life Editor. He asked if I would like to direct a film based on the Benn diaries for Channel 4. If I could have picked my dream job, this would be it. Of course I said yes.

Tony and I were and remain good friends but that did not mean that there were not some difficult moments. Ray assigned a researcher to the programme, Mark Hollingsworth, and he soon got stuck into the phenomenal archive that Tony has in his house in Holland Park, London. We were frequent visitors and Tony decided to call us M&M. We appeared in his diaries on and off for the next few years. The major disagreement that could have caused serious problems was over editorial control. Tony felt strongly that, as the elected representative of the people, he should be allowed to say what he liked in the film. I felt equally strongly that, as the director appointed by a public service television channel, I could not cede editorial control to anyone. Indeed, it was in the guidelines for producers and there was no negotiating on the issue. This resulted in a summons by Tony to the commissioning editor for Channel 4 and Ray, my editor from Granada, to attend a meeting at Tony's house for him to explain his strong feelings on the issue to them and hope to shift me from my entrenched position.

Ray and David Lloyd, titans both of the world of serious television journalism, said next to nothing as Tony and I traded arguments in a fairly robust manner. Eventually, Tony asked them whose argument they supported and naturally they said mine. Somewhat to my surprise, he then conceded. He had put his case as strongly as possible but been unable to conquer the vested interests of public service television. In the end I put to him a set of rules drawn up by the veteran American film-maker, Roger Graef. We agreed to show Tony the film before transmission and we agreed to make any factual alterations if we had made mistakes. Otherwise, he had the right to refuse to do anything that made him uncomfortable or give us information he did not want us to have.

This worked out fine in the end because, on the whole, we were in agreement about most things and it was a pleasant enough experience, I think, for both sides. Tony wanted to centre the first programme around issues to do with the monarchy, the royal prerogative, and we agreed. The second programme looked at the 'winter of discontent', when a series of strikes devastated the economy and the then Labour government lost the election and allowed in the government of Margaret Thatcher. We had a certain amount of trouble getting other people featured in the diaries to take part. Some had political differences but most were worried that what they thought they had said in a privileged situation, for example a Cabinet meeting, would now be exposed on television. It is one thing to be quoted in a political book, another to have the whole discussion aired on network TV.

At the time of filming the first of the two programmes, it was still illegal to interview MPs in the parliamentary buildings. I had got permission from the Office of the Sergeant at Arms, in charge of security in the building, to film in Central Hall. I also had permission to film Tony in a room off Central Hall. But I could not get permission to film my interview with Tony in Central Hall. I thought this was absurd, so we set up the camera to start the interview right by the statue of Charles I, who had been beheaded by the Parliamentary allies of Cromwell in 1649. As we started filming, we were stopped by an officer from the Sergeant at Arms' Office. I refused to be bullied and off he went to collect reinforcements. Tony then recorded a perfect piece to camera which became the opening of the film. 'We have been told we cannot film in this place because this is the Palace of Westminster, a royal palace. And that tells you all you need to know about the royal prerogative.'

Tony went on throughout the film to draw attention to the power that the monarchy still holds, often in an amusing, even anarchic, way. In one sequence, he read out the oath of the Privy Council. He is himself a Privy Councillor, which means, in effect, an adviser to the Queen, through his many years as a Cabinet Minister. The oath is secret and should never be revealed. Absurd, says Tony. When I showed the rough cut to David at Channel 4, he said, 'You are being a little naughty here, aren't you?' and that was the end of that.

In one of my own favourite reviews ever, Nancy Banks-Smith of *The Guardian*, a woman who could give Dorothy Parker a run for her money any day, wrote, 'No sooner had they started filming than a man in a flat cap came up and told them to stop . . . A typically subversive film from Maxine Baker.' My dad enjoyed the films; they were definitely better than *The King and I*, in his eyes anyway.

Lessons from Benn:

1 Always guard jealously your editorial control.
2 Know the law but also know when you can push your luck – like we did over the Privy Council Oath or filming in St Stephen's Hall.
3 Call in the big guns to support you when you need backup, but accept that you will probably end up having to fight the battle yourself.

CASE STUDY 4: Real Life (Rigside, Glasgow, 1993)

I went to Scottish Television in 1992 as Executive Producer and Commissioning Editor for Documentary Programmes. It was great fun because I was allowed to take the kind of risks we are not normally allowed, on one condition: that I brought in the ratings. *Real Life* was one of the first series I commissioned.

It had its fair share of controversy. It was only transmitted by Scottish and Grampian Television because the English network controllers are convinced that the audience south of the border cannot understand Scottish accents. This is one of the more bizarre forms of racism, in my view. The programmes were phenomenally successful in ratings terms, drawing more than 50 per cent of the available audience on transmission of the first episode and getting bigger every week. The series also gave me, the commissioning editor, one of the biggest ethical dilemmas of my working life.

The programmes followed the lives of four families, drawn from different economic groups, over a period of six weeks. Four crews were assigned, each to one family. They lived with the people from early morning till late at night and filmed their every move, however mundane. We shot on Hi8, the forerunner of mini-DV, and thus were able to afford to shoot as much as we wished. Our idea was to show programmes which reflected the state of Scotland at that time. The inspiration for us was the Mass Observation movement in the 1930s, which attempted to document the lives of people all over the United Kingdom in an anthropological way, allowing the people to speak for themselves as much as possible.

In *Real Life* we wanted to know what our families talked about, what they watched on television, which newspapers they read, what was their ambition for the future. One programme centred on the Scottish Football Cup. The wealthy family were at the match and at the post-match party, dressed up to the nines. Two of the families watched on television, supporting different sides. The fourth family was originally from England and did not watch at all. Editorially, we were aware that we might have a copyright problem which might make the programme untransmittable. The Scottish Football Association are notoriously unhelpful in granting television rights to their matches and we knew they might not give permission. So we asked the crews to film in such a way that we could not see the television screen all the time. That would give us room for manoeuvre if permission was not granted. In the end we were allowed to use the sound of the match but not the picture. This was considered to be a major concession.

The genre of documentary to which *Real Life* belongs has since been dubbed 'the docusoap'. Since then, there have been many different films and series using the same idea but, so far, none have been so up to date because they have all edited their films some time after they were shot. Following the example of *The Family*, Paul Watson's seminal series, we decided to take a huge gamble and edit the programmes and transmit them in the week of filming. This was only possible because we were shooting on tape and editing on the digital system, Avid. So unless we would have been able to afford three cutting rooms working at once and huge overtime bills – which the BBC in the old days could but we could not – the series would not have been possible before digital technology was invented. We were pioneering a whole new way of working.

As commissioning editor, I had to accept the programmes as good enough for transmission and so I involved myself closely in the final edit. Weaving the four storylines together to make entertaining viewing while at the same time sticking to our serious sociological intentions was not easy, and the editors and producers had a nerve-wracking time. There were massive amounts of tape arriving from the embedded crew on a daily basis, so it would not have been possible to review them all. Instead, the crews sent their recommendations for which were the best scenes, or those which most typified the lives and attitudes of the families. It was a great team effort, with every single member of the staff taking some editorial responsibility.

The series hit the headlines the first week of transmission. We were congratulating ourselves on the spectacular overnight ratings and huge amount of press coverage when I received a call from the series producer, Derek Guthrie, asking for an important policy decision. The crew covering one of the families had phoned in to say that remarks made by the wife in the programme transmitted the night before had so incensed members of the community where they lived that angry crowds were gathering outside their house, threatening both the family and the crew. It was a notoriously tough housing estate and the woman had casually remarked, 'You can get anything stolen for you round here. Videos, bikes, anything. Just order it.' There was no doubt that she was right but the neighbours felt that she was demeaning them and their village, so they decided to get their revenge. The crew kept filming as the crowds gathered. Police were called and recommended that the crew withdraw. The crew did not want to abandon the family so, through their producer, they asked my permission to stay.

I had to consider the safety of the family and the people who were working for me. Our presence could, arguably, be making the situation worse. But the family were genuinely frightened and our programme had put them into this situation. I felt very strongly that the woman had a right to express her views in a free country without being intimidated by a mob. We had discussed including the line when we were editing the programme and realized it would not make her popular in her community, but could not have anticipated such a violent reaction. While I was trying to decide what to do, I also could not ignore the fact that it would all make riveting television. In the end, the police agreed to escort both family and crew out of the house and they were driven away together to a safe house, with our people still filming.

The next day, we were the subject of massive newspaper coverage. The *Sun* newspaper had a photographer on the scene and they covered four pages with the story. The English papers picked it up and ran with the story, concentrating on the question of editorial fairness. The Channel 4 programme *Right to Reply* investigated and criticized us for not having enough regard for the local population in Rigside. They claimed that we were deliberately creating a crisis for the sake of ratings, a claim which Derek Guthrie, who was interviewed in the programme, calmly and comprehensively refuted. The Independent Television Commission also investigated and concluded that we were not at fault, particularly as it emerged that local journalists had been going from house to house the morning after the programme asking contentious questions. Anything for a good story.

The following week's programme naturally opened with the beleaguered family being escorted away from their home. It was good television all right. The decision to include the offending lines was made very late on the night before transmission. I still think we were right and could never have expected such a violent response to a plain statement of fact. The crew had been marvellous throughout the sorry affair. The family stayed in the series and never expressed any criticism of the programmes. All of the families said that they enjoyed the experience.

Recently, programmes like *Big Brother* use the same techniques of editing their 'reality' shows and I admire the skill that goes into the editing, having experienced for myself the difficulty of making complex decisions in a very short time, knowing that millions of people will be watching and judging you for it. But they have at least the safeguard of having chosen the characters primarily for their entertainment value and also manipulating the situation through the control of the Big Brother character. We had no control over anything. Because we were quite genuinely dealing with 'real life'.

Lessons from *Real Life*:

1 Protect your characters. You put them in that position, you get them out.
2 Know your media law. The Scottish Football Association could have sued if we had failed to get their permission.

3 Watch out for dodgy journalists who will exploit any 'telly' story to their own advantage. Especially, in the UK, the Murdoch press.
4 Be ready to defend your work in public. *Real Life* was subject to massive scrutiny in the English press, although it was not transmitted there. It was also blasted on Channel 4's *Right to Reply*. We defended it and were not castigated by the regulator as a result.
5 My old rule from way back applied in this case more than most. Eat healthy food and get plenty of sleep. Because, one day, you may need to stay up all night to cope with a crisis. Keep fit!

People tell me that they had no idea how they wanted to spend their working life, often up to and even after finishing their formal education. I knew from a very young age that I wanted to work in both film and journalism. Documentary was the obvious choice for me and I tailored my own education to make sure it would happen for me. I got some very good advice when I was about 16. I had always assumed that it would be important for me to study serious subjects like economics or politics at university, but I was told that the best thing is to study something you enjoy and make sure you get a degree. The most important thing is to choose a university with a good student paper. Volunteer for the paper on day one of your first term and write lots of copy that you can show to future employers. Also, foreign languages are a good bet. I followed this advice to the letter and got a job as a documentary researcher, straight out of university.

I have always loved my work. Even now, I sometimes wonder how I got to be so lucky. The genuine priviledge of having a licence to pry into other people's lives, fly around the world, meet the most interesting people and – as Norma Percy puts it – actually get paid for doing it, still delights me. And of course I am always learning. For the last few years I have done more executive producing than directing and I also teach at two major film schools. But I suppose I have missed the thrill of authoring my own films, however much I enjoy helping young film-makers to find their own voice. So, now that the DV technology makes it possible to shoot and edit your own films, and do so very cheaply,

I have decided to follow the example of the young people I work with and buy my own equipment. That is my next big project. Of course, I will have to go back to film school myself now and get some training from the technical experts. I am really looking forward to it. Like so many of my contemporaries, I am starting out on the documentary adventure, again.

FILMOGRAPHY

After several years as a researcher at Tyne Tees Television, CBC Toronto, BBC TV London and Thames Television, I joined Granada Television, where I worked from 1977 to 1990. Credits include, as series producer with Gus Macdonald, two series called *Camera*, the first dealing with Victorian photography, 13 programmes transmitted on network ITV in 1979. The second *Camera*, 'Moving Pictures', told the story of the first 20 years of cinema. It was transmitted on ITV in 1981.

In 1980 I produced a series about local business for Granada Television in the north of England. It was called *The Survivors*. I then produced a series called *Victorian Values*, a response to the Thatcher government's inaccurate version of Victorian history. There were six programmes, networked by ITV at 7 p.m.

In 1984–5 I worked on the series *End of Empire*, made by Granada for Channel 4. I produced the film about the battle for independence by Kwame Nkrumah in Ghana. The second film chronicled the freedom struggles in the Central African Federation, now broken up into the separate countries, Zimbabwe, Malawi and Zambia.

In 1986, I produced and directed a fluffy little series called *Village Show*, also for Channel 4 – great fun, but not particularly mind-stretching. Then, in 1987–8, I directed two films for Channel 4 about the leader of the British left, Tony Benn, *The Benn Diaries*.

In 1989–90, I produced the studio show *What The Papers Say* for the BBC and made a *World in Action* investigation called *The Curse of the Superbug*, about the dangers to public health of the hospital superbug, MRSA – a warning that, sadly, was not heeded by the authorities.

In 1991, I directed programme two of the international co-production, *The Prize*, about the history of the oil industry.

From 1991 to 1993, I was Head of Documentaries and Commissioning Editor, Factual, at Scottish Television. Then, in 1993–4, I took over the Documentary Department at the National Film and Television School, where the new director, Henning Camre, wanted a new curriculum and more integration with the rest of the school. This we finally achieved. From 1995 to 1997 I was director of the Scottish Film Council, where I worked closely with the government's Scottish Office in setting up Scottish Screen.

From 1998 to the present, I have divided my time between teaching assignments at the National Film and Television School and the International School for Cinema and Television, Cuba (the EICTV) and I also executive produce and work with young directors to help them develop their projects successfully.

Appendix 1 International documentary film festivals

DOCUMENTARY FILM FESTIVALS

At festivals which feature documentaries either exclusively or primarily, documentary film-makers are most likely to find audiences, colleagues, potential employers and buyers for their films. The most important documentary festivals have international pitching forums, sales markets and competitions. These should be prioritized, and special attention given to their submission requirements, because many prefer or even require a national or continental premiere. IDFA (Amsterdam) and HotDocs are most important; Marseilles, Munich, Visions du Réel (Nyon) and Yamagata should also be prioritized. Still, one should be realistic: such festivals are very selective. Film-makers should of course pursue festivals in their home countries or regions as well. Even if not of international importance, such festivals are important meeting places for documentary makers and industry executives. Many young festivals, such as Encounters in South Africa and It's All True in Brazil, are rapidly gaining recognition as the most important in their respective regions. Since many documentaries never make it to television, minor and local festivals may be the best opportunity for public screenings.

Aarhus Filmfestival
Jaegergaardsgade 152
8000 Aarhus C
Denmark
Tel: +45-8732-1156
E-mail: mail@aarhusfilmfestival.dk
Website: www.aarhusfilmfestival.dk
Runs in October
Submissions deadline: contact festival

Big Sky Documentary Film Festival
131 South Higgins Avenue,
   Suite 201
Missoula, MT 59802
USA
Tel: +1-406-728-0753

E-mail: bigsky@highplainsfilms.org
Website: http://www.bigskyfilmfest.org
Runs in February
Submissions deadline: November

**Bilbao International Festival of
   Documentary and Short Films**
Colón de Larreátegui 37-4 Dcha
48009 Bilbao
Spain
Tel: +34-94-424-86-98
Fax: +34-94-424-56-24
E-mail: info@zinebi.com
Website: http://www.zinebi.com
Runs in November
Submissions deadline: September

Chicago International Documentary Festival
1112 North Milwaukee Avenue
Chicago, IL 06022
USA
Tel: +1-773-486-9612
Fax: +1-773-486-9613
E-mail: info@chicagodocfestival.org
Website: www.chicagodocfestival.org
Runs in April
Submissions deadline: January

Cinéma du Réel
BPI, 25 rue du Renard
Centre George Pompidou
75197 Paris Cedex 04
France
Tel: +33-1-44-78-44-21
Fax: +33-1-44-78-12-24
E-mail: cinereel@bpi.fr
Website: www.bpi.fr
Runs in March
Submissions deadline: December

CPH:DOX – Copenhagen International Documentary Festival
St. Kannikestr. 6
DK-1169 Copenhagen K
Denmark
Tel: +45-3312-0005
E-mail: info@cphdox.dk
Website: http://www.cphdox.dk
Runs in November
Submissions deadline: August

DocAviv International Documentary Film Festival
Tel Aviv Cinematheque
2 Shprintzak St.
P.O. Box 20370
61203 Tel Aviv
Israel
Tel: 972-3-691-7181
Fax: 972-3-696-2841
E-mail: docaviv@netvision.net.il
Website: www.DocAviv.co.il

Runs in April
Submissions deadline: January

Docfest – New York International Documentary Festival
The New York Documentary Center
159 Maiden Lane
New York, NY 10038
USA
Tel: +1-212-668-1100
Fax: +1-212-943-6396
E-mail: docfest@aol.com
Website: www.docfest.org
Runs in June
Submission by invitation (must send synopsis, press materials and CV first)

DocPoint – Helsinki Documentary Film Festival
Perämiehenkatu 11 C
00150 Helsinki
Finland
Tel: +358-967-2472
Fax: +358-967-3998
E-mail: info@docpoint.info
Website: http://www.docpoint.info
Runs in January
Submissions deadline: contact festival

Docudays – Beirut International Documentary Festival
PO Box 113-7222
Hamra, Beirut
Lebanon
Tel: 961-3-771-880
Fax: 961-1-352-256
E-mail: docudays@docudays.com
Website: www.docudays.com
Runs in November
Submissions deadline: contact festival

Documenta Madrid
Area de Gobierno de Las Artes
Direccion General de Actividades Culturales
C/ Conde Duque, 11
28015 Madrid
Spain

Tel: +34-91-540-40-10
Fax: +34-91-588-58-39
E-mail: info@documentamadrid.com
Website: www.documentamadrid.com
Runs in May
Submissions deadline: December

Docupolis International Documentary Festival
CCCB
C/ Montalegre 5
08001 Barcelona
Spain
Tel: +34-93-306-41-00
Fax: +34-93-302-24-23
E-mail: info@docupolis.org
Website: http://www.docupolis.org
Runs in October
Submissions deadline: June

Dokument ART
Grosse Krauthoferstr. 16
D-17033 Neubrandenburg
Germany
Tel: +49-(0)39-55-66-61-09
Fax: +49-(0)39-55-66-66-12
E-mail: dokumentart@latuecht.de
Website: http://www.latuecht.de/dokart
Runs in October
Submissions deadline: June

DOXA Documentary Film and Video Festival
1112-207 West Hastings
Vancouver, BC
Canada V6B 1H7
Tel: +1-604-646-3200
E-mail: programming@doxafestival.ca
Website: http://www.doxafestival.ca
Runs in May
Submissions deadline: November/December

Encontros Internacionales de Cinema Documental
Centro Cultural Malaposta
Rua Angola-Olival Basto
2675 Odivelas

Portugal
Tel: +351-21-938-8570
Fax: +351-21-938-9347
E-mail: amascultura@mail.telepac.pt
Runs in November
Submissions deadline: September

Encounters – South African International Documentary Festival
PO Box 16191
Vlaeberg 8018
South Africa
Tel: +27-21-426-0405
Fax: +27-21-426-0577
E-mail: info@encounters.co.za
Website: http://www.encounters.co.za
Runs in July/August
Submissions deadline: June

Festival dei Popoli
Istituto Italiano per il Film di
    Documentazione Sociale ONLUS
Borgo Pinti 82 rosso
50121 Firenze
Italy
Tel: +39-055-244778
Fax: +39-055-241364
E-mail: festivaldeipopoli@festivaldeipopoli.
    191.it
Website: www.festivaldeipopoli.org
Runs in November
Submissions deadline: contact festival

Festival International du Documentaire
Vue sur les Docs
14, allees Leon Gambetta
13001 Marseilles
France
Tel: +33-4-95-04-44-90
Fax: +33-4-95-04-44-91
E-mail: welcome@fidmarseille.org
Website: http://www.fidmarseille.org
Runs in June/July
Submissions deadline: March

Festival San Benedetto del Tronto
Premio Bizzarri
CP 207 – Via Mario Curzi 24
63039 San Benedetto del Tronto (AP)
Italy
Tel: +39-0735-582-992
Fax: +39-0735-577-252
E-mail: bizzarridoc@libero.it
Website: http://www.ildocumentario.it/
  bizzarri
Runs in October
Submissions deadline: January

Full Frame Documentary Film Festival (formerly Doubletake)
212 West Main Street, Suite 104
Durham, NC 27701
USA
Tel: +1-919-687-4100
Fax: +1-919-687-4200
E-mail: info@fullframefest.org
Website: www.fullframefest.org
Runs in April
Submissions deadline: November (late
  entry in December)

HotDocs
517 College Street, Suite 420
Toronto, Ontario
Canada M6G 4A2
Tel: +1-416-203-2155
Fax: +1-416-203-0446
E-mail: info@hotdocs.ca
Website: www.hotdocs.ca
Runs in April
Submissions deadline: January

Human Right Watch International Film Festival
33 Islington High Street
London N1 9LH
UK
Tel: +44-20-7713-1995
Fax: +44-20-7713-1800
E-mail: hrwuk@hrw.org
Website: www.hrw.org/iff

Runs in March
Submissions deadline: December

International Belgrade Festival of Documentary and Short Film
Majke Jevrosime 20
11000 Belgrade
Serbia and Montenegro
Tel: +381-11-334-6946
Fax: +381-11-334-6837
E-mail: kratkimetar@fest.org.yu
Runs in March
Submissions deadline: February

International Documentary Filmfestival Amsterdam
Kleine Gartmanplantsoen 10
1017 RR Amsterdam
The Netherlands
Tel: +31-20-627-33-29
Fax: +31-20-638-53-88
E-mail: info@idfa.nl
Website: www.idfa.nl
Runs in November/December
Submissions deadline: September

International Leipzig Festival for Documentary and Animated Film
Dokfestival Leipzig
Grosse Fleischergasse 11
04109 Leipzig
Germany
Tel: +49-34-19-80-39-21
Fax: +49-34-19-80-61-41
E-mail: info@dokfestival-leipzig.de;
  presse@dokfestival-leipzig.de
Website: http://www.dokfestival-
  leipzig.de
Runs in October
Submissions deadline: August

Iowa City International Documentary Festival
P.O. Box 10008
Iowa City, IA 52240
USA

Tel: +1-319-335-3258
E-mail: info@icdocs.org
Website: www.icdocs.org
Runs in April
Submissions deadline: February

Ismailia International Film Festival for Documentary and Short Films
Egyptian Film Center
City of Arts
Pyramids Ave, Giza
12111 Ismailia
Egypt
Tel: +202-58-51-613
Fax: +202-58-54-701
E-mail: egyptianfilmcenter@hotmail.com
Website: www.egyptianfilmcenter.org.eg/
    indexen.html
Runs in September
Submissions deadline: contact festival

It's All True International Documentary Festival
Rua Euclides de Andrade 55
05030-030 Pompéia
São Paulo
Brazil
Tel: +55-11-3868-3277
Fax: +55-11-3873-7296
E-mail: info@itsalltrue.com.br
Website: www.itsalltrue.com.br
Runs in March/April
Submissions deadline: January

Kalamata International Documentary Festival
125–127 Kifissias Avenue
115 24 Athens
Greece
Tel: +30-210-884-7893
Fax: +30-210-884-7038
E-mail: info@docfeskalamata.gr
Website: www.docfeskalamata.gr
Runs in October
Submissions deadline: June

Kasseler Dokumentarfilm und Video Fest
Goethestrasse 31
34119 Kassel
Germany
Tel: +49-561-188-44
Fax: +49-561-188-34
E-mail: dokfest@filmladen.de
Website: www.filmladen.de/dokfest
Runs in November
Submissions deadline: August

Margaret Mead Film and Video Festival
American Museum of Natural History
79th Street at Central Park West
New York, NY 10024
USA
Tel: +1-212-769-5305
Fax: +1-212-769-5329
E-mail: meadfest@amnh.org
Website: www.amnh.org/Mead
Runs in November
Submissions deadline: contact festival

Message to Man, St Petersburg International Film Festival
Karavannaya 12
191011 St Petersburg
Russia
Tel: +7-812-230-2200
Fax: +7-812-235-3995
Tel/fax: +7-812-235-2660
E-mail: info@message-to-man.spb.ru
Website: www.message-to-man.spb.ru
Runs in June
Submissions deadline: April

Mumbai International Film Festival
Films Division
Ministry of Information and Broadcasting
Govt. of India
24, Mumbai 400 026
India
Tel: +91-22-381-0176/386-0931/386-1421
    (5 lines)/386-1461
Fax: +91-22-380-0308/386-8492/386-7068

Website: http://www.filmsdivision.com
Runs in January
Submissions deadline: September

Munich International Documentary Film Festival

Landwehrstrasse 79
80336 Munich
Germany
Tel: +49-89-5139-9788
Fax: +49-89-5156-3936
E-mail: info@dokfest-muenchen.de
Website: www.dokfest-muenchen.de
Runs in April/May
Submissions deadline: January

Nordisk Panorama

Georgernes Vreft 12
N-5011 Bergen
Norway
Tel: +47-55-32-74-08
E-mail: elin@bergenmediaby.no
Website: www.nordiskpanorama.com
Runs in September
Submissions deadline: contact festival

Norwegian Documentary Film Festival

Myrane Studentheilm Apartment MB-206
6100 Volda
Norway
E-mail: siri@dokfilm.com
Website: www.dokfilm.com
Runs in April
Submissions deadline: February

One World – International Human Rights Documentary Film Festival

People in Need/One World
Sokolska 18
120 00 Prague 2
Czech Republic
Tel: +420-226-200-468
Fax: +420-226-200-401
E-mail: program@oneworld.cz
Website: http://www.oneworld.cz
Runs in April
Submissions deadline: November

Pärnu International Documentary and Anthropology Film Festival

Pärnu Filmifestival
PO Box A
80011 Pärnu
Estonia
Tel: +372-443-0772
Fax: +372-443-0774
E-mail: aip@chaplin.ee; docfest@chaplin.ee
Website: http://www.chaplin.ee/english/
  filmfestival/
Runs in July
Submissions deadline: March

Punto de Vista – Documentary Film Festival of Navarra

C/ Navarrería, 39
31001 Pamplona (Navarra)
Spain
Tel: +34-848-42-46-84
Fax: +34-848-42-46-24
E-mail: puntodevista@cfnavarra.es
Website: http://www.cfnavarra.es/
  puntodevista
Runs in February
Submissions deadline: September

RAI International Festival of Ethnographic Film

50 Fitzroy Street
London W1T 5BT
UK
Tel: +44-20-7387-0455
Fax: +44-20-7383-4235
E-mail: film@therai.org.uk
Website: www.therai.org.uk
Runs in September
Submissions deadline: March

Shadow Festival

Ceintuurbaan 13, Third Floor
1072 ER Amsterdam
The Netherlands
E-mail: info@shadowfestival.nl
Website: www.shadowfestival.nl
Runs in November
Submissions deadline: August

Sheffield International Documentary Festival
15 Paternoster Row
Sheffield S1 2BX
UK
Tel: +44-114-276-5141
Fax: +44-114-272-1849
E-mail: info@sidf.co.uk
Website: www.sidf.co.uk
Runs in November
Submissions deadline: June

Silverdocs
American Film Institute
8633 Colesville Road
Silver Spring, MD 20910
USA
Tel: +1-301-495-6776
Fax: +1-301-495-6798
E-mail: info@silverdocs.com
Website: www.silverdocs.com
Runs in June
Submissions deadline: March

Taiwan International Documentary Festival
4F-8
No. 7 Ching-Tao E. Rd.
Taipei 100
Taiwan
Tel: +886-2-2396-2001
Fax: +886-2-2396-2117
E-mail: info@tidf.org.tw
Website: http://www.tidf.org.tw
Runs in December, biennially (even years)
Submissions deadline: August

Thessaloniki Documentary Festival
9 Alexandras Avenue
GR-11473 Athens
Greece
Tel: +30-210-8706000
Fax: +30-210-6456251
E-mail: newhorizons@filmfestival.gr
Website: www.filmfestival.gr
Runs in April
Submissions deadline: February

Viewpoint Documentary Filmfestival 2002
Sint-Annaplein 63 – De Filmplanet VZW
9000 Gent
Belgium
Tel: +32-(0)9-225-08-45
Fax: +32-(0)9-233-75-22
E-mail: viewpoint@studioskoop.be
Website: www.viewpointdocfest.be
Runs in February/March
Submissions deadline: December

Visions du Réel
CP 593 18, Rue Juste-Olivier
1260 Nyon
Switzerland
Tel: +41-22-365-4455
Fax: +41-22-365-4450
E-mail: docnyon@visionsdureel.ch
Website: www.visionsdureel.ch
Runs in April
Submissions deadline: January

Voicingsilence
#17 Shan Sultan Complex
Cunningham Road
Bangalore 560052
India
Tel: 0091-80-51235233
Fax: 0091-80-22088234
E-mail: info@voicingsilence.com
Website: http://www.voicingsilence.com
Runs in December
Submissions deadline: November

Yamagata International Documentary Film Festival
2-3-25 Hatago-machi
990-8540 Yamagata City
Japan
Tel: +81-23-624-8368
Fax: +81-23-624-9618
E-mail: info@yidff.jp
Website: www.city.yamagata.yamagata.jp/
yidff/
Runs in October, biennially
Submissions deadline: December (late
deadline in April)

GENERAL FILM FESTIVALS

In general, most film festivals screen documentaries alongside fiction, animation and experimental films. It is worth investigating and pursuing such festivals, as they may be prestigious and high profile, or might be local to you or your production. There exist over 1600, too many to list here, and new ones are being founded every year. The Internet remains the best source for finding such festivals: www.filmfestivals.com and www.britfilms.com have excellent databases, and www.filmmaking.net and www.insidefilm.com are also useful.

Many film festivals of international prominence have documentary programmes and competitions which are as important as documentary-exclusive festivals. A premiere or even a prize at such festivals could lead to a sale of the film. These festivals often have marketplaces as well, which have become important places for film-makers to sell their work. For film-makers hoping for international sales, the Berlin, Sundance and Toronto Film Festivals should be prioritized alongside the documentary festivals HotDocs, IDFA, Marseilles, Munich, Visions du Réel and Yamagata.

Berlin International Film Festival
Internationale Filmfestspiele Berlin
Potsdamer Strasse 5
D-10785 Berlin
Germany
Tel: +49-30-25-92-00
Fax: +49-30-25-92-04-99
E-mail: program@berlinale.de
Website: www.berlinale.de
Runs in February
Submissions deadline: November

Brisbane International Film Festival
Level 3, Hoyts Regent Building
167 Queen Street Mall
Brisbane 4001
Queensland
Australia
Tel: +61-7-3007-3003
Fax: +61-7-3007-3030
E-mail: biff@biff.com.au
Website: www.biff.com.au
Runs in July/August
Submissions deadline: April

Cork Film Festival
10 Washington Street
Cork
Ireland
Tel: +353-21-427-1711
Fax: +353-21-427-5945
E-mail: info@corkfilmfest.org
Website: www.corkfilmfest.org
Runs in October
Submissions deadline: July

Edinburgh International Film Festival
Filmhouse
88 Lothian Road
Edinburgh EH3 9BZ
Scotland, UK
Tel: +44-(0)131-228-4051
Fax: +44 (0)131-229-5501
E-mail: info@edfilmfest.org.uk
Website: www.edfilmfest.org.uk
Runs in August
Submissions deadline: April

Galway Film Fleadh
Cluain Mhuire
Monivea Road
Galway
Ireland
Tel: +353-91-751-655
Fax: +353-91-735-831
E-mail: gafleadh@iol.ie

Website: www.galwayfilmfleadh.com
Runs in July
Submissions deadline: April

Goteborg Film Festival
Olof Palmes plats
413 04 Goteborg
Sweden
Tel: +46-31-339-30-00
Fax: +46-31-41-00-63
E-mail: goteborg@filmfestival.org
Website: www.goteborg.filmfestival.org
Runs in January/February
Submissions deadline: November

Helsinki International Film Festival
P.O. Box 889
FI-00101 Helsinki
Finland
Tel: +358-968-435-230
Fax: +358-968-435-232
E-mail: office@hiff.fi
Website: www.hiff.fi
Runs in September
Submissions deadline: contact festival

Hong Kong International Film Festival
22/F
181 Queen's Road Central
Hong Kong
Tel: +852-2970-3300
Fax: +852-2970-3011
E-mail: info@hkiff.org.uk
Website: www.hkiff.org.uk
Runs in March
Submissions deadline: December

International Film Festival Rotterdam
P.O. Box 21696
3001 AR Rotterdam
The Netherlands
Tel: +31-10-890-9090
Fax: +31-10-890-9091
E-mail: tiger@filmfestivalrotterdam.com
Website: www.filmfestivalrotterdam.com
Runs in January/February
Submissions deadline: November

Jerusalem International Film Festival
Jerusalem Cinemateque
11 Hebron Road
P.O. Box 8561
Jerusalem 91083
Israel
Tel: +972-2-565-4333
Fax: +972-2-565-4334/5
E-mail: Festival@jer-cin.org.il
Website: www.jff.org.il
Runs in July
Submissions deadline: April

Karlovy Vary International Film Festival
Film Servis Festival, a.s.
Panska 1
110 00 Prague 1
Czech Republic
Tel: +420-221-411-001
Fax: +420-221-411-033
E-mail: festival@kviff.com
Website: www.kviff.com
Runs in July
Submissions deadline: April

London Film Festival
National Film Theatre
South Bank
London SE1 8XT
UK
Tel: +44-0207-815-1322/3
Fax: +44-0207-633-0786
Website: www.lff.org.uk
Runs in October/November
Submissions deadline: July

Melbourne International Film Festival
First Floor, 207 Johnston Street
Fitzroy 3065
Victoria
Australia
Tel: +61-3-9417-2011
Fax: +61-3-9417-3804
E-mail: miff@melbournefilmfestival.com.au

Website: www.melbournefilmfestival.
com.au
Runs in July/August
Submissions deadline: March

Montréal World Film Festival
1432 Rue De Bleury
Montréal, Québec
Canada H3A 2J1
Tel: +1-514-848-3883
Fax: +1-514-848-3886
E-mail: info@ffm-montreal.org
Website: www.fmm-montreal.org
Runs in August/September
Submissions deadline: June

Munich Film Festival
Internationale Muenchner Filmwochen
GmbH
Sonnenstrasse 21
D-80331 Munich
Germany
Tel: +49-89-38-19-04-64
Fax: +49-89-38-19-04-61
E-mail: fachsbesucherakkreditierung@
filmfest-muenchen.de
Website: www.filmfest-muenchen.de
Runs in June/July
Submissions deadline: April

Natfilm Festival
St. Kannikestr. 6
DK-1169 Copenhagen K
Denmark
Tel: +45-3312-0005
Fax: +45-3312-7505
E-mail: info@natfilm.dk
Website: www.natfilm.dk
Runs in March/April
Submissions deadline: January

Pusan International Film Festival
Annex 2-1
139 Woo 1-Dong Yachting Center
Haeundae-Gu
Busan
Korea

Tel: +82-51-747-3010
Fax: +82-51-747-3012
E-mail: program@piff.org
Website: www.piff.org
Runs in October
Submissions deadline: July

Rencontres Internationales Paris/Berlin
roARaTorio
51 rue Montorgueil
75002 Paris
France
Tel: +33-1-40-26-66-34
Fax: +33-1-42-33-36-44
E-mail: info@art-action.org
Website: http://art-action.org
Runs in November
Submissions deadline: contact festival

São Paulo International Film Festival
Rua Antonio Carlos
288 Second Floor
01309-010 São Paulo SP
Brazil
Tel: +55-11-3141-0413
Fax: +55-11-3266-7066
E-mail: info@mostra.org
Website: www.mostra.org
Runs in October/November
Submissions deadline: August

Sundance Film Festival
8857 West Olympic Blvd., Suite 200
Beverly Hills, CA 90211-3605
USA
Tel: +1-310-360-3605
E-mail: festivalinfo@sundance.org
Website: www.sundance.org
Runs in January
Submissions deadline: September

Stockholm International Film Festival
Box 3136
S-103 62 Stockholm
Sweden
Tel: +46-8-677-50-00
Fax: +46-8-20-05-90

E-mail: info@filmfestivalen.se
Website: www.filmfestivalen.se
Runs in November
Submissions deadline: September

Sydney Film Festival
PO Box 96
Strawberry Hills
NSW 2012
Australia
Tel: +61-2-9280-0511
Fax: +61-2-9280-1520
E-mail: info@sydneyfilmfestival.org
Website: www.sydneyfilmfestival.org
Runs in June
Submissions deadline: February

**Toronto International Film Festival
(Real to Reel programme)**
2 Carlton Street, West Mezzanine
Toronto, Ontario
Canada M5B 1J3
Tel: +1-416-967-7371
Fax: +1-416-967-3598
E-mail: tiffg@torfilmfest.ca
Website: www.bell.ca/filmfest
Runs in September
Submissions deadline: June

Valladolid International Film Festival
Teatro Calderon
Calle Leoplodo Cano
s/n, 4.planto
Apartado de Correos 646
47003 Valladolid
Spain
Tel: +34-983-42-64-60
Fax: +34-983-42-64-61
E-mail: festvalladolid@seminci.com

Website: www.seminci.com
Runs in October
Submissions deadline: June

Vancouver International Film Festival
Vancouver International Film Centre
1181 Seymour Street
Vancouver, BC
Canada V6B 3M7
Tel: +1-604-685-0260
Fax: +1-604-688-8221
E-mail: viff@viff.org
Website: www.viff.org
Runs in September/October
Submissions deadline: July

**Viennale – Vienna International Film
Festival**
Siebensterngasse 2
A-1070 Vienna
Austria
Tel: +43-1-5265947
Fax: +43-1-5234172
E-mail: office@viennale.at
Website: www.viennale.at
Runs in October
Submissions deadline: August

Warsaw International Film Festival
P.O. Box 816
00-950 Warsaw 1
Poland
Tel: +48-22-621-46-47
Fax: +48-22-621-62-68
E-mail: kontakt@wff.pl
Website: www.wff.pl
Runs in October
Submissions deadline: June

Appendix 2 Sources of funding for documentaries

In the UK and Europe, most documentary films are funded by television. Film-makers may take their ideas directly to a broadcaster's commissioning editors or, more effectively, to an independent production company that already has relationships with broadcasters. In the UK, there also exists public money, from the Film Council, Regional Screen Agencies and from National Lottery Funds. Further, money exists from the European Union in the form of MEDIA Plus, which also advises on pan-European co-productions. If your documentary might appeal to audiences in other countries, you should pursue international co-production financing. The pitching forums at IDFA (Amsterdam), HotDocs (Toronto) and Discovery Campus are the best venues for exploring this possibility.

Non-profit organizations and foundations also fund documentaries, particularly in the USA, where it is more difficult for independent producers to receive television commissions. Many such funds are limited to US residents or citizens, but others are international. Some will grant money only to non-profit organizations; many documentary non-profits will provide 'fiscal sponsorship' to a project, so the producer can pursue these monies.

BROADCASTERS IN THE UK AND IRELAND

British Broadcasting Corporation
BBC Television Centre
London W12 7RJ
UK
Tel: +44-208-743-8000
Fax: +44-208-752-6060
Website: www.bbc.co.uk/commissioning

Channel 4 Television
124 Horseferry Road
London SW1P 2TX
UK

Tel: +44-207-396-4444
Fax: +44-207-306-8351
Website: www.channel4.com/4producers

Channel Five
22 Long Acre
London WC2E 9LY
UK
Tel: +44-207-550-5555
Fax: +44-207-836-1273
Website: www.five.tv/accessibility/
aboutfive/corporate/producersnotes/

Discovery Channel
160 Great Portland Street
London W1W 5QA
UK
Tel: +44-207-462-3600
Fax: +44-207-462-3700
Website: http://producers.discovery.com

ITV
ITV Network Centre, 200 Gray's Inn Road
London WC1X 8HF
UK
Tel: +44-207-843-8000
Fax: +44-207-843-8157
Website: www.itv.com

S4C
Parc Ty Glas, Llanishen
Cardiff CF14 5DU
Wales, UK
Tel: +44-29-2074-7444
Fax: +44-29-2075-4444
Website: www.s4c.co.uk

**The History Channel/The Biography
  Channel**
Grant Way, Isleworth
Middlesex TW7 5QD
UK

Tel: +44 207-941-5185
Fax: +44-207-941-5187
Website: www.thehistorychannel.co.uk

**National Geographic Channels
  International**
1145 17th Street NW
Washington, DC 20036
USA
Tel: +1-202-912-6500
Fax: +1-202-912-6694
Website: www.ngcideas.com

Radion Telefis Eireann
RTE 1 and RTE 2
Donnybrook
Dublin 4
Ireland
Tel: +353-1-208-3111
Fax: +353-1-208-3080
Website: www.rte.ie/tv

TG4
Baile na hAbhann
Co. na Gailimhe
Ireland
Tel: +353-91-50-50-50
Fax: +353-91-50-50-21
Website: www.tg4.ie

UK FUNDING

Arts Council England

National Office:
14 Great Peter Street
London W1P 3NQ
Tel: 0207-333-0100
Fax: 0207-973-6581
E-mail: enquiries@artscouncil.org.uk
Website: www.artscouncil.org.uk

Regional Offices:
Arts Council England, East
Eden House
48–49 Bateman Street

Cambridge CB2 1LR
Tel: 0845-300-6200
Fax: 0870-242-1271

Arts Council England, East Midlands
St Nicholas Court
25–27 Castle Gate
Nottingham NG1 7AR
Tel: 0845-300-6200
Fax: 0115-950-2467

Arts Council England, London
2 Pear Tree Court
London EC1R ODS

Tel: 0845-300-6200
Fax: 0207-608-4100
E-mail: London@artscouncil.org.uk

Arts Council England, North East
Central Square
Forth Street
Newcastle upon Tyne NE1 3PJ
Tel: 0845-300-6200
Fax: 0191-230-1020

Arts Council England, North West
Manchester House
22 Bridge Street
Manchester M3 3AB
Tel: 0845-300-6200
Fax: 0161-834-6969

Arts Council England, South East
Sovereign House
Church Street
Brighton BN1 1RA
Tel: 0845-300-6200
Fax: 0870-242-1257

Arts Council England, South West
Bradnich Place
Gandy Street
Exeter
Devon EX4 3LS
Tel: 0845-300-6200
Fax: 01392-229-229
E-mail: southwest@artscouncil.org.uk

Arts Council England, West Midlands
   Arts
82 Granville Street
Birmingham B11 2LH
Tel: 0121-631-3121
Fax: 0121-643-7239
E-mail: info@west-midlands.arts.org.uk

Arts Council of England, Yorkshire
21 Bond Street
Dewsbury
West Yorkshire WF13 1AX
Tel: 01924-455555

Fax: 01924-466522
E-mail: Yorkshire@artscouncil.org.uk

Arts Council of Northern Ireland
Arts Development Department
MacNeice House, 77 Malone Road
Belfast BT9 6AQ
Tel: 028-9038-5200
Fax: 028-9066-1715
Website: www.artscouncil-ni.org

Arts Council of Wales
9 Museum Place
Cardiff CF10 3NX
Tel: 029-20-376-500
Fax: 029-20-396-284
E-mail: info@artswales.org.uk
Website: www.artswales.org.uk

Scottish Arts Council
12 Manor Place
Edinburgh EH3 7DD
Tel: 0845-603-6000
Fax: 0131-225-9833
E-mail: Help.desk@scottisharts.org.uk
Website: www.sac.org.uk

Awards for All
Tel: 0845-600-2040
E-mail: info@awardsforall.org.uk
Website: www.awardsforall.org.uk

Awards for All in England
Ground Floor, St Nicholas Court
25–27 Castle Gate
Nottingham NG1 7AR

Awards for All in Scotland
Highlander House
58 Waterloo St
Glasgow

British Council
Films and Literature Department
10 Spring Gardens
London SW1A 2BN
Tel: 0207-389-3166

Fax: 0207-389-3175
E-mail: Filmliterate@britishcouncil.org
Website: www.britishcouncil.org
      or
      www.britfilms.com
Provides distribution of British films to
  international film festivals.

The Carnegie United Kingdom Trust
Comley Park House
Dunfermline, Fife
KY12 7EJ
Scotland
Tel: 01383-721445
Fax: 01383-620682
Website: www.carnegieuktrust.org.uk

Cineworks
Glasgow Media Access Centre
Third Floor, 34 Albion Street
Glasgow G1 1LH
Tel: 0141-553-2620
Fax: 0141-553-2660
E-mail: info@cineworks.co.uk
Website: www.cineworks.co.uk

Community Fund
St Vincent House
16 Suffolk Street
London SW1Y 4NL
Tel: 0207-747-5299
E-mail: enquiries@community-fund.org.uk
Website: www.community-fund.org.uk

Edingburgh Mediabase
25a South West Thistle Street Lane
Edinburgh EH2 1EW
Tel: 0131-220-0220
Fax: 0131-220-9158
E-mail: info@edinburghmediabase.com
Website: www.edinburghmediabase.com

The First Film Foundation
9 Bourlet Close
London W1P 7PJ
Tel: 0207-580-2111

Fax: 0207-580-2116
Website: www.firstfilm.co.uk

Isle of Man Film and Television Fund
Isle of Man Film Commission
Department of Trade and Industry
Hamilton House, Peel Road
Douglas
Isle of Man
Tel: 01624-687173
Fax: 01624-687171
E-mail: filmcomm@dti.gov.im
Website: www.gov.im/dti/iomfilm

Northern Ireland Community Relations Council
Publications and Media Grant Scheme
6 Murray Street
Belfast BT1 6DN
Tel: 028-90-227-500
Fax: 028-90-22-7551
E-mail: info@community-relations.org.uk
Website: www.community-
  relations.org.uk

Northern Ireland Film and Television Commission
Third Floor, Alfred House
21 Alfred Street
Belfast BT2 8ED
E-mail: info@niftc.co.uk
Website: www.niftc.co.uk

Scottish Screen
Second Floor, 249 West George Street
Glasgow G2 4QE
Tel: 0141-302-1700
Fax: 0141-302-1711
E-mail: info@scottishscreen.com
Website: www.scottishscreen.com

Sgrin Cymru Wales
The Bank
10 Mount Stuart Square
Cardiff Bay
Cardiff CF10 5EE
Tel: 029-2033-3300

Fax: 029-2033-3320
E-mail: sgrin@sgrin.co.uk
Website: www.sgrin.co.uk

UK Film Council
10 Little Portland Street
London W1N 7JG

Tel: 0207-861-7861
Fax: 0207-861-7862
E-mail: info@filmcouncil.org.uk
Website: www.filmcouncil.org.uk

Regional Screen Agencies

East London Moving Image Initiative
E-mail: elmii@filmlondon.org.uk
Website: www.elmii.org.uk

EM-MEDIA
35–37 St Mary's Gate
Nottingham NG1 1PU
Tel: 0115-934-9090
Fax: 0115-950-0988
Website: www.em-media.org.uk

Film London
20 Euston Centre
Regent's Place
London NW1 3JH
Tel: 0207-387-8787
Fax: 0207-387-8788
E-mail: info@filmlondon.org.uk
Website: www.filmlondon.org.uk

Northern Film and Media
Central Square
Forth Street
Newcastle upon Tyne NE1 3PJ
Tel: 0191-269-9200
Fax: 0191-269-9213
E-mail: info@northernmedia.org
Website: www.northernmedia.org

North West Vision
233 Tea Factory
82 Wood Street
Liverpool L1 4DQ
Tel: 0151-708-2967

Fax: 0151-708-2984
Website: www.northwestvision.co.uk

Screen East
Anglia House
Norwich NR1 3JG
Tel: 0845-601-5670
Fax: 01603-767-191
E-mail: info@screeneast.co.uk
Website: www.screeneast.co.uk

Screen South
Folkestone Enterprise Centre
Shearway Business Park
Shearway Road
Folkestone
Kent CT19 4RH
E-mail: info@screensouth.org
Website: www.screensouth.org

Screen West Midlands
31–41 Bromley Street
Birmingham B9 4AN
Tel: 0121-766-1470
Fax: 0121-766-1480
E-mail: info@screenwm.co.uk
Website: www.screenwm.co.uk

Screen Yorkshire
Studio 22
46 The Calls
Leeds LS2 7EY
Tel: 0113-294-4410
Fax: 0113-294-4989

E-mail: info@screenyorkshire.co.uk
Website: www.screenyorkshire.co.uk

South West Screen
St Bartholomews
Lewins Mead

Bristol BS1 5BT
Tel: 0117-952-9982
Fax: 0117-952-9988
Website: www.swscreen.co.uk

EUROPEAN FUNDING SOURCES

Eurimages
Council of Europe
Palais de l'Europe
67075 Strasbourg Cedex
France
Tel: +33-3-88-41-26-40
Fax: +33-3-88-41-27-60
Website: www.coe.int/T/E/
    Cultural_Co-operation/Eurimages

MEDIA Programme
MEDIA Plus Programme
European Commission, Directorate
    General X
Education and Culture
Rue de la Loi, 200
1049 Brussels
Belgium
Tel: +32-2-299-11-11
Fax: +32-2-299-92-14
E-mail: Eac-media@cec.eu.int
Website: Europa.eu.int/comm./avpolicy/
    media/index_en.html
Provides training, development, distribution
    and promotion programmes, particularly
    for pan-European co-productions.
    Film-makers should contact their national
    or regional MEDIA Desk office.

UK MEDIA Desk
Fourth Floor, 66–68 Margaret Street
London W1W 8SR

Tel: 0207-323-9733
Fax: 0207-323-9747
E-mail: England@mediadesk.co.uk
Website: www.mediadesk.co.uk

MEDIA Service Northern Ireland
Third Floor, Alfred House
21 Alfred Street
Belfast BT2 8ED
Tel: 02890-232-444
Fax: 02890-239-918
E-mail: media@niftc.co.uk
Website: www.mediadesk.co.uk

MEDIA Antenna Scotland
249 West George Street
Glasgow G2 4QE
Tel: 0141-302-1776
Fax: 0141-302-1778
E-mail: Scotland@mediadesk.co.uk
Website: www.mediadesk.co.uk

MEDIA Antenna Wales
The Bank
10 Mount Stuart Square
Cardiff Bay
Cardiff CF10 5EE
Tel: 02920-333-304
Fax: 02920-333-320
E-mail: antenna@sgrin.co.uk
Website: www.mediadesk.co.uk

CANADIAN FUNDING

Canada Council for the Arts
350 Albert Street
P.O. Box 1047
Ottawa, Ontario
K1P 5V8
Tel: 1-800-263-5588 or 613-566-4414
Fax: 613-566-4390
Website: http://www.conseildesarts.ca/

Canadian Television Fund
111 Queen Street East, Fifth Floor
Toronto, Ontario
M5C 1S2
Tel: 416-214-4400 or 1-877-975-0766
or
407 McGill Street, Suite 811
Montréal, Québec
H2Y 2G3
Tel: 514-499-2070 or 1-877-975-0766
Website: www.canadiantelevisionfund.ca

National Film Board of Canada
Many offices worldwide support
national film-makers and international
co-productions. See website for
details.
Tel: 1-800-267-7710 or 1-514-283-9000
Fax: 1-514-283-7564
Website: www.nfb.ca/documentary/

Rogers Documentary and Cable Network Fund
333 Bloor Street East, Ninth Floor
Toronto, Ontario
M4W 1G9
Tel: 416-935-2526
Fax: 416-935-2527
Website: www.rogers.com/english/
aboutrogers/communitysupport/
rogers_ documentary_fund.html

US FUNDING

Anthony Radziwill Documentary Fund
IFP/New York
104 West 29th Street
New York, NY 10001
Tel: 212-465-8200 ext 830
E-mail: docfund@ifp.org
Website: http://www.ifp.org/docfund

Arthur Vining Davis Foundations
111 Riverside Ave., Suite 130
Jacksonville, FL 32202-4921
Tel: 904-359-0670
Fax: 904-359-0675
E-mail: arthurvining@msn.com
Website: www.jvm.com/davis/

The Corporation for Public Broadcasting
The Program Challenge Fund
401 Ninth Street, N.W.

Washington, DC 20004-2129
E-mail: programming@cpb.org
Website: http://www.cpb.org/grants/ list.html

Creative Capital
65 Bleecker Street, Seventh Floor
New York, NY 10012
Tel: 212-598-9900
Fax: 212-598-4934
E-mail: info@creative-capital.org
Website: www.creative-capital.org

Experimental Television Center
109 Lower Fairfield Rd.
Newark Valley, NY 13811
Tel: 607-687-4341
Fax: 607-687-4341
E-mail: etc@experimentaltvcenter.org
Website: http://www.experimentaltvcenter.
org/

Film Arts Foundation
145 Ninth Street, #101
San Francisco, CA 94103
E-mail: info@filmarts.org
Website: http://www.filmarts.org/grants/
index.html

ITVS
51 Federal Street, Suite 100
San Francisco, CA 94107
Tel: 415-356-8383
Fax: 415-356-8391
Website: www.itvs.org

Latino Public Broadcasting
6777 Hollywood Blvd., Suite 500
Los Angeles, CA 90028
Tel: 323-466-7110
Fax: 323-466-7521
Website: www.lpbp.org/

**National Black Programming
Consortium**
4802 Fifth Avenue
Pittsburgh, PA 15213
Tel: 412-622-6443
Fax: 412-622-1331
E-mail: info@nbpc.tv
Website: http://nbpc.tv/

National Endowment for the Arts
1100 Pennsylvania Avenue N.W.,
Suite 726
Washington, DC 20506
Tel: 202-682-5452
Fax: 202-682-5721
Website: www.arts.gov

**National Endowment for
the Humanities**
Division of Public Programs
1100 Pennsylvania Avenue N.W.,
Room 426
Washington, DC 20506
Tel: 202-606-8267
Fax: 202-606-8557

E-mail: publicpgms@neh.gov
Website: www.neh.gov

**National Foundation for Jewish
Culture**
330 Seventh Avenue, 21st Floor
New York, NY 10001
Tel: 212-629-0500
Fax: 212-629-0508
E-mail: grants@jewishculture.org
Website: www.jewishculture.org

**Native American Public
Telecommunications**
1800 North 33rd St.
P.O. Box 83111
Lincoln, NB 68501
Tel: 402-472-3522
Fax: 402-472-8675
E-mail: native@unl.edu
Website: www.nativetelecom.org

Pacific Islanders in Communications
1221 Kapiolani Blvd., Suite 6A-4
Honolulu, HI 96814
Tel: 808-591-0059
Fax: 808-591-1114
E-mail: info@piccom.org
Website: www.piccom.org

Playboy Foundation
680 North Lake Shore Drive
Chicago, IL 60611
Tel: 312-751-8000
Fax: 312-751-2818
E-mail: giving@playboy.com
Website: www.playboy.com/corporate

**Wallace Alexander Gerbode
Foundation**
470 Columbus Avenue, Suite 209
San Francisco, CA 94133
Tel: 415-391-0911
Fax: 415-391-4587
E-mail: maildesk@gerbode.org
Website: www.fdncenter.org/grantmaker/
gerbode

INTERNATIONAL FUNDING

Alter-Ciné Foundation
5371 avenue de l'Esplanade
Montréal, Québec
Canada H2T 2Z8
Tel: +1-514-273-7136
Fax: +1-514-273-8280
E-mail: altercine@ca.tc
Website: http://www.sextans.com/
 altercine/index2.html

Annie E. Casey Foundation
701 St Paul Street
Baltimore, MD 21202
USA
Tel: 410-547-6600
Fax: 410-547-6624
Website: www.aecf.org

Ford Foundation
320 East 43rd Street
New York, NY 10017
USA
Tel: 212-573-5000
Fax: 212-351-3677
Website: www.fordfound.org

Herbert Bals Fund
International Film Festival Rotterdam
P.O. Box 21696
3001 AR Rotterdam
The Netherlands
Tel: +31-108-909-090
Fax: +31-108-909-091
E-mail: hbf@filmfestivalrotterdam.com
Website: www.filmfestivalrotterdam.com
Film-maker must reside in a developing
 country.

Jan Vrijman Fund
IDFA
Kleine-Gartmanplantsoen 10
1017 RR Amsterdam
The Netherlands
Tel: +31-206-273-329
Fax: 31-206-385-388

E-mail: info@idfa.nl
Website: www.idfa.nl
Film-maker must be based in a developing
 country.

John D. and Catherine T. MacArthur Foundation
Office of Grants Management
140 South Dearborn Street
Chicago, IL 60603
USA
Tel: 312-726-8000
Fax: 312-920-6258
E-mail: 4answers@macfound.org
Website: www.macfound.org

John D. Rockefeller Foundation
420 Fifth Avenue
New York, NY 10018
USA
Tel: 212-869-8500
Fax: 212-852-8438
E-mail: creativity@rockfound.org
Website: www.rockfound.org

John Simon Guggenheim Memorial Foundation
90 Park Avenue
New York, NY 10016
USA
Tel: 212-687-4470
Fax: 212-697-3248
E-mail: fellowships@gf.org
Website: www.gf.org

Lucius and Eva Eastman Fund
5926 Fiddletown Place
San Jose, CA 95120
or
48 Lakeshore Drive
Westwood, MA 02090
USA
Tel: CA, 408-268-2083; MA, 781-326-7922
Fax: CA, 408-268-2083
E-mail: leastman@best.com

Nordic Film and TV Fund
Skovveien 2
0257 Oslo
Norway
Tel: +47-23-283-939
Fax: +47-22-561-223
E-mail: nftf@nftf.net
Website: www.nftf.net

**Paul Robeson Fund for Independent
 Media**
Funding Exchange
666 Broadway, Suite 500
New York, NY 10012
USA
Tel: 212-529-5300
Fax: 212-982-9272
Website: www.fex.org/grantmaking.shtml

Roy W. Dean Grant
From The Heart Productions
1455 Mandalay Beach Rd.
Mandalay Shores, CA 93035
USA
Tel: 805-984-1768
Website: www.fromtheheartproductions.
 com

Sundance Documentary Fund
8857 West Olympic Blvd.
Beverly Hills, CA 90211
USA
Tel: +1-310-360-1981
Fax: +1-310-360-1969
E-mail: sdf@sundance.org
Website: http://institute.sundance.org

CONFERENCES, MARKETPLACES, PITCHING AND CO-FINANCING FORUMS

The following forums are excellent venues to find financing for your project in development, buyers for a finished film, or co-financing for a partially financed project. Many are attached to important documentary festivals, like HotDocs or IDFA. Discovery Campus offers training initiatives and mentorships to emerging film-makers.

**Australian International Documentary
 Conference**
12 King William Road
Unley, SA 5061
Australia
Tel: +61-8-9322-6906
Fax: +61-8-9322-1734
E-mail: aidc2004@aidc.com.au
Website: www.aidc.com.au
Runs in February

Discovery Campus
Einsteinstrasse 28
D-81675 Munich
Germany
Tel: +49-89-410-739-30
Fax:+49-89-410-739-39
E-mail: info@discovery-campus.de

Website: www.discovery-campus.de
Runs programmes year-round in various
 European cities

DocsBarcelona
Terrassa
Barcelona
Spain
Tel: +34-93-453-00-25
Fax: +34-93-323-93-30
Website: www.docsbarcelona.com
Runs in November
Submissions deadline: October

Documentary in Europe
Via C. Lombroso 26
10125 Torino
Italy
Tel: +39-011-6694924

Fax: +39-011-6694908
E-mail: documentary@docineurope.org
Website: www.docineurope.org
Runs in July

The FORUM for International Co-financing of Documentaries

Part of International Documentary
   Festival Amsterdam
   (same contact)
E-mail: theforum@idfa.nl
Website: www.idfa.nl
Runs in November
Submissions deadline: September

Forum for International Co-financing in Israel

P.O. Box 14581
61143 Tel Aviv
Israel
Tel: 972-3-685-0315
Fax: 972-3-686-9248
E-mail: ornayarm@copro.co.il
Website: www.copro.co.il
Runs in April
Submissions deadline: December

IFP Market

104 West 29th Street, 12th Floor
New York, NY 10001
USA
Tel: +1-212-465-8200
Fax: +1-212-465-8525
E-mail: marketinfo@ifp.org
Website: www.ifp.org
Runs in September

Nordisk Forum for Co-financing of Documentaries

Vognmagergade 10
1120 Reykjavik
Iceland
Tel: +45-33-11-51-52
Fax: +45-33-11-21-52
E-mail: mail@filmkontakt.dk
Website: www.filmkontakt.com

Runs in September
Submissions deadline: June

Sunny Side of the Doc

23 rue Francois Simon
13003 Marseilles
France
Tel: +33-4-95-04-44-80
Fax: +33-4-91-84-38-34
E-mail: contact@sunnysideofthedoc.com
Website: www.sunnysideofthedoc.com
Runs in June

Thessaloniki Pitching Forum

10 Aristotelous Str.
546 23 Thessaloniki
Greece
Tel: +45-3313-1122
Fax: +45-3313-1144
Website: www.filmfestival.gr
Runs in March

Toronto Documentary Forum

Part of HotDocs Festival
Tel: +1-416-203-2155
Fax: +1-416-203-0446
E-mail: info@hotdocs.ca
Website: www.hotdocs.ca
Runs in April

Transit Zero

International Documentary Conferences in
   the Baltic Region
Tel: +46-485-36660
Fax: +46-485-36670
E-mail: info@transitzero.org
Website: www.transitzero.org

Verticalplus

Trufanowstrasse 33
04105 Leipzig
Germany
Tel: +49-30-285-290-90
E-mail: info@vertical-strategy.com
Website: www.verticalstrategies.de
Runs in March
Submissions deadline: February

OTHER FUNDING OPPORTUNITIES

These lists are not exhaustive. Indeed, there are many foundations and grant-giving institutions that fund documentaries, or could be persuaded to do so if the topic falls within their area of interest. One should explore the following resources and databases for other possibilities and ideas:

The Council on Foundations
Website: www.fundfilm.org

Korda
Database for public funding of film in Europe
Website: http://korda.obs.coe.in

The Foundation Center
Website: www.fdncentre.org

UK Fundraising
Website: www.fundraising.co.uk

Documentary makers should bear in mind that they are eligible for many arts grants and, indeed, documentary is increasingly prominent in the world of galleries and museums. Film-makers are eligible for many artists' residencies, which may provide studio space, equipment, living arrangements and even a stipend for a period of weeks or months.

Artquest
Provides information and support to London artists. Its website and e-newsletter has invaluable listings of funding and residence opportunities, and includes legal and managerial advice for freelancers.
Website: www.artquest.org.uk

Worldwide Network of Artist Residencies
Website: www.resartis.org

ORGANIZATIONS AND RESOURCES

The following are professional networks and associations. They organize or participate in festivals, marketplaces, training sessions and pitching forums; they publish magazines, newsletters, helpful websites and indispensable guidebooks; they provide their members with a host of discounts and opportunities. They are non-profit and often charge a membership fee. Some provide fiscal sponsorships to independent film-makers so that they may apply for funds that are granted only to non-profit organizations.

Association of Independent Video and Filmmakers
304 Hudson Street, Sixth Floor
New York, NY 10013
USA
Tel: 212-807-1400
Fax: 212-463-8519

E-mail: info@aivf.org
Website: www.aivf.org

Documentary Filmmakers Group
225a Brecknock Road
London N19 5AA

UK
Tel: 0207-428-0882
E-mail: info@dfglondon.com
Website: www.dfglondon.com

European Documentary Network
Vognmagergade 10
1120 Copenhagen K
Denmark
Tel: +45-3313-1122
Fax: +45-3313-1144
E-mail: edn@edn.dk
Website: www.edn.dk

Film/Video Arts
462 Broadway, Suite 520
New York, NY 10013
USA
Tel: 212-941-8787
Website: www.fva.com/

Independent Feature Project
104 West 29th Street, 12th Floor
New York, NY 10001

USA
Tel: +1-212-465-8200
Fax: +1-212-465-8525
E-mail: ifpny@ifp.org
Website: www.ifp.org

International Documentary Association
1201 West Fifth Street, Suite M320
Los Angeles, CA 90017-1461
USA
Tel: +1-213-534-3600
Fax: +1-213-534-3610
E-mail: info@documentary.org
Website: www.documentary.org

Women Make Movies
462 Broadway, Suite 500WS
New York, NY 10013
USA
Tel: 212-925-0606
Fax: 212-925-2052
E-mail: info@wmm.com
Website: www.wmm.com

Index

Index

300

301

303

Index